Island Hopping across the Pacific Theater
America's Victorious Leapfrogging Strategy against Imperial Japan

By Charles River Editors

A Japanese cruiser under attack during the Battle of Leyte Gulf

About Charles River Editors

Charles River Editors provides superior editing and original writing services across the digital publishing industry, with the expertise to create digital content for publishers across a vast range of subject matter. In addition to providing original digital content for third party publishers, we also republish civilization's greatest literary works, bringing them to new generations of readers via ebooks.

[Sign up here to receive updates about free books as we publish them](), and visit [Our Kindle Author Page]() to browse today's free promotions and our most recently published Kindle titles.

Introduction

A picture of a Japanese plane being shot down during the Mariana Islands Campaign

Island Hopping

"Should we lose in the Philippines operations, even though the fleet should be left, the shipping lane to the south would be completely cut off so that the fleet, if it should come back to Japanese waters, could not obtain its fuel supply. If it should remain in southern waters, it could not receive supplies of ammunition and arms. There would be no sense in saving the fleet at the expense of the loss of the Philippines." – Soemu Toyoda, Combined Fleet Chief of the Imperial Japanese Navy

The waters of the Pacific Ocean – stretching deep blue under the tropical sun, or scourged by typhoons – provided World War II's most far-flung battlefield. Two of the world's premier mid 20th century maritime powers, the United States of American and the Empire of Japan, grappled for supremacy across that vast expanse.

By the time the Battle of Midway was over in June 1942, the defeat was so devastating for Japan that it was actually kept secret from all but the highest echelons of the Japanese government. Along with the loss of hundreds of aircraft and over 3,000 men killed, the four Japanese aircraft carriers lost, when compared to America's one lost carrier, was critical considering America's huge shipbuilding superiority. The protagonists at Midway were putting into practice a newly emerging naval doctrine, one which ultimately meted out a terrible punishment to the side that miscalculated. Carrier versus carrier combat had come of age.

From that point forward, it would be the Americans who operated aggressively across the Pacific. The Guadalcanal Campaign, which ran from August 1942 to February 1943, was a bitter and protracted struggle that also happened to be a strange and transitional confrontation quite unlike any other in the long Pacific War. In conjunction with the American victory at the Battle of Midway, Guadalcanal represented the crucial moment when the balance of power in the Pacific tipped in favor of the Allies, but the idea that Guadalcanal would be such a significant battle would have come as a surprise to military strategists and planners on both sides.

Nonetheless, by the time the Guadalcanal campaign was underway, it was a confrontation that neither side actively sought, but that both sides came to believe they could not afford to lose. When Allied forces landed on the island, it was an effort to deny the Japanese the use of the island and other nearby islands, but the Japanese defenders fought bitterly in an effort to push them off the island, resulting in a rather unique battle that consisted mostly of a Japanese offensive against Americans that invaded amphibiously and dug in. While the Americans closed the campaign with a substantial material advantage, the American garrison on Guadalcanal was initially undermanned and terribly undersupplied.

Eventually, nearly 100,000 soldiers fought on the island, and the ferocity with which the Japanese fought was a fitting prelude to campaigns like Iwo Jima and Okinawa. The campaign would include six separate naval battles, three large-scale land clashes, and almost daily skirmishing and shelling. Not surprisingly, the campaign exacted a heavy toll, with more than 60 ships sunk, more than 1200 aircraft destroyed, and more than 38,000 dead. While the Japanese and Americans engaged at sea and in the skies, of the 36,000 Japanese defenders on the ground, over 30,000 of them would be dead by the end of the Guadalcanal campaign, while the Americans lost about 7,000 killed.

By the end of the fighting, the Guadalcanal Campaign had unquestionably become a turning point in the Pacific War, representing both the last gasp of the Japanese offensive and the first stirrings of the American onslaught. In the wake of the Japanese defeat, Major General Kiyotake Kawaguchi asserted, "Guadalcanal is no longer merely a name of an island in Japanese military history. It is the name of the graveyard of the Japanese army."

By the spring of 1943, American military planners had begun to create a plan to dislodge Japan from east and southeast Asia. To do so, parts of the Philippines were considered main strategic points in the potential Allied attack in the Pacific. The end goal of the Allied plan was an invasion of the Japanese home islands, in which heavy aerial bombardment would precede a ground assault. In order for this to occur, Allied forces would have to occupy areas surrounding Japan, with China adding to Luzon (the largest island in the Philippines) and Formosa (a large island off the coast of China) to create a triangle from which they could launch their bombers.

The Allied advance across the Pacific was based on this 1943 plan, with General MacArthur and his forces moving to the north through New Guinea, then Morotai Island, and then to Mindanao, which was the southernmost major island in the Philippines chain. At the same time, Admiral Chester Nimitz sent his fleet through the central Pacific, where they engaged Japanese forces at the Gilbert, Marshall, Marianas and Palau Islands en route to Mindanao. As the Allies advanced, American strategists became embroiled in a discussion over whether to stick to the 1943 plan, or whether to focus their efforts on seizing Formosa, from which they would be able to create a supply link to China and would also be able to cut Japanese communication lines to the south. By the time the campaign for the Philippines started, Japan was on the defensive, but as they would prove in other places like Iwo Jima and Okinawa, Japanese soldiers would act fanatically before admitting defeat or surrendering. During this second major Philippines campaign, an estimated 330,000 Japanese died, and only about 10,000 were willing to be taken prisoner. In fact, some Japanese soldiers engaged in guerrilla warfare on the Philippines well after the campaign had ended and even after Japan had formally surrendered, prompting the Japanese emperor to personally make a visit and intervene to end the fighting.

Meanwhile, when Admiral Nimitz was directed to capture an island in the Bonin group, Iwo Jima stood out for its importance in making progress against the mainland, with three airfields that would allow American air forces to attack the Japanese mainland. But the Japanese were also well aware of how important Iwo Jima was, and they fought desperately in bunkers and tunnels that required the Americans to carefully clear them out gradually. Less than 5% of the Japanese soldiers on Iwo Jima were taken alive, and American casualties were estimated at 26,000, with 6,800 killed or captured. A month later at Okinawa, which lasted from April-June, the Americans suffered an estimated 62,000 casualties, with 12,000 Americans killed or captured. These deadly campaigns came after widely-held predictions that taking these islands would amount to no more than a brief footnote in the overall theater. However, the national character of the Empire was equally misunderstood. Following the month of Iwo Jima, "commentator after commentator in the Anglo-American camp agreed that the Japanese were more despised than the Germans…uncommonly treacherous and savage…alluding to their remarkable tenacity…refused to give up any territory and incurred thousands of losses daily without any possibility of surrender."

Near the end of 1944, as Allied forces were pushing across the Pacific and edging ever closer to Japan, plans were drawn up to invade the Ryuku islands, the most prominent of them being Okinawa. Military planners anticipated that an amphibious campaign would last a week, but instead of facing 60,000 Japanese defenders as estimated, there were closer to 120,000 on the island at the beginning of the campaign in April 1945. The Battle of Okinawa was the largest amphibious operation in the Pacific theater, and it would last nearly 3 months and wind up being the fiercest in the Pacific theater during the war, with nearly 60,000 American casualties and over 100,000 Japanese soldiers killed. In addition, the battle resulted in an estimated 40,000-150,000 Japanese civilian casualties.

Given the horrific nature of the combat put up by the Japanese, it's no surprise that the final campaigns had a profound psychological effect on the men who fought, but it also greatly influenced the thinking of military leaders who were planning subsequent campaigns, including a potential invasion of the Japanese mainland. The casualty tolls ultimately helped compel President Truman to use the atomic bombs on Hiroshima and Nagasaki in an effort to end the war before having to attempt such an invasion.

Island Hopping across the Pacific Theater in World War II: The History of America's Victorious Leapfrogging Strategy against Imperial Japan analyzes the American offensives across the Pacific as they turned the tide of the war against the Japanese. Along with pictures of important people, places, and events, you will learn about the island hopping campaigns like never before.

Island Hopping across the Pacific Theater in World War II: The History of America's Victorious Leapfrogging Strategy against Imperial Japan

About Charles River Editors

Introduction

The Guadalcanal Campaign

The Marianas

The Philippines and Leyte Gulf

Iwo Jima

Okinawa

Dropping the Atomic Bombs

Further Reading

Free Books by Charles River Editors

Discounted Books by Charles River Editors

The Guadalcanal Campaign

Although they did not yet know it during the Battle of Midway, the Americans had wiped out the Japanese offensive air arm with the loss of only one carrier, and while the Japanese would subsequently have some successes in the north, the Battle of Midway ensured the center of the action in the Pacific would subsequently move south. Within three months of Midway, the Americans would launch their first real counter-offensive with the amphibious invasion of Guadalcanal in the Solomon Islands. The tide had truly turned.

In the middle of 1942, both sides would end up focusing on the Solomons, a long chain of mostly volcanic islands stretching nearly a thousand miles from the southeast to the northwest. The western edge of the Solomons is about 600 miles due east from the coast of New Guinea, and as much as a thousand miles northeast from the coast of Australia. The indigenous population consisted of about 100,000 people, largely Christian and overwhelmingly Melanesian, and they had been subjects of a British protectorate since the 1890s.

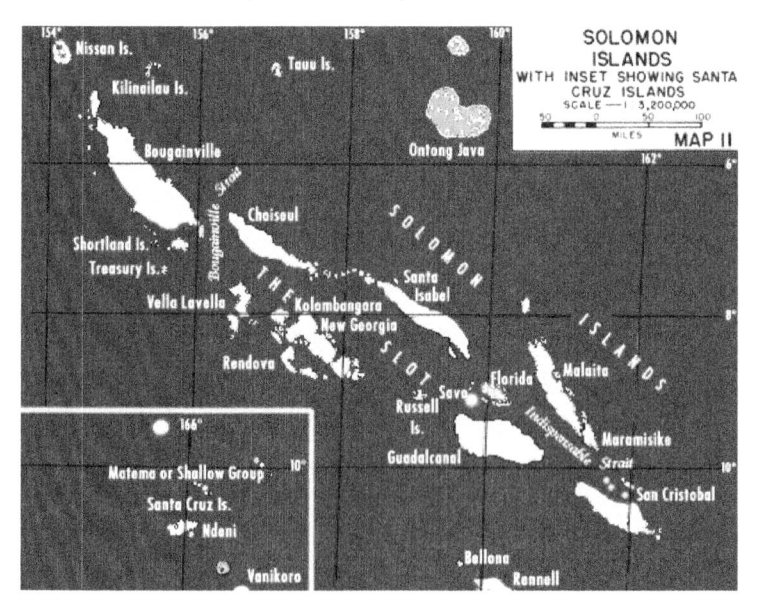

A map of the Solomons

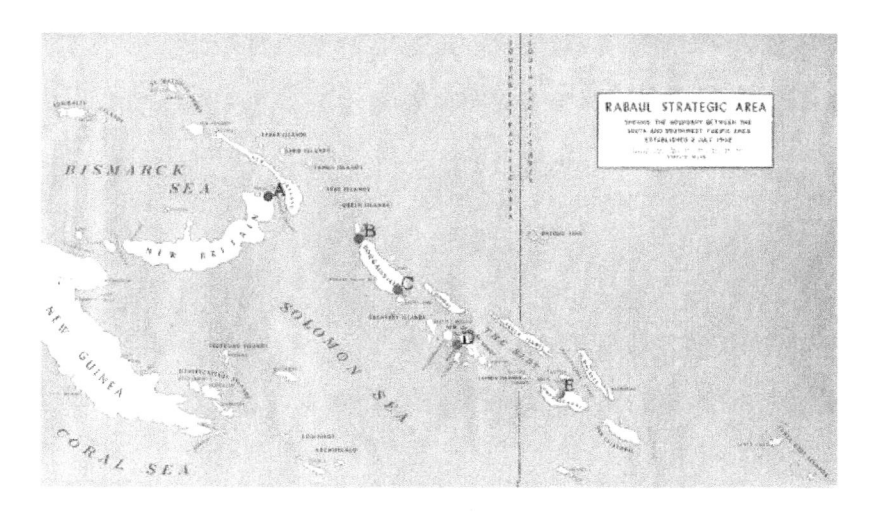

A map of Japanese bases on the Solomons, including one (E) on Guadalcanal

Guadalcanal itself is a mid-sized island just over 2,000 square miles near the southeastern end of the chain. Honiara, on the island's north coast, is today the capital and largest city of the independent Solomon Islands, but the interior of Guadalcanal is highly mountainous, and the terrain that greeted the combatants was largely dense tropical rainforest, buzzing with insects and crawling with lizards and rodents. The climate is punishingly hot and extremely humid year-round, with some of the world's heaviest rain falls and daytime temperatures ranging from 77-90 degrees Fahrenheit. August, when combat began, is somewhat cooler and drier than average, but as the campaign wore on, soldiers and sailors on both sides were subjected to the tropical wet season, with warmer temperatures, more frequent rains, and occasional cyclones in the Coral Sea.

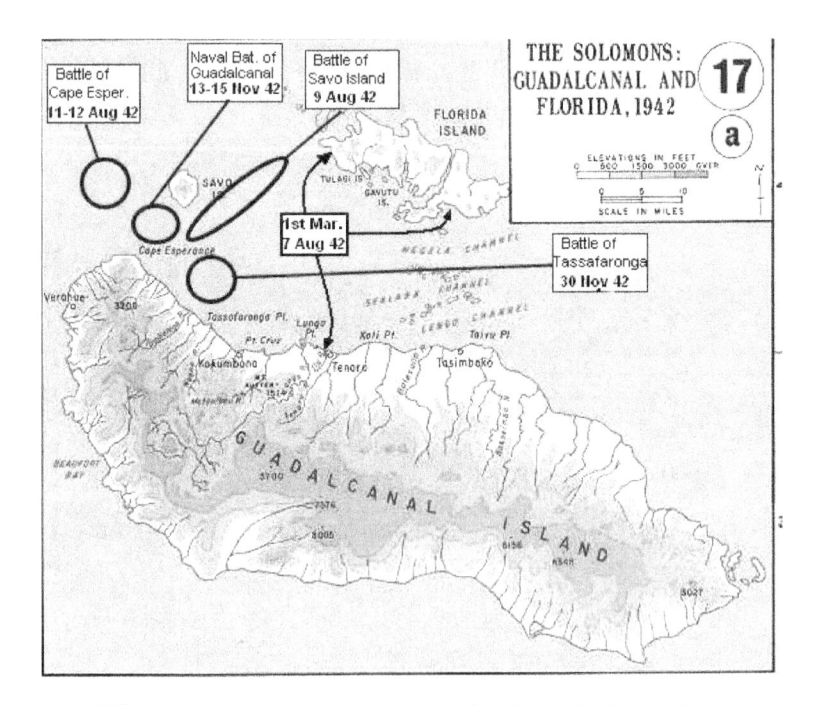

A map of Guadalcanal Island and nearby naval battles fought during the campaign

Prior to the Guadalcanal Campaign, few in either Japan or the United States had envisioned a major confrontation in the Solomons. Within the Imperial Japanese Navy, strategic doctrine had held that upon the outset of hostilities with America, the Navy would seize the Philippines and the Western Pacific. The American fleet would then be forced to steam west to confront Japan's combined fleet in a decisive battle. Interestingly enough, the US Navy's Plan Orange for war with Japan outlined essentially the same sequence of events. Neither side had imagined a conflict to the south in Melanesia; in fact, at the outset of the war, the US Navy did not even have detailed nautical charts of the region.

As it happened, however, while Japanese forces did indeed overrun Southeast Asia and the Western Pacific, no decisive fleet engagement came, in part because the Americans, focused on Atlantic convoys and the European theater, were in no position to dispatch a major offensive battle fleet across the Pacific. The Japanese, having won a Pacific empire on the cheap, were not disposed to risk their precious aircraft carriers in any but the most advantageous circumstances.

The results at Midway created space for the Americans to begin their cautious advance back across the Pacific, and this directed new attention to the South Pacific, where the situation was more ambiguous. In January and February of 1942, Japanese forces under Vice Admiral Inoue Shigeyoshi and Major General Horii Tomitaro had overtaken Rabaul on the island of New Britain, part of Australian New Guinea. At Rabaul, Inoue took advantage of the caldera-formed deepwater harbor to establish a major naval and air base as his headquarters, and from there, the Japanese proceeded to invade the north and west of mainland New Guinea and bombard Australian forces in Darwin.

Inoue

The Battle of the Coral Sea had forced Inoue to abandon his plans for a seaborne invasion of Port Moresby on New Guinea's southeast coast. It did not, however, prevent him from occupying the capital of the British Solomon Islands Protectorate: Tulagi, a small island no more than 3 miles wide and just off the southern coast of the larger Florida Island (now called Nggela Sule). Tulagi is about 25 miles north across the Savo Sound from the much larger island of Guadalcanal. On June 8, a Japanese construction battalion from Tulagi landed on the north shore of Guadalcanal, established a small outpost, and began construction of an airstrip.

Picture of the construction of the airstrip on Guadalcanal

When it reached American war planners through radio intercepts and Australian coastwatchers, news of the Guadalcanal airstrip was greeted with alarm. With control of the skies over and around the Solomons, the Japanese could strike shipping to and from Australia, potentially dividing the United States from its most significant Pacific ally and setting the stage for a further advance southeast. Thus, denying the Japanese use of the Guadalcanal airstrip became a top priority for American military planners in the Pacific.

As a target, Guadalcanal had other attractions as well. Control of the island might represent a valuable first step in an offensive operation aimed at taking Rabaul and driving the Japanese out of the southwest Pacific. Such a prospect, however, inspired conflict and rivalry among American commanders nearly as heated as that between the contending militaries.

Command of the American war effort in the southwest Pacific was a cumbersome hybrid that was split by service and geography and beset by rivalry and miscommunication. On one side was the Navy, commanded in Washington by Admiral Ernest J. King, Commander-in-Chief of the US Fleet. King was a loner, an only child raised by his Ohio father after his mother had been institutionalized. A top graduate of the United States Naval Academy at Annapolis in 1901, King had experience in both surface ships and submarines, and he was qualified as a naval aviator in 1927. President Roosevelt, who appreciated King's drive and initiative, appointed him overall commander of the US fleet in December 1941, as well as one of the four members of the newly-established Joint Chiefs of Staff. King was abrasive, hot-tempered, and stubborn, but he had a penetrating grasp of naval strategy. He is reputed (perhaps anachronistically) to have said of himself, "When they get in trouble they send for the sonsabitches."

Admiral King

According to one of his assistants, the belligerent King frequently locked horns with General H. H. Arnold, another member of the Joint Chiefs. The two managed to avoid blow-ups only because of the urgency of the military situation: "King knew he had to get along. That was the compelling influence on all of them. They knew they had to get along." (Conolly, 375-76)

Arnold

On the other side, simultaneously cooperating and competing with the Navy, was the Army, still led by General Douglas MacArthur. This arrangement meant that any American offensive against the Japanese in the Solomons, New Britain and New Guinea would fall awkwardly between the army and navy, and thus the commands of MacArthur and King. Both officers yearned to go on the offensive and resented Allied war planners' "Europe-first strategy," which prioritized men and materiel for commanders preparing for the North Africa Campaign. For MacArthur, the motivations were personal; his retreat from the Philippines, after loudly proclaiming that he would turn the Japanese back from the beaches, was a humiliation that only victory could erase. For King, the notion of a defensive naval war was an absurdity. Strategic doctrine in the US Naval Academy, inspired by the theorist Alfred Thayer Mahan, stressed the need for offense to establish dominance of the seas. According to Mahan, "the nation that would rule upon the sea must attack" (Mahan, 68).

Thus, both King and MacArthur pushed hard for a southwest Pacific advance, albeit advances very different in character. King, in March 1942, argued for a naval advance along the Solomons chain and up to Rabaul and northern New Guinea. MacArthur, on the other hand, advocated a quick strike against Rabaul itself, claiming that he could capture the Japanese headquarters in three weeks if provided with a division of amphibious assault troops and a navy task force with two aircraft carriers. The argument, which was more about who would command the offensive than over how it would proceed, roiled the Joint Chiefs of Staff. In fact, King went so far as to threaten General George Marshall that the navy would proceed with its advance on the Solomons "even if no support of army forces in the southwest Pacific is made available." MacArthur, for his part, claimed that King's obstinacy was part of a navy conspiracy aimed at "the complete absorption of the national defense function by the Navy, the Army being relegated to merely base, training, garrisoning, and supply purposes" (Hayes, 208-9). At its heart, this was merely a bureaucratic dispute over America's limited war supplies, and for all their mutual recriminations, both King and MacArthur agreed that it was essential the forces in the Pacific get their fair share. As an assistant with the Joint Chiefs of Staff described the controversies of the time, "They were fighting for men and supplies. The money was insignificant. You could get all the money you wanted but there were just so much supplies in the US." (Silverthorne, 265).

George Marshall

After considerable acrimony, the Joint Chiefs managed to hammer out a compromise. The advance would be divided into three phases: an occupation of Tulagi, including the airstrip on nearby Guadalcanal, followed by a simultaneous advance up the Solomon chain and along the northern coast of New Guinea, and finally an all-out attack on the Japanese regional headquarters in Rabaul. The final two phases would be under MacArthur's command, but the first, even where it extended into the army's "Southwest Pacific Area," would be controlled by the navy. King, who managed the naval war from the yacht *Dauntless*, which rode at anchor in the Washington Navy Yard, delegated command of the Pacific theater to Admiral Chester Nimitz, a quiet and capable West Texan of German ancestry. Nimitz, in turn, delegated the southwest Pacific area to the command of Rear Admiral Robert L. Ghormley.

Portrait of Nimitz

Ghormley

Ghormley would probably have been an ideal commander to oversee the defensive operations American war planners had initially assigned to the navy in the southwest Pacific. He was a skilled diplomat who could be expected to manage tensions among his Australian, New Zealand, and New Caledonian Free French allies, all while organizing, training, and equipping his troops for the large-scale advance to come. Ghormley was not, however, well-suited to the aggressive, improvisatory, shoestring operation which he suddenly found himself leading. Doubtful about the strategy in general, Ghormley besieged his superiors with requests to postpone the mission until his troops were reinforced and better-supplied. Expected by King and Nimitz to command the operation on site, Ghormley chose instead to remain at his area headquarters at Noumea, in New Caledonia. As the violence on Guadalcanal escalated through August and September, Ghormley became vacillating and despondent, hardly an ideal commander.

As for the Japanese, tensions between the Imperial Japanese Army and the Imperial Japanese Navy were even more bitter and longstanding than on the American side. Naval operations in the Pacific were overseen by Admiral Isoroku Yamamoto, Commander of the Combined Fleet. Yamamoto was, perhaps, a curious choice to manage Japan's war against America. He had advocated against going to war with the United States against the Axis alliance, opposed the

Japanese Army's invasion of China, and was in favor of naval arms limitation treaties. Yamamoto was by no means a pacifist, but he had a more realistic grasp than most of his colleagues of Japan's relative position in the world. Having spent time in Britain and America, Yamamoto understood that Japan had no hope of prevailing in a long war of attrition with the United States. Having lost the political battle over whether or not to go to war, however, Yamamoto acquiesced and threw himself into preparations for the war he had sought to avoid. The brilliant tactical success at Pearl Harbor had largely been his doing.

Yamamoto

Japanese army operations in the southwest Pacific were under the command of General Hyakutake Harukichi, who operated out of Rabaul on the island of New Britain. Hyakutake had been a part of the radical Kwantung Army during the "Manchurian Incident" of September 1931, in which radical junior officers deliberately precipitated a Japanese invasion of Manchuria, supposedly to defend Japan's South Manchurian Railway against "Chinese bandits." As commander of the Seventeenth Army, Hyakutake was primarily concerned with Japanese operations on New Guinea. He was slow to credit Yamamoto's increasing alarm about the American garrison on Guadalcanal, and he frequently discounted estimates of American strength as exaggerations.

Harukichi at his headquarters in Rabaul

A picture of equipment being prepared in New Zealand ahead of the invasion

Howitzers on the deck of transport ships

Picture of Marines entering transport ships in a landing rehearsal ahead of the invasion

Phase one of the new American offensive began in the predawn hours of August 7 when troops from the First Marine Division, under Major General Archer Vandegrift, landed on Tulagi and the north shore of Guadalcanal. The Marines were undertrained, consisting mostly of young post-Pearl Harbor recruits, and they were also poorly equipped. They had arrived in New Zealand in June as a small, forward-positioned contingent not expected see actual combat until sometime in 1943, and their transports had not even been "combat loaded," meaning they could not be unloaded rapidly in support of an amphibious landing. Upon learning of their new mission, the Marines rushed to reload the transports, dramatically cutting stocks of food, supplies, and even ammunition to save time.

Photo # 80-CF-112-4-63   RAdm. Turner & MGen Vandegrift aboard USS McCawley, July-Aug. 1942

Picture of amphibious crafts headed towards Guadalcanal

While this rush to battle left the Americans dangerously under-supplied, it also helped them to seize an advantage that had done so much for the Japanese in their six-month advance: surprise. The Japanese construction troops on Guadalcanal, unaware of the American landing until the moment that covering fire from naval guns began raining down upon them, initially offered little resistance. Most simply retreated into the jungle. On Tulagi and the nearby islands of Gavutu and Tanambogo, however, the main Japanese force pushed back tenaciously against the Marines. Outnumbered and taken by surprise, the Japanese defenders fought virtually to the last man, extracting the maximum possible price for control of the islands. Altogether, only three of the 350 Japanese soldiers on Tulagi survived, and only 20 of the roughly 500 on Gavutu and Tanambogo survived, a grim taste of the brutal combat that would come to characterize the Guadalcanal Campaign and the war in the Pacific as a whole.

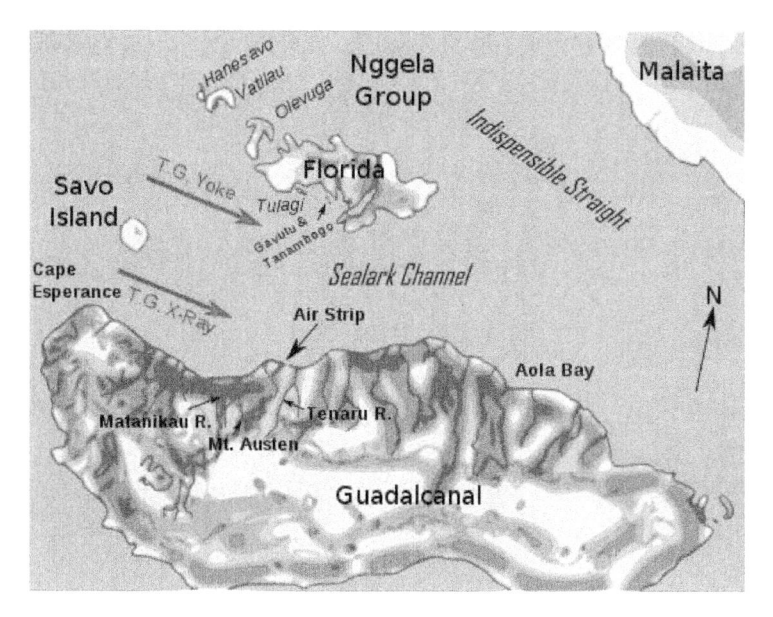

A map of Guadalcanal and direction of the landings

A picture of Marines coming to shore on Guadalcanal on August 7

Aerial photo of Tanambogo and Gavutu Islands during the invasion

Aerial photo of Tulagi during the invasion

By August 8, the Marines had secured Guadalcanal, but even by then, ominous strains and fractures had begun to show within the American coalition before the first Marine waded ashore. The Guadalcanal invasion fleet initially consisted of 76 ships assembled piecemeal from Australia, New Zealand, Pearl Harbor, and San Diego, and at the heart of the force were three of the navy's four remaining aircraft carriers - *Enterprise*, *Wasp*, and *Saratoga* - under the command of Vice Admiral Frank Jack Fletcher. As operational commander of the US fleet at the battles of Midway and the Coral Sea, Fletcher had proven himself a daring and capable officer, but he was skeptical of the Guadalcanal operation and believed that so modest a prize was not worth the risk of bringing three precious carriers within range of Japanese air power. Even before the operation began, the dispute between Fletcher and Rear Admiral Richmond Kelly Turner, who commanded the transports and cargo ships, grew heated and personal, to the extent that Turner's chief of staff reported he "was amazed and disturbed by the way these two admirals talked to each other. I had never heard anything like it." (Dyer, 301). In the end, Fletcher insisted that his carriers would stay to cover the landings for no more than three days, enraging General Vandegrift, who argued that his Marines would require five days at the least to unload their supplies and equipment.

Fletcher

That would not be the end of the matter either. On the afternoon of August 8, not quite two full days into the operation, Fletcher received word of Japanese torpedo planes in the area. Convinced that large numbers of Japanese aircraft could be preparing to strike, and that the risk of losing his carriers outweighed all other factors, Fletcher sent a terse message to Admiral Ghormley in Noumea: "Fighter strength reduced from 99 to 78. In view of large numbers of enemy torpedo planes and bombers in this area, I recommend the immediate withdrawal of my carriers. Request tankers be sent forward immediately as fuel running low." (Dyer, 383). Fletcher didn't bother waiting for a reply; he readied his ships and departed at 6:30 that evening, leaving Vandegrift with his Marines only partly deployed and Turner with only a few surface ships for protection.

As a result of those decisions, the American forces found themselves in an incredibly vulnerable position when they encountered the first devastating Japanese counter-strike. Informed of the American incursion by the Japanese garrison at Tulagi, Admiral Yamamoto ordered Vice Admiral Mikawa Gun'ichi, commander of the Eighth Fleet (based in Rabaul), to assemble a group of five heavy and two light cruisers and steam southeast to destroy the American transport ships. Given that Mikawa's small force had no air support, the move was daring, if not reckless, but Fletcher's untimely departure considerably evened the odds, and the Japanese sailors were also well-trained in night-time operations.

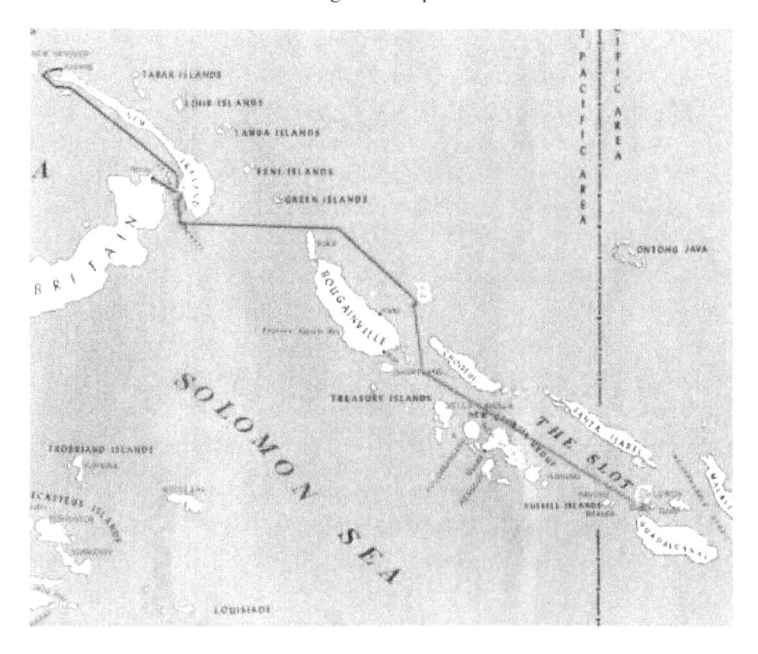

The route of the Japanese airstrike

As it happened, Mikawa's small attack group arrived just as Turner was convening a conference of his officers to discuss whether or not they could continue to unload Vandegrift's Marines without air support. This meant that the perimeter of Savo Sound, where Turner's transports and cargo ships rode at anchor, was even more lightly defended than usual. Mikawa took advantage of his adversaries' lack of readiness, as well as the cloudy and moonless conditions, to launch what naval historian Samuel Eliot Morison labeled "the worst defeat ever suffered on the high seas by the US Navy." (Morison, 167). Mikawa's squadron slipped completely undetected through the south entrance to Savo Sound about 1:30 a.m., and by communicating via a system of hooded blinkers arranged so that they would only be visible to his own ships, Mikawa launched a furious assault on the ships patrolling the southern entrance. The Japanese sank the Australian cruiser *Canberra* and damaged *Chicago*, the flagship of the officer in command, Captain Howard D. Bode. In the confusion, Bode failed to alert his ships in the north entrance to the Savo Sound about the Japanese assault. As a result, 15 minutes later, when Mikawa swung around Savo Island and came up behind the heavy cruisers *Quincy*, *Astoria*, and *Vincennes* at the north entrance, he caught them completely by surprise. Under punishingly accurate fire from Mikawa's squadron, *Quincy* sank almost immediately, as did *Astoria* a few minutes later. *Vincennes* lasted through the night, heavily damaged, but slipped beneath the waters the next morning. Having sustained only minor damage to his ships, Mikawa steamed out of Savo Sound and back to Rabaul, leaving behind him four destroyed cruisers and almost 2,000 dead and wounded.

A picture of the *Quincy* on fire and sinking

The *Canberra* before being sunk

The Battle of Savo Island, as it was called, was a defeat for the Americans, and the damage was immediately recognized as such by Admiral Turner, who blamed overconfidence on the part of the Navy: "The Navy was still obsessed with a strong feeling of technical and mental superiority over the enemy. In spite of ample evidence as to enemy capabilities, most of our officers and men despised the enemy and felt themselves sure victors in all encounters under any circumstances. The net result of all this was a fatal lethargy of mind which induced a confidence without readiness, and a routine acceptance of outworn peacetime standards of conduct. I believe that this psychological factor, as a cause of our defeat, was even more important than the element of surprise."

Historian Richard B. Frank would later cite that battle as the point after which "the United States picked itself up off the deck and prepared for the most savage combat in its history," but the next morning, August 9, was a dark one for the Americans. While rescue ships plucked bodies and desperate survivors out of the sea and medics tended to the hundreds of wounded,

Turner and Vandegrift reconsidered their position. The only bright spot from the previous night was that in his hurry to leave the Sound before the Americans could mount any sort of adequate response to his incursion, Mikawa had failed to strike his main target: the transports and supply ships. Since those were still manned and intact, they could continue loading Marines and supplies onto Guadalcanal. Indeed, when Mikawa returned to Rabaul and sent his report to Yamamoto, the admiral was furious. The whole point of the operation had been to destroy the transports and prevent the Americans from landing any further troops on Guadalcanal, so Yamamoto questioned the value of a victory over the cruisers if the treasure they guarded remained unclaimed.

On the American side, however, the catastrophe of the previous night had driven home to Turner his fleet's alarming vulnerability. He decided that without air cover, he could not afford another night in Savo Sound. His crews worked feverishly throughout the day to unload everything they could onto Guadalcanal, but as the sun went down, they weighed anchor, turned south, and set off for Ghormley's headquarters in Noumea. Nearly 2,000 Marines who had not been able to unload in time sailed off with Turner.

The Marines who remained, about 11,000 on Guadalcanal and another 6,000 on Tulagi, could have been forgiven for feeling abandoned. In the rush to reload at Wellington, their supplies had been drastically scaled back, and in his own rush to leave Savo Sound with most of his fleet intact, Turner had only managed to unload about half of the little he had brought. Young, poorly-trained, isolated and alone, the remaining Marines were an obvious target for Japanese counter-strikes, and to top it off, they had no radio equipment, no radar, no construction equipment, and no barbed wire. They had no more than four days' worth of ammunition and ate only two simple meals per day. In the words of one officer, "We had no idea what was going to happen. We were all wondering where our planes were. The Navy had left, their carriers had left. We didn't have a thing there." (Pollock, 130-32)

From those inauspicious beginnings, conflict over control of the island and its airstrip would drag on for half a year.

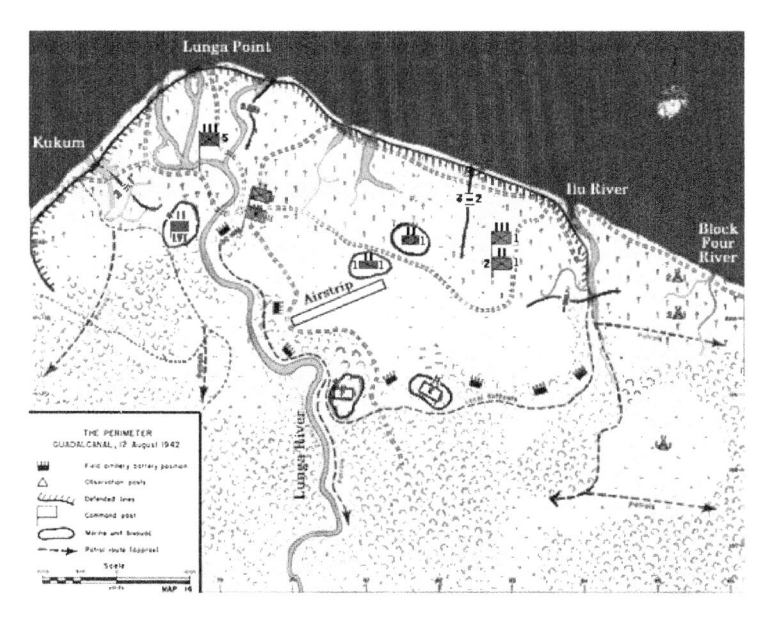

The Marines' defensive perimeter in early August

Japan's greatest strategic failure in the early stages of the Guadalcanal Campaign was to misjudge the Americans' intentions and capabilities. The Battle of Midway had been a major setback, but even so, a great many Japanese officers believed that the dynamic of the conflict was still one of Japanese advance and American response. Even canny strategists like Yamamoto, who understood and respected the war-making potential of the "sleeping giant," believed that the Americans could not possibly initiate a major offensive until 1943.

To be fair, these were hardly unreasonable expectations, because most American strategists held more or less the same opinion. Without the stubborn, reckless determination of King and MacArthur to seize the initiative at any cost, the Americans would never have launched a Solomons campaign so early. Indeed, had Roosevelt and his other Joint Chiefs understood just how expensive the Guadalcanal Campaign would end up being, they probably would never have even agreed to it in the first place.

Moreover, Mikawa's easy success in the Battle of Savo Island suggested that the Americans were not fully committed to holding Guadalcanal, and Fletcher and Turner's hasty retreats to Noumea implied the same. On that basis, even astute Japanese strategists like Admiral Yamamoto concluded that there could be no more than 10,000 Marines on Guadalcanal and perhaps as few as 2,000. Yamamoto further assumed that these Marines were likely isolated, undersupplied, and demoralized. The American garrison was badly undersupplied and, for a time, cut off from headquarters in Noumea. Nonetheless, Vandegrift's Marines were closer to 20,000 strong and by no means ready to surrender.

Making matters worse, Army General Hyakutake, at Rabaul, was at this time still more focused on the New Guinea operation, and he considered Guadalcanal the navy's problem. Even when he began receiving reports that thousands of Americans were on the island and that the Japanese contingent was threatened with total defeat, he did not believe them.

In addition to being underestimated, the Marines held one key asset: the airstrip. The Japanese construction troops had nearly completed it before the August 7 invasion, and Vandegrift's men used captured equipment to rush the airstrip to completion. The airstrip was renamed Henderson Field in honor of Lofton Henderson, a Marine major who had died at the Battle of Midway. On August 15, a small contingent of destroyer-transports managed to deliver equipment, including aviation fuel and bombs, as well as a team of badly-needed aircraft technicians. Within the week, 19 fighters and 12 dive-bombers managed to fly into Henderson Field from the escort carrier *Long Island*. These were the beginnings of the so-called "Cactus Air Force," a name based off the Allied codeword for Guadalcanal ("cactus"). The Cactus Air Force maintained American control of the air around Guadalcanal, an essential advantage in the months ahead.

Aircraft at Henderson Field

Since all these warning signs went unread, it was unsurprising that the Japanese response was initially piecemeal and somewhat half-hearted. Admiral Yamamoto did detach a number of destroyers from Rear Admiral Tanaka Raizo's Destroyer Squadron Two to form the Guadalcanal

Reinforcement Force, and this force, which American Marines would soon be referring to as the "Tokyo Express," was tasked with transporting men and supplies to the beleaguered Japanese troops on Guadalcanal. Admiral Tanaka reportedly considered the assignment beneath his dignity, but he would eventually learn to his dismay that the mission was also beyond his abilities. In addition, Yamamoto persuaded General Hyakutake to begin assembling a 6,000 man force to retake the island.

Tanaka

Before this full force was prepared, however, Yamamoto and Hyakutake dispatched Colonel Ichiki Kiyonao, with just over 900 men, to strike the Americans. On the night of August 18, Ichiki and his men landed at Taivu on the north coast of Guadalcanal, just east of the American garrison, and began marching through the jungle. Expecting to encounter a small contingent of malnourished soldiers, Ichiki was surprised on August 21 when his men clashed with a large, heavily-armed Marine force. The Battle of the Tenaru, fought at the mouth of Alligator Creek, was a bloodbath, and when Ichiki mounted a foolish frontal assault, the Americans, armed with machine guns and light tanks, virtually annihilated his invasion force. Nearly 800 of the Japanese soldiers were killed, with most of the rest of the survivors fleeing back into the jungle. Only one surrendered, and Ichiki himself committed suicide when he saw that the battle was lost. It was a moment full of added significance because Ichiki had commanded the Japanese troops in the 1937 Battle of Lugou Bridge, also known as the "Marco Polo Bridge Incident," the opening of Japan's invasion of coastal China and widely considered an event that truly marked the beginning of World War II.

Ichiki

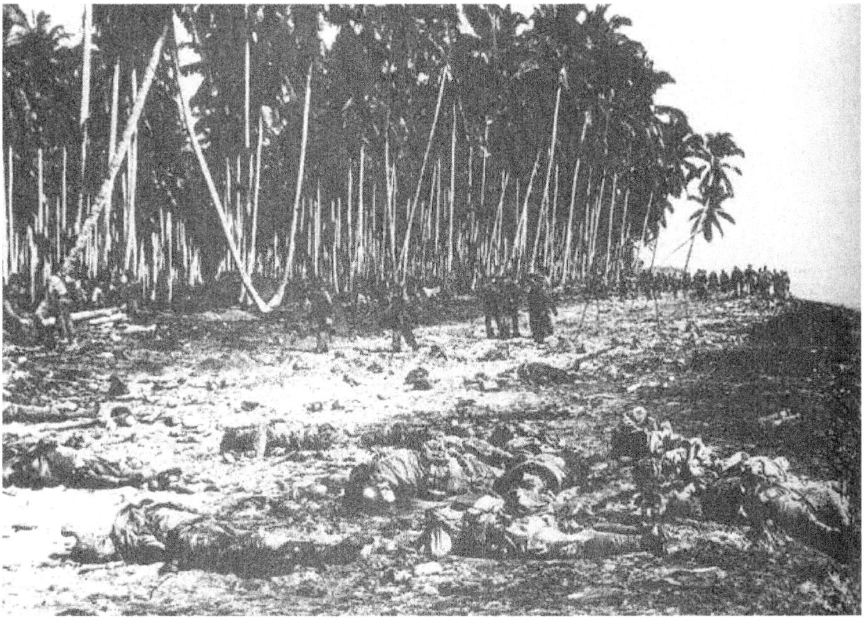

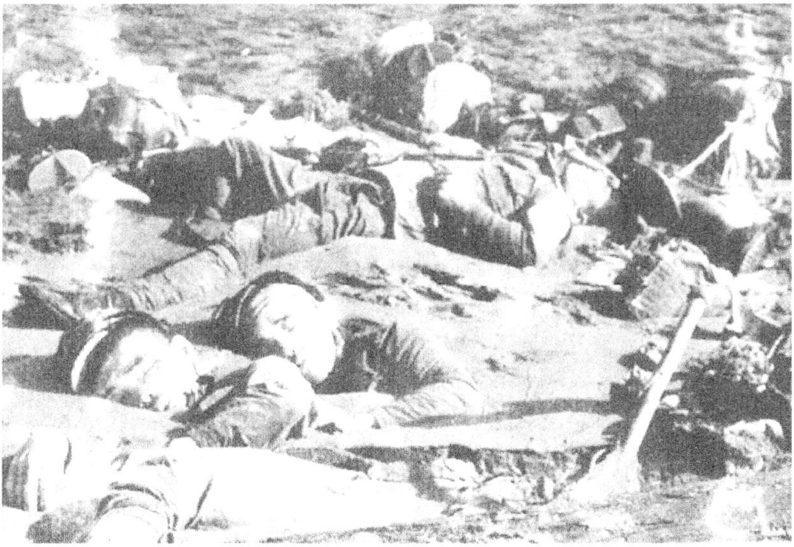

Dead Japanese soldiers after the battle

Following the disaster of the Ichiki mission, the Japanese navy turned its attentions more seriously toward dislodging the Americans from Guadalcanal. For Admiral Yamamoto in particular, conflict over the Solomons appeared to be not just a threat but an opportunity to finally lure the American fleet into the long-awaited "decisive battle" advocated by naval doctrine. On August 24, the Battle of the Eastern Solomons was an evenly-matched carrier confrontation between Fletcher and Admiral Nagumo Chuichi, who had been the operational commander of the Pearl Harbor attack. Nagumo's fleet, including the heavy carriers *Shokaku* and *Zuikaku* and the light carrier *Ryujo*, was providing air support for a convoy landing reinforcements for General Hyakutake's troops on Guadalcanal. Reports of the large-scale Japanese action had brought Fletcher's fleet, including the carriers *Enterprise*, *Wasp*, and *Saratoga*, up from Noumea. On Fletcher's approach, Nagumo immediately broke off from supporting the convoy to strike at the American carriers, a far larger prize, in his eyes, than recapturing Guadalcanal.

The *Enterprise* during the battle

The outcome, yet again, was less than decisive. American pilots managed to sink the light carrier *Ryujo*, but bombers and torpedo-planes from *Shokaku* and *Zuikaku* returned the favor, damaging *Enterprise* so badly that she had to be sent back to Pearl Harbor for repairs. As historian Richard B. Frank put it, "The Battle of the Eastern Solomons was unquestionably an American victory, but it had little long-term result, apart from a further reduction in the corps of trained Japanese carrier aviators. The (Japanese) reinforcements that could not come by slow transport would soon reach Guadalcanal by other means."

Following the exchange, both carrier groups retreated, anxious to avoid any further losses, but in one bright spot for the Americans, the convoy of Japanese troop transports and destroyers was now bereft of air support. The next day, Marine dive-bombers from Henderson Field and B-17 bombers from Espiritu Santo managed to locate and destroy the convoy before it could land reinforcements on Guadalcanal.

Still, while the flow of Japanese reinforcements had been delayed, it was not stopped. Yamamoto's Reinforcement Force under Admiral Tanaka began running regular convoys from Rabaul through the Solomon chain ("up the slot") and onto Guadalcanal. The "Tokyo Express" operated largely by night and frequently attempted to dampen American air power by bombarding Henderson Field. By the end of August, having taken advantage of dark, moonless nights, Tanaka managed to convoy nearly 6,000 well-armed reinforcements under General Kawaguchi Kiyotake onto Guadalcanal.

Japanese troops climb aboard a destroyer on the Tokyo Express

The Cactus Air Force over Henderson Field

  After the fiasco that was the Battle of the Tenaru, Kawaguchi's orders, from General Hyakutake, were cautious and ambiguous. He was to reconnoiter Henderson Field, try to determine the enemy's strength, and estimate whether he would need further reinforcements before mounting an assault. Kawaguchi, however, threw caution to the wind and decided to attack immediately without sending out scouts or reconnoitering the area. On the night of September 13, after marching through dense jungle, his troops crawled up a low ridge about a thousand yards south of Henderson Field. Attempting to overrun and outflank the Marine perimeter, Kawaguchi's troops, supported by heavy mortar fire, launched at least a dozen charges up the face of the ridge. The Marine defenders, led by Lieutenant Colonel Merritt Edson, slowly pulled back but managed to hold the final knoll of the ridge. By morning, the ridge was littered with dead bodies, lending the battle its name, "Bloody Ridge." 20% of Edson's Marines were dead or wounded, but Kawaguchi had fared even worse, losing more than half of his men. He retreated back into the jungle, with the Marines too weak to pursue.

Edson

Dead Japanese soldiers after the battle

In both Washington and Tokyo, news of Kawaguchi's defeat at Bloody Ridge merely bolstered each side's determination to make a stand at Guadalcanal and thus accelerated the steady buildup of forces on both sides.

On September 18, a convoy under Admiral Fletcher managed to land the entire Seventh Regiment, 4,000 thousand Marines with all their weapons and equipment, in the face of Japanese air and submarine attacks. Meanwhile, the "Tokyo Express" ensured a steady flow of Japanese reinforcements, including General Hyakutake, who arrived on October 9 to personally direct the Japanese offensive. Meanwhile, Admirals Ghormely and Turner resisted calls from their subordinates on Guadalcanal to direct all their resources to the campaign, but they did eventually agree to reinforce the Marines with the 3,000 former Dakota National Guardsmen of the 164th Regiment, who arrived on October 13. Their escort of surface ships, under Rear Admiral Norman Scott, had managed a few days earlier to beat back Tanaka's "Tokyo Express" in the Battle of Cape Esperance.

As the conflict expanded, the popular press in the United States had begun to invest Guadalcanal with an outsized psychological importance, portraying it as a chance to redeem the many humiliating losses of before. A *New York Herald Tribune* editorial of October 16 stated, "The shadows of a great conflict lie over the Solomons." On October 24, President Roosevelt, a keen judge of popular opinion, directed the Joint Chiefs of Staff to "make sure that every possible weapon gets into that area to hold Guadalcanal." (Frank, 405) Despite the reinforcements, these raised expectations proved too much for Admiral Ghormely in Noumea, who complained to Nimitz, "My forces [are] totally inadequate to meet [the] situation." Concluding at last that it was Ghormley who was inadequate to the situation, Nimitz replaced him with the aggressive and determined Vice Admiral William "Bull" Halsey, already something of a legend in the navy. Meeting with Vandegrift in Noumea for the first time, Halsey was blunt: "Go on back. I'll give you everything I've got." With that, the Guadalcanal Campaign had entered a new phase.

Halsey

After the first few weeks, the action at Guadalcanal fell into a regular pattern that held for several months. Each side struggled to supply and reinforce its own forces on the island, while simultaneously attempting to interdict the supply convoys of its enemy. While control of Henderson Field gave the Americans a built-in advantage in the air, Japanese mastery of night operations meant that Tanaka's "Tokyo Express" could maintain a steady flow of Japanese troops and supplies onto the island. Air and naval battles frequently revolved around attempts at resupply on one side or the other.

For troops on Guadalcanal itself, the environment could be just as threatening as the enemy. Aside from the narrow beaches, the island was covered with a profusion of giant hardwood trees, creeping vines, twisting roots, and undergrowth. Visibility was often as low as a yard or two, and soldiers would be lucky to march a mile or two in a day. Furthermore, both Japanese and Americans were largely unused to the tropical climate, which bred fungus, skin infections, jaundice, and acute attacks of dysentery. Of course, the jungles were crawling with spiders, leeches, giant ants and wasps. Worst of all was the malarial mosquito; as dedicated as each side may have been to eliminating the other, malaria was often a greater threat than enemy action.

As bad as the environment was, the supply situation wasn't much better. Soldiers on both sides lived in tents if they were lucky and muddy dugouts if they were not. The Marines, for the most part, subsisted on canned C-rations, dehydrated meats and vegetables, and, when they could get it, captured Japanese rice. The Japanese, particularly as the conflict dragged on, often found their rations sharply reduced or even eliminated, surviving where they could on roots, coconuts, and moss.

Naturally, the stress and anxiety of the conflict weighed heavily on Japanese and American soldiers alike. Marines often spoke of "going Asiatic," which would now be called battle psychosis. As one Marine described the Japanese to John Hersey, a war correspondent: "They hide up in the trees like wildcats. Sometimes when they attack, they scream like a bunch of terrified cattle in a slaughter house. Other times they come so quiet they wouldn't scare a snake. One of their favorite tricks is to fire their machine guns off to one side. That starts you shooting. Then they start their main fire under the noise of your own shooting. Sometimes they use firecrackers as a diversion. Other times they jabber to cover the noise of their men cutting through the underbrush with machetes. You've probably heard about their using white surrender flags to suck us into traps. We're onto that one now." (Hersey, 20).

American soldiers, particularly those stationed at or around Henderson Field, frequently suffered through nightly bombardments by the "Tokyo Express." One Marine, recalling a particularly extensive episode in mid-October, wrote, "It was the most tremendous thing I've ever been through in all my life. Anyone who says a naval bombardment isn't worse than any artillery shelling is absolutely crazy….There was one big bunker near our galley in the First Marines…a shell dropped right in the middle of it and practically everybody in the hole was killed. We tried to dig the men out but it wasn't any use." (Pollock, 117).

Japanese bombardment of Henderson Field in October 1942

For the American pilots at Henderson Field, the stresses of the Guadalcanal Campaign could be extreme. They faced many of the same challenges as other soldiers, including heat, humidity, disease, insects, poor diet, and uncertainty, but in addition to those problems, the "Cactus Air Force" struggled with shortages of fuel, spare parts, and ammunition, not to mention the poor condition of the airfield and almost nightly Japanese bombardments of it. The average flier could only last 30 days on Guadalcanal before being judged physically or psychologically unfit to fly. For example, Marine Air Group Twenty-Three was the first contingent of dive-bombers to operate from Guadalcanal, but of that group's pilots, "only one would eventually be able to walk to the plane that carried him away from Henderson Field." (Merrillat, 103).

One particular stress for American pilots was the fact that during the Guadalcanal Campaign, Japanese fliers still enjoyed a technological edge. The Mitsubishi Zero fighter was substantially faster, more maneuverable, and more reliable than both the Marine Wildcat fighter and the Army Air Force P-40 fighter. Indeed, the Wildcats had immense difficulty just making their way up to combat altitude, often requiring 35-40 minutes of advance warning in order to engage incoming Japanese bombers. In addition, the B-17 bombers, which military planners had hoped to use against enemy ships, proved nearly worthless. Nonetheless, American control of Henderson Field proved invaluable because the Japanese Zeroes, forced to fly in from Rabaul, could only afford to spend a few minutes at a time over Guadalcanal before returning to base to refuel.

General Hyakutake had arrived on Guadalcanal to personally oversee a massive Japanese offensive aimed at capturing Henderson Field, and he believed his men were ready by mid-October. The plan was for a three-pronged land offensive, with elements from the Combined Fleet prepared to intercede to prevent American warships from reaching and supporting the

Marines. On October 16, some 20,000 Japanese troops began struggling through the dense jungle to position themselves for the assault, and with a 30 mile trek ahead of them, the soldiers each carried a full ammunition pack, 12 days of rations, and an artillery shell.

Perhaps not surprisingly, while contending with heat, insects, rough terrain, and anxiety, the three "prongs" lost track of each other and the detailed timetable they had worked out in advance. According to the plan, Lieutenant General Maruyama Masai's Second Division was meant to strike from the south, but it was repeatedly delayed, and when a communications failure prevented Major General Sumiyoshi Tadashi (to the west) from learning of the postponement, he launched his assault as originally scheduled on October 23. Without support from the other two "prongs" of the attack, Sumiyoshi's forces faced the full brunt of the Marines arrayed against them. His troops, already tired and weak from their march through the jungle, fell into line behind their nine light tanks, but the Marine artillery were already sighted and prepared for the assault. They quickly knocked the tanks out of commission, after which Sumiyoshi's force was virtually annihilated.

Dead Japanese soldiers and disabled tanks

A Marine howitzer defending on the western side of the perimeter

At the very least, Sumiyoshi's ordeal did keep the Americans focused on the west while the main body of the assault formed up unobserved to the south, along Bloody Ridge. In fact, with one Marine battalion reassigned west to support the action against Sumiyoshi, defenses on the south side of Henderson Field were relatively light. Just one unit, the First Battalion, Seventh Marines, under Lieutenant Colonel Lewis "Chesty" Puller, manned the 4,000 yard perimeter to the south of the airfield.

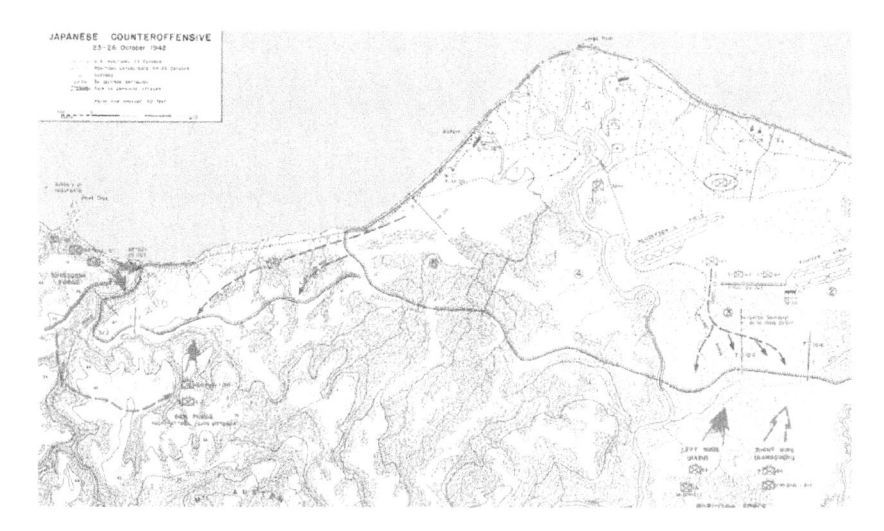

Map of the three prongs

General Hyakutake launched his major assault late on the night of October 23 in the midst of a major rainstorm. Hitting all along the southern side of the perimeter at once, the Japanese threatened to overwhelm and outflank Puller's Marines, and they did manage to break through the defensive line in a few places, but these holes were rapidly filled. As Puller's Marines fell back, from the force of the Japanese assault, they were reinforced by elements of the 164th Regiment. The Dakota National Guardsmen, though considerably older than the Marines, managed to hold their own.

While Hyakutake's march through the jungle had secured him the element of surprise, he made poor use of such a hard-won prize. Wave upon wave of poorly-trained rural recruits were ordered to make pointless and suicidal "*banzai*" charges, running up the ridge directly only to be mown down by disciplined automatic fire. By morning, the assault had broken off, leaving more than a thousand Japanese dead.

Hyakutake struck the next night as well, again attempting to charge up Bloody Ridge to break the Marine perimeter and take Henderson Field, but with no better results. Altogether, as many as 3,500 Japanese may have died in this, the Second Battle of Bloody Ridge.

Dead Japanese soldiers after the attacks on October 25-26

On October 26, Hyakutake's support fleet, which was stationed to the northeast off the Santa Cruz Islands, clashed with an American carrier task force under Admiral Thomas Kinkaid. The Japanese fleet, under Vice Admiral Kondo Nobutake, managed to sink one American carrier, *Hornet*, and badly damage another, *Enterprise*. On the flip side, Kinkaid's men damaged two carriers, *Zuiho* and *Shokaku*, but were not able to knock them out of the fight. The Americans ultimately had to withdraw, but while Kondo had shown that Japanese naval aviators could still hold their own against the Americans in an equally-matched contest, the Japanese were perpetually harassed by ground-based aircraft out of the invaluable Henderson Field. Unable to strike Henderson, running short on aircraft and experienced pilots, and worried about his carriers' vulnerability after learning that Hyakutake's ground assault had been a failure, Kondo figured he had no operational justification for continuing to risk the safety of his ships. As a result, Kondo withdrew his forces.

Combined, the Second Battle of Bloody Ridge on land and the Battle of the Santa Cruz Islands at sea marked an important watershed. Though few suspected it at the time, the operations turned out to be Japan's last major attempt to claim Henderson Field from the Marines. Furthermore, Kondo's dilemma off the Santa Cruz Islands demonstrated just what a valuable prize the Americans had claimed. With more than 100 aircraft operating out of Henderson Field, the Americans held unquestioned mastery of the air in the eastern Solomons, which ensured that Guadalcanal would remain a secure beachhead and jumping-off point for further incursions into Japanese-held territory. Finally, the steep losses the Japanese suffered at Bloody Ridge and the Santa Cruz Islands demonstrated to Japanese military planners that they could no longer afford to mount offensive operations. The loss of so many aircraft and experienced pilots was particularly alarming. The Americans, with their massive industrial and population base, might have made up for such losses, but the Japanese could not.

The final major phase of the Guadalcanal Campaign after the Second Battle of Bloody Ridge was a grim war of attrition. This was precisely the sort of war that Japanese military planners, especially Admiral Yamamoto Isoroku, had desperately sought to avoid, a contest of brute numbers in which America's massive industrial economy, now fully mobilized for war production, would slowly grind down Japan's much more limited material base. In a sense, the final phase of the Guadalcanal campaign was a preview of the Pacific War battles yet to come: brutal contests of strength in which American numbers would ultimately overwhelm Japan's desperate, determined resistance.

In retrospect, the outcome was probably never in doubt after October, but for the Japanese military command, however, the Guadalcanal Campaign did not yet seem a lost cause. As one officer at the Imperial General Headquarters put it, "We must be aware of the possibility that the struggle for Guadalcanal in the southeast area may develop into the decisive struggle between America and Japan." (Hattori, 21). Indeed, even Admiral Yamamoto, who had warned against descending into just such a conflict with the Americans and ought to have known better, sometimes fantasized that the struggle at Guadalcanal might still be used to draw the Americans into the long-awaited "decisive battle."

Early in November, the new Eighth Area Army, under General Imamura Hitoshi, took command in Rabaul and began overseeing Army operations in both New Guinea and the Solomons. In a good omen for the Japanese effort in Guadalcanal, Imamura and Admiral Yamamoto enjoyed a far better relationship than those between most generals and admirals. In their youths, the two had served together in London, where they frequently played bridge together, but while meeting with Imamura, Yamamoto warned his old friend that American war mobilization, finally kicking into high gear, was badly hurting Japan's prospects in the southwest Pacific. In the air, the Americans already enjoyed a 3:1 advantage. In addition, American pilots and sailors were becoming better trained and better equipped as the war progressed. "Our emphasis on intensive training and discipline isn't wrong," Yamamoto argued, "but we should have made sure it was accompanied by scientific and technological improvements as well. I have a strong sense of responsibility for our failure in that regard." (Agawa, 342).

Imamura

Throughout November, the Japanese continued to pour men and material - resources they could scarce afford to lose - into the forlorn cause of retaking the island. Admiral Tanaka's "Tokyo Express" continued to dispatch men and supplies to Guadalcanal, but increasing American control of the air and sea gradually constricted the flow to an irregular trickle. Meanwhile, Admiral Yamamoto, who had moved his headquarters to the Micronesian island of Truk in order to be closer to the action in the Solomons, prepared for one last major offensive in mid-November. A large convoy of 11 high-speed transports carrying 3,000 naval landing troops and a full army division would land at Tassafaronga, to the east of the American garrison. Simultaneously, a task force of battleships and cruisers would bombard Henderson Field to prevent the Americans from using their "Cactus Air Force" to interdict the reinforcements.

Unfortunately for the Japanese, by this point the Americans had cracked Japan's naval code (the "Magic" decrypts), so Halsey had advance warning of the operation and enough time to put together a strong response force of his own, including the carrier *Enterprise*, which had just returned from the naval repair yards at Pearl Harbor. The conflict, now referred to as the Naval Battle of Guadalcanal, began on November 12 when the Japanese task force (two battleships, a light cruiser, and six destroyers) under Vice Admiral Abe Hiroaki steamed down the "slot" of the Solomons chain to bombard Henderson Field and cover the landing at Tassafaronga. Admiral Turner, alerted to the impending Japanese operation, spotted Abe early and dispatched Rear Admiral Daniel J. Callaghan with five cruisers and eight destroyers to confront him. The Americans also had the advantage of functioning radar systems, which detected the Japanese task force early, but the officials were so unused to the new technology that Callaghan held his fire for too long, giving Japanese lookouts a chance to spot him and thus conceding the element of surprise.

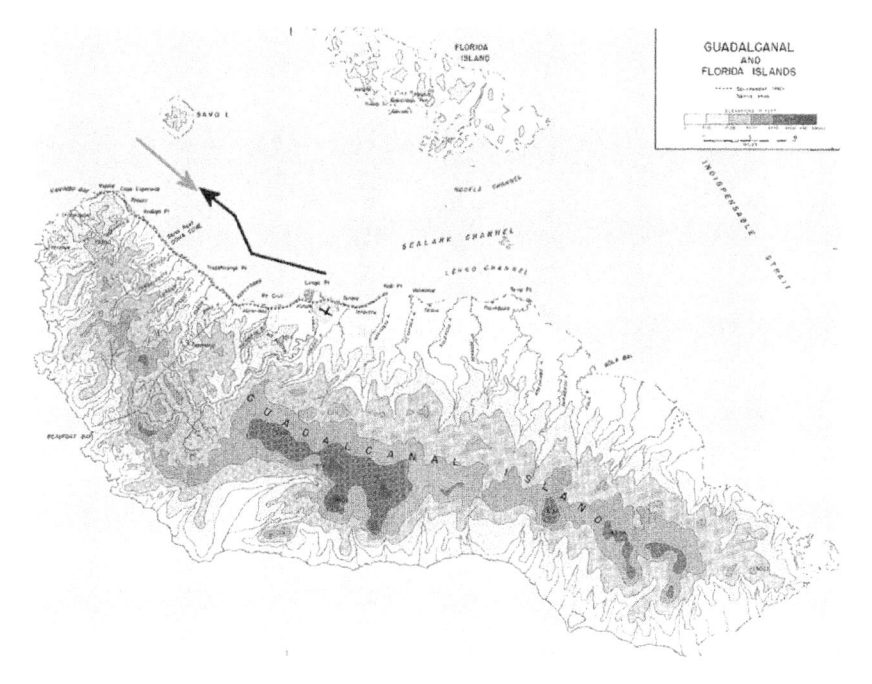

The arrows represent the routes taken by the fleets toward each other.

Nevertheless, while the engagement proved a costly victory for the Americans, it was a victory. Abe managed to sink the cruiser *Atlanta*, as well as three of Callaghan's destroyers. In addition, the cruisers *Portland* and *San Francisco* were heavily damaged, and Admiral Callaghan himself was killed. The exchange was relentless and at very close range, at times so close that Callaghan reportedly could not even lower his big guns to fire on the enemy. One Marine described the action, "The star shells rose, terrible and red. Giant tracers flashed across the night in orange arches ... the sea seemed a sheet of polished obsidian on which the warships seemed to have been dropped and were immobilized, centered amid concentric circles like shock waves that form around a stone dropped in mud."

In the end, Abe's force sustained so much damage that he was forced to call a retreat, and his flagship, the battleship *Hiei*, was so badly damaged that it could barely limp back up the slot. The next morning, aircraft from Henderson Field - the very aircraft that Abe's bombardment had been designed to keep out of the air at all costs - located the *Hiei* and finished the job Callaghan had started, sending it to the bottom of the sea.

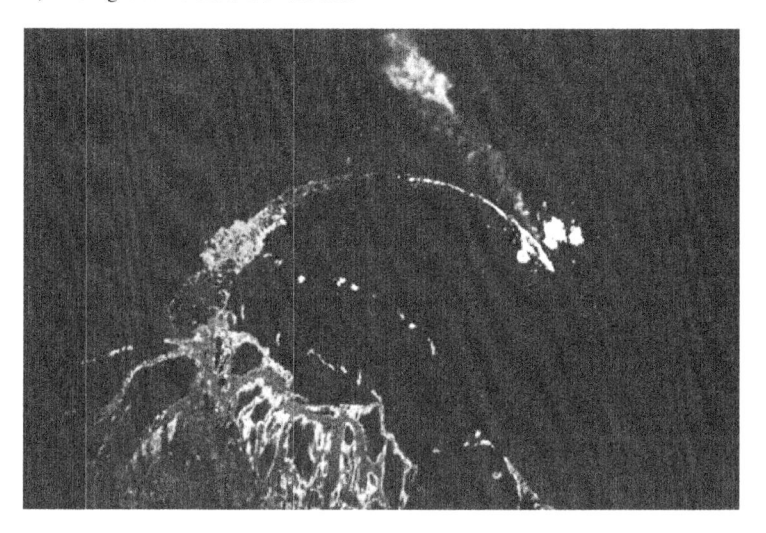

Aerial photo of the bombing of the *Hiei*

Without any relief from American air power based out of Henderson Field, the resupply and reinforcement convoy under Tanaka was dangerously exposed. Even so, the convoy continued on toward Guadalcanal. On the night of August 14, a small group of Japanese cruisers did manage to bombard Henderson Field, but not badly enough to do any significant damage. The next morning the Cactus Air Force was back in the air, sinking six of Tanaka's precious transport ships, as well as one of his cruisers.

The night of November 15, Kondo dispatched his remaining forces, the battleship *Kirishima* along with four cruisers, in one final attempt to knock Henderson Field and its aircraft out of the fight. Unbeknownst to Kondo, however, the *Kirishima* would face a new and dangerous foe. Rear Admiral Willis A. Lee had just arrived at Guadalcanal with two battleships from Admiral Kinkaid's task force. The battleships, *Washington* and *South Dakota*, were new models, faster, more maneuverable, and more heavily armored. They were perfect examples of the technological superiority that America was beginning to enjoy as the conflict wore on. Moreover, unlike most of his peers, Admiral Lee understood and appreciated the value of radar, a tool he believed could make up for the long-standing Japanese advantage in naval night-fighting. As historian Eric Hammel noted, "On November 12, 1942, the (Japanese) Imperial Navy had the better ships and the better tactics. After November 15, 1942, its leaders lost heart and it lacked the strategic depth to face the burgeoning U.S. Navy and its vastly improving weapons and tactics. The Japanese never got better while, after November 1942, the U.S. Navy never stopped getting better."

With the help of radar, the confrontation between Lee and Kondo was a hard-fought but decisive American victory. As the clash began, the power system on *South Dakota* failed, leaving it separated from *Washington* and helplessly exposed to enemy fire. However, the new battleship's improved armor proved its worth. Suffering no fewer than 42 large-caliber hits, *South Dakota* simply continued steaming ahead, damaged but unbowed. Shortly after that, *Washington* used its radar to direct a highly accurate rain of shells onto the deck of *Kirishima*. Within minutes, Kondo's battleship was sinking, one of his destroyers was maimed, and the rest of his task force was in retreat. At the cost of three American destroyers (and the damaged *South Dakota*), Admiral Lee had saved Henderson Field from bombardment.

The *Washington* firing at the Japanese during the battle

With no protection from American air power, Tanaka's transports suffered through a rain of fire in their attempts to land at Guadalcanal. Four of the transports did manage to beach themselves on a point near Tassafaronga, but aircraft based on Henderson Field and *Enterprise* strafed and bombed their decks mercilessly as the hapless soldiers attempted to disembark. In all, no more than 2,000 Japanese reinforcements made it onto Guadalcanal, and they were already traumatized, isolated, and poorly supplied. In Washington the next day, Navy Secretary Knox told reporters, "We can lick them. I don't qualify that. We'll defeat them." (Griffith, 205).

Pictures of wrecked Japanese transport ships on the beach

In the weeks following the Naval Battle of Guadalcanal, the Americans finally wrested full control of the sea lanes in the southeastern Solomons from the Japanese and the garrison around Henderson Field expanded steadily. By the end of the year, there were more than 60,000 airmen, Marines, soldiers, sailors, and other personnel on the island. By contrast, after their last major successful convoy in October, the Japanese struggled to land reinforcements and supplies on Guadalcanal. By December, American control of the sea had advanced so far that an increasingly desperate Japanese Navy had begun running stealth groups of high-speed destroyers up to the coast at night to hurl drums of rice and other supplies overboard and speed off before the Americans could detect them. Responding to the new supply tactics, American pilots and PT-gunners took to searching out and sinking the drums before Japanese shore parties could recover them.

With all of this occurring, the remaining Japanese troops on Guadalcanal found their position rapidly deteriorating. Outnumbered nearly two to one, isolated from headquarters in Rabaul, and with little to no air or sea support, they found themselves reduced to increasingly depleted rations. By the end of the year, malnutrition and starvation had set in, accompanied as always by tropical diseases that wracked the bodies of the already weakened soldiers. In some, dysentery and malnourishment had proceeded so far that their hair and nails stopped growing. The commander of one division of 6,000 soldiers estimated that only about 250 of his men were actually fit enough for combat, and one officer observed the precarious mortality of his troops as follows:

> "Those who can stand -- 30 days
>
> Those who can sit up -- 3 weeks
>
> Those who cannot sit up -- 1 week
>
> Those who urinate lying down -- 3 days
>
> Those who have stopped speaking -- 2 days
>
> Those who have stopped blinking – tomorrow" (Frank, 527).

As the Japanese capacity to mount offensive operations collapsed, the initiative passed to Vandegrift and his Marines. In the wake of the Second Battle of Bloody Ridge, he had begun pushing his defensive perimeter slowly and patiently outward while sending out teams to locate and destroy any isolated Japanese detachments that still clung to survival in the jungle. Finally, after four months of the most punishing jungle combat of the war thus far, Vandegrift and his long-suffering First Marine Division were transferred out of Guadalcanal in early December, replaced by the Second Marine Division under Army Lieutenant General Alexander M. Patch.

Altogether, Vandegrift's Marines had lost 650 dead and 1,300 wounded. About half of his men had contracted some tropical disease, usually malaria. For this steep price, however, Vandegrift could claim to have purchased a stunning success. In the first weeks after his men had waded onto the shores of Guadalcanal, they had been severely undersupplied and undermanned, an isolated garrison with a barely-functioning airstrip that struggled to keep more than a dozen planes in the sky. By December, there were more than 35,000 Americans on Guadalcanal, and more than 200 planes on Henderson Field. They controlled the air and increasingly the sea lanes as well. The Japanese forces on the island, while by no means negligible, were outnumbered and barely supplied. The tide had turned.

By the time General Patch took over command of the Guadalcanal Campaign on December 9, the Japanese had been decisively defeated in the Solomons. As the closing years of the war would demonstrate with horrible clarity, however, defeat and surrender are two completely different things. While the Japanese had no realistic prospects of retaking Guadalcanal, the task of dislodging them completely from the island would be a long and costly one. Early in December, Japanese destroyers covertly running supplies and equipment to their beleaguered ground forces on Guadalcanal were challenged by a group of American cruisers. The Japanese sunk one and damaged three others, and while these victories were growing increasingly rare, they made clear that Guadalcanal was not yet safe for the Americans.

Undeterred, General Patch was determined to complete the job of driving the Japanese from the island. He planned to spend the remainder of December neutralizing dangerous Japanese positions on the high ground overlooking Henderson Field. With that work accomplished, in early January, he would begin an all-out advance across the island west from the Marine garrison. He hoped to clear Guadalcanal of all Japanese forces by April.

As it happened, however, the campaign ended sooner than even the most optimistic American military planners had expected. In the wake of their crushing defeat in the Naval Battle of Guadalcanal, Japan's military leaders made the highly uncharacteristic decision of choosing to pull back. The Emperor approved the decision on December 31, and in February 1943, the Japanese demonstrated that despite all the setbacks they had suffered in the Solomons, they were still capable of executing complex, demanding military operations in complete secrecy and in the dead of night. Over the course of about a week, they evacuated more than 10,000 men from Guadalcanal. American leaders were so unfamiliar with the concept of a Japanese retreat that when Admiral Halsey noted the increased activity, he assigned extra forces to guard Henderson Field because he feared yet another attack was coming. By February 8, an advance force of Patch's Marines marched west across the island, encountering nothing but a few abandoned boats and supplies on the far western coast. The next day, Patch radioed to Admiral Halsey, "Tokyo Express no longer has terminus on Guadalcanal." After a grueling campaign that took almost half a year, the Guadalcanal campaign had ended with an American victory.

The significance of the campaign, launched by both the Japanese and the Americans on a shoestring and escalated in an unsteady, piecemeal, tit-for-tat pattern, came as a surprise to military planners and observers on both sides. Barely aware of the Solomon Islands prior to the Pacific War, both nations found themselves committed to triumphing in a contest of wills whose import at times seemed just as much psychological as practical. In the end, Guadalcanal represented the inevitable point where the military balance in the Pacific tipped in favor of the Americans. As strategists like Admiral Yamamoto Isoroku well understood, given the time and determination necessary to mobilize its massive population and industrial economy for war, the United States was bound to crush Japan. The remainder of the Pacific War was merely the working out of that destiny.

When King and MacArthur had won the Joint Chiefs' approval for the Guadalcanal operation in mid-1942, it had been conceived as merely the first and smallest phase of a campaign to capture Japan's southwestern Pacific headquarters in Rabaul. As the Guadalcanal conflict metastasized into an essential win-at-all-costs campaign, however, concern with the prize of Rabaul gradually withered away. In the end, King and MacArthur elected to bypass Rabaul.

Effectively cut off from contact with the rest of the Japanese war effort, frequently bombarded, alone and impotent, Rabaul was never actually invaded. Instead, the Americans turned their attentions to the north and west, to the Philippines, the Central Pacific, and beyond. Having reached the practical outer limits of their Asian-Pacific empire, and having gambled away so much at Midway and Guadalcanal, the Japanese hunkered down behind an extensive defense perimeter, awaiting the inevitable American advance. Conversely, the Americans, having finally succeeded in mobilizing their massive population and industrial economy on behalf of the war effort, began to overwhelm their Japanese opponents with men and materiel. The next few years would be marked by incredibly deadly campaigns like Iwo Jima and Okinawa, with poorly-supplied Japanese island garrisons attempting to hold out against a much larger American invasion force. These confrontations often proved unprecedentedly brutal, with desperate suicide tactics on the Japanese side and indiscriminate area bombing on the American side.

The tide had turned, but there was still plenty of bloody war ahead.

The Marianas

By the spring of 1943, American military planners had begun to create a plan to dislodge Japan from east and southeast Asia. To do so, parts of the Philippines were considered main strategic points in the potential Allied attack in the Pacific. The end goal of the Allied plan was an invasion of the Japanese home islands, in which heavy aerial bombardment would precede a ground assault. In order for this to occur, Allied forces would have to occupy areas surrounding Japan, with China adding to Luzon (the largest island in the Philippines) and Formosa (a large island off the coast of China) to create a triangle from which they could launch their bombers.

The Allied advance across the Pacific was based on this 1943 plan, with General MacArthur and his forces moving to the north through New Guinea, then Morotai Island, and then to Mindanao, which was the southernmost major island in the Philippines chain. At the same time, Admiral Chester Nimitz sent his fleet through the central Pacific, where they engaged Japanese forces at the Gilbert, Marshall, Marianas and Palau Islands en route to Mindanao. As the Allies advanced, American strategists became embroiled in a discussion over whether to stick to the 1943 plan, or whether to focus their efforts on seizing Formosa, from which they would be able to create a supply link to China and would also be able to cut Japanese communication lines to the south.

Military officials like General George C. Marshall, Lieutenant General Joseph McNarney, and General Henry Arnold all seemed to favor bypassing the Philippines for Formosa during late 1943 and early 1944, while others like Lieutenant General Brehon Somervell argued that it was important to take the entire Philippines before moving on to Formosa and China. For his part, MacArthur was very vocal in his belief that the American army and navy needed to liberate the Philippines before moving on to other portions of the plan.

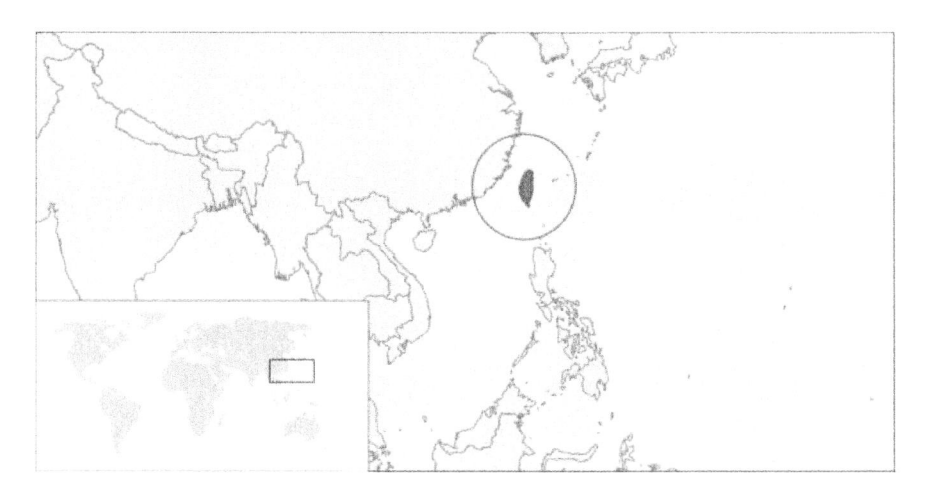

A map showing the location of Formosa

By March 1944, the Joint Chiefs decided to prepare for both options for the Allied attack and instructed MacArthur to prepare his men to move into the southern Philippines by the end of the year, and then into Luzon by early 1945. They also ordered Admiral Chester Nimitz to prepare for an assault on Formosa for early 1945.

Nimitz

Meanwhile, between March and June of 1944, American intelligence had learned that Japan was in the process of reinforcing areas under their control in the western Pacific, especially Formosa. This meant that the longer it took for the Americans to begin their attack on the island, the better-prepared Japanese forces would be to defend it. For the Joint Chiefs, this meant that in order to attack Formosa, they would have to move up their timetable to the fall of 1944 if they wanted to carry out an assault on the island.

Another complicating factor was the belief by American strategists that the Chinese resistance was in danger of collapsing against Japanese pressure. This would nullify one of the major reasons for privileging Formosa over the Philippines (aiding in the supply of Chinese forces on the mainland). By this time, both MacArthur and Nimitz were advocating the need to take the

Philippines to secure air bases from which the Allies could launch further operations across the Pacific. In July 1944, Roosevelt sailed to Pearl Harbor to discuss strategy. Although often cited as the key event in the lead up to the invasion of the Philippines, the truth is that the meeting was indecisive. It was not until September 1944 that President Roosevelt, the Joint Chiefs, MacArthur and Nimitz were all committed to the plan of invading the Philippines before engaging in further attacks on Japan. This made sense mostly in terms of aircraft ranges and the imperative to keep ground forces under the umbrella of short range fighters, but as MacArthur was soon to discover, the carriers were not up to the job on their own.

Once military leaders settled on the Philippines-first plan, they began to prepare for the upcoming campaign. The Allied strategy would comprise of four phases. First, naval and ground units would establish a foothold on southeastern Mindanao, where they could establish airfields that would support further operations. Next, Allied units would move into the central Philippines at Leyte, where MacArthur would set up air and supply bases for the attack on Luzon. The third phase involved taking Luzon, and then the fourth phase would involve dislodging Japanese troops from the minor Philippines islands that had been bypassed during the first three phases.

Before they could advance on the Philippines, however, American forces would have to take the Mariana Islands to the east.

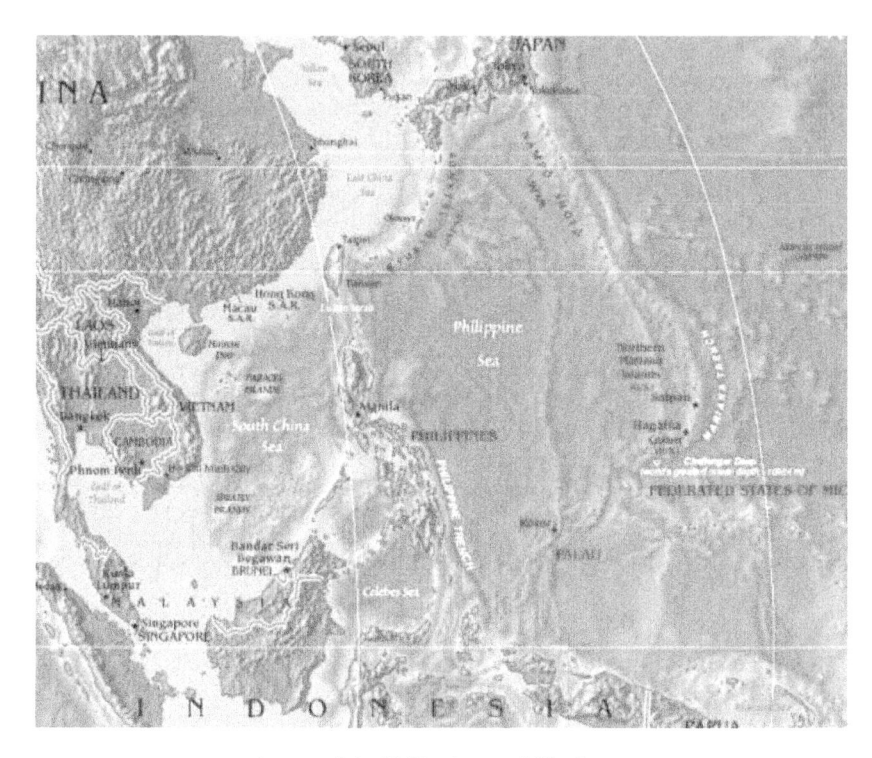

A map of the Philippines and Marianas

The operation against the Marianas, codenamed Operation Forager, involved the largest amphibious invasion in the Pacific Theater to date. Another unusual feature of the operation lay in the close cooperation of US Marine Corps (USMC) and US Army units, a fact reflected in the force's name, the Joint Expeditionary Force. This arrangement led to bitter inter-service rivalry, much of it traceable to USMC General Holland "Howlin' Mad" Smith – whose trouble-making lost him command of the subsequent invasion of Okinawa.

Smith

The Americans set a D-Day of June 15, 1944 for Saipan, but not for the other two islands' landing dates – "J-Day" for Tinian and "W-Day" for Guam. Though this fell within the wet season of the southern Marianas' generally mild climate, the rain would not peak until August, providing an urgent timetable for the Americans to observe. Lingering over the conquest might also expose the supporting fleet to the danger of typhoons.

Estimating the number of defenders at 18,000 rather than the actual 30,000, the Americans committed 66,779 troops to the push against Saipan. The Joint Expeditionary Force assembled in Hawaii prior to moving to Eniwetok for the jump-off to the Marianas. The Landing Ship – Tank (LST) group left first due to the slow speed of the vessels, departing Hawaii on May 25th. Troop transports packed with Marines and Army National Guard soldiers began sailing from Hawaii four days later on May 29th, with the last transports launching the following day. The ships of Task Force 58 steamed out of Majuro in the Marshall Islands in support.

American warships arrived off the Marianas first and launched heavy attacks against Saipan and Tinian, in the form of both naval bombardment by destroyers, cruisers, and battleships, and massive carrier aircraft strikes against airfields and installations. F6F Hellcats also located Japanese convoys, both attempting to escape the islands and trying to slip in with supplies. The American pilots attacked, sending over a dozen ships, totaling more than 30,000 tons, to the bottom.

On the afternoon of June 11th, 15 American aircraft carriers of Task Force 58 launched 225 Grumman F6F Hellcat fighters against the three islands. Out of the aircraft the Japanese managed to scramble in defense, the tough, burly-looking F6Fs shot down 89, while suffering only 11 losses in return. The Hellcats also destroyed 29 Japanese aircraft on the ground. A man from the Japanese 9th Tank Regiment on Saipan, Matsuya Tokuzo, described the American air superiority: "At a little after 1300, I was awakened by the air raid alarm […] Scores of enemy Grumman fighters began strafing and bombing Aslito Airfield and Garapan. For about two hours, the enemy planes ran amuck and finally left leisurely amidst the unbelievably inaccurate anti-aircraft fire. All we could do was watch helplessly." (Denfeld, 1997, 46).

216 carrier aircraft came on June 12th, along with waves of B-24 bombers, which bombed gun emplacements, anti-aircraft batteries, and airfields on the three target islands on June 13th and 14th also. Some aircraft also dropped white phosphorous and the new, experimental napalm bombs on the numerous sugar cane fields in the southern area of Saipan. The Americans hoped to burn off the cane to deny the Japanese cover during the coming invasion, but most of the fields remained intact, the green cane and the rainy, moist conditions preventing widespread fires.

Seven fast USN battleships arrived on June 13th and began a shore bombardment with their heavy guns. Though the Japanese found the shelling alarming, with seasoned soldiers put into a mood of samurai fatalism and recruits terrified, the fire did little damage. The training of the fast battleship gunners emphasized firing on rapidly moving targets, rendering them poorly suited to attacking fixed positions. Additionally, the Navy forbade the ships from approaching the coast nearer than five nautical miles lest they run afoul of mines. Firing at such a distance rendered the guns even more inaccurate.

On June 14th, several old battleships, plus 11 cruisers and 27 destroyers, arrived off the southern Marianas and launched a furious bombardment. With minesweepers confirming the absence of mines in the waters off Saipan and Tinian, the USN ships moved in closer and successfully pulverized numerous machine gun positions and anti-aircraft batteries. However, as one Captain Shimamura later reported, "Beach positions withstood four days of bombardment. Those observation posts and gun emplacements that were protected by splinter-proof shelters were able to withstand the bombardment. Dummy positions proved very effective. […] Communication lines were cut frequently, and the need for repair and messengers was great."

(Crowl, 1994, 76).

On the night of the 14th, immediately before the landings, Underwater Demolition Teams 5, 6, and 7, each consisting of 16 officers and 80 enlisted men, scouted the approaches to the landing beaches on Saipan's southwest coast. The frogmen successfully reconnoitered the approaches, confirming the lack of mines and obstacles. Working rapidly and skillfully, these forerunners of the Navy SEALs dynamited gaps in the reef to admit DUKW amphibious trucks and marked out tank routes with buoys. However, the Japanese spotted UDT 7 and opened fire before they could complete their task, killing four men, wounding seven more, and compelling the rest to retreat.

In the early morning of June 15th, a gigantic convoy of troop transports and LSTs (Landing Ship – Tank) sailed past the southern coast of Saipan and took up positions off the island's southwest beaches. Crammed onto these vessels, the men of the 2nd Marine Division and the 4th Marine Division watched the colors of dawn spread behind the blunt 1,554-foot limestone cone of Mount Tapochau.

A picture of the transports heading for the shore

Fire splotched the black outline of Saipan's shore where white phosphorous shells had ignited targets, and clouds of smoke and dust rose murkily against the dawn. Light trade winds blew from the northeast, partly alleviating the sticky warmth of the 83 Fahrenheit morning. At 5:30 AM, two battleships, a pair of cruisers, and seven destroyers began hammering the beach in preparation for the assault.

While the Japanese command brushed off this preparatory bombardment in a rather blasé manner, the ordinary Japanese troops found it harrowing. A shell plunged into a fuel and ammunition dump, setting off a series of violent, fiery detonations. At least one Japanese officer steadied his nerves, according to his diary, by swigging at a quart bottle of alcohol during the shelling.

At 7 AM, 34 LSTs swung into line abreast nearly three miles offshore and anchored. Opening their bow doors and lowering their ramps, these vessels disgorged 719 amphibious tractors and tanks, many filled with Marines from the assault battalions. A second line of 12 LSTs formed further offshore, preparing to launch DUKWs with light artillery pieces and their crews on board. Further out lay two dock landing ships filled with LCMs that would bring non-amphibious tanks and other vehicles ashore, and beyond them, close to six miles out, a line of troop transports. The ships ceased fire and a mix of carrier aircraft and bombers took their turn, pummeling Saipan's defenders for half an hour. After these airstrikes, the naval bombardment recommenced.

As the huge flotilla of amphibious vehicles moved forward in unison at 8:40 AM – a postponement of almost an hour due to deployment problems – several battalions from the USMC 2nd Division circled in the ocean off the town of Garapan, serving as a feint. Though the Japanese believed it a diversion, they left considerable numbers of troops in place at Garapan nevertheless, removing them from the following struggle.

In fact, all the landings occurred south of Garapan. The 2nd Division landed north of Afetna Point, on Green and Red beaches, while the 4th division's beaches, Blue and Yellow, lay south of the Point. Though the Japanese opened fire with artillery and mortars as soon as the amphibious vehicles advanced over the fringing reefs, only three vehicles failed to reach shore, and of those only one suffered a direct hit from a Japanese weapon.

A picture of American soldiers coming ashore

American soldiers on Red Beach

The Marines managed to put 8,000 men ashore in just 20 minutes, though this caused congestion problems, particularly in the north, where the terrain severely hampered the tractors and tanks from moving inland. In the south, the somewhat easier terrain enabled the 4th Marine Division to push forward hundreds of yards into the interior. All the while, the Japanese maintained heavy fire against the beachheads with light artillery and mortars from the high ground inland, cutting down Marines by the score. Though the tanks returned fire and the destroyers and cruisers offshore directed deadly fire at the Japanese positions, their aim now greatly assisted by forward observers, shells burst constantly among the Marines up and down the beaches.

Moreover, Japanese infantry also provided a dogged defense. IJA riflemen and machine-gunners stubbornly contested every yard of territory, even on the beach, from spider-holes, camouflaged trenches, and even from behind small piles of coral. The incessant roar of combat rolled along the beach front, blending the chatter of machine guns, the crack of rifles, the crash of shells, and the thunderous reports of American tank guns firing inland. The freight-train howl of 14 and 16 inch shells from the ships, passing overhead, only added to the din.

The Marines fought their way tenaciously inland, but much slower than projected. Over the course of the day, 2,000 men on the American side suffered wounds or died, approximately 25% of the initial assault force, though reinforcements continued coming ashore all day long through the increasingly heavy surf. Only a few scattered battalions pushed forward to the 1,000 yard 0-1 Line designated for the first day's advance, and the USMC commanders ordered these units pulled back to establish a firmer perimeter at 600 yards from the waterline.

With the Japanese fleet reported on the move from Mawi Mawi to attack the Marianas expeditionary force, Admiral Raymond A. Spruance ordered the Army National Guard 27th Division close inshore to Saipan. Lieutenant General Holland "Howlin' Mad" Smith also wanted the 27th available in consideration of the powerful resistance offered by the Japanese.

Spruance

As the transports moved close to Saipan early on June 16th, First Lieutenant George O'Donnell witnessed a spectacular sight: "It was the huge explosion of a Jap aviation gas dump. The flames seemed to leap about 10,000 feet in the air, and to burn instantaneously. About ten seconds later we heard the report; it almost knocked us off our feet." (O'Brien, 2003, 85).

The Japanese still hoped to throw the Marines back into the sea on the first night, and as they did throughout the war, the Emperor's soldiers preferred nighttime as moment for their counterattacks. Units of the Japanese 31st Army struck south along the road from Garapan against the USMC 2nd Division's left flank. Tanks rolled forward through the dark, supported by swarms of Japanese infantry. However, the Japanese threw away any element of surprise they might have gained through their nocturnal advance by screaming furiously and blowing bugles loudly as they moved forward.

The Marines had only 75mm pack howitzers ashore in this area, but a quick radio signal to the destroyers offshore brought tremendous fire support to bear. The destroyers fired star shells over the action to provide both their gunners and the Marine marksmen a clear view of the attacking 135th Regiment. The Japanese unit's official account stated that "as soon as the night attack units go forward, the enemy points out targets by using the large star shells which practically turn night into day. Thus the maneuvering of units is extremely difficult." (Denfeld, 1997,54). Indeed, the Marine riflemen and machine gunners, along with the destroyer crews, shot the attacking force to pieces. By the time the remnants pulled back, 700 Japanese troops lay dead in front of the Marine positions. One group slipped through to the 2nd Division's headquarters, but most of them quickly died amid rifle fire and a tank sweep.

The Japanese attempted counterattacks and infiltrations at other areas along the line on the night of June 15th-16th. All came to grief, including one during which the Japanese drove women and children ahead of them to simulate a surrender. This maneuver got the Japanese soldiers quite close to the Marine positions before the men spotted armed IJA troops just behind the civilian human shields and found themselves forced to open fire.

On the following day, the Marines resumed their advance. Lieutenant General Saito Yoshitsugo had committed only part of his available forces to the counterattacks, hoping to conserve men, but in fact lost most of the attack parties while accomplishing nothing. Now the Japanese found their 75mm and 150mm guns on the high ground in danger of being overrun, due to their complete lack of suitable vehicles to move them.

Yoshitsugo

The Americans spent much of June 16th strengthening their beachhead, bringing the rest of the Marine division strength ashore. That night, General Saito sent 37 tanks of the Japanese 9th Tank Regiment and 1,000 infantry of the 135th Infantry Regiment forward in an attack aimed at the USMC radio station. The chaotic advance of this force, which simply rushed forward in disorder in the radio station's general direction, quickly drew a storm of fire. Once again picked out by star shells, the incompetently led Japanese suffered tremendous losses, including many of the tanks (though probably less than the two dozen vehicles claimed by the Marines). On top of that, Japanese attempts to reinforce Saipan from the other Marianas failed, with only a handful of men getting through.

On June 17th, the Marines pushed forward strongly, doubling the size of their beachhead and taking the high ground immediately inland from which considerable Japanese artillery fire had come. Early in the morning of June 18th, 35 barges packed with Japanese infantry sailed from Tanapag Harbor, attempting an amphibious landing against the rear of the Marine positions. However, a group of LCI(G)s, Landing Craft Infantry gunboats modified to carry three 40mm Bofors L/60 autocannons, intercepted this flotilla and sank a number of barges, chasing the survivors back to Tanapag Harbor.

The Marines drove eastward across the island again on June 18th, now strengthened by the 27th Infantry Division. The rugged terrain, with ridges and valleys, the latter choked with thick tangles of vines, delayed the Americans more than Japanese resistance. Nevertheless, by the end of the 18th, Marines and the 165th Infantry reached Magicienne Bay on the east side of Saipan, taking most of the southern third of the island. A force of Japanese found themselves penned on Nafutan Point in Saipan's extreme southeast.

With the situation obviously deteriorating quickly, Prime Minister Tojo in Japan, speaking for the Emperor, sent an encouraging message to Saipan's defenders. The response struck a note of resigned fatalism indicating the mood of the local command: "Have received your honorable Imperial words. By becoming the bulwark of the Pacific with 10,000 deaths we hope to acquire Imperial favor." (Rottman, 2004, 59).

Most of the American forces now wheeled north to conquer the central highlands of Saipan, a formidable obstacle heavily defended by the Japanese. Major General Ralph Smith, commander of the 27th Infantry Division, committed four battalions of his men to reduce the holdouts on Nafutan Point on June 20th, while the rest of his men swung north. However, General "Howlin' Mad" Smith soon diverted all but one of these battaltions northward also, leaving the remaining battalion in a desperate struggle against 1,500 Japanese soldiers over Nafutan Point's nearly impossible terrain.

Smith

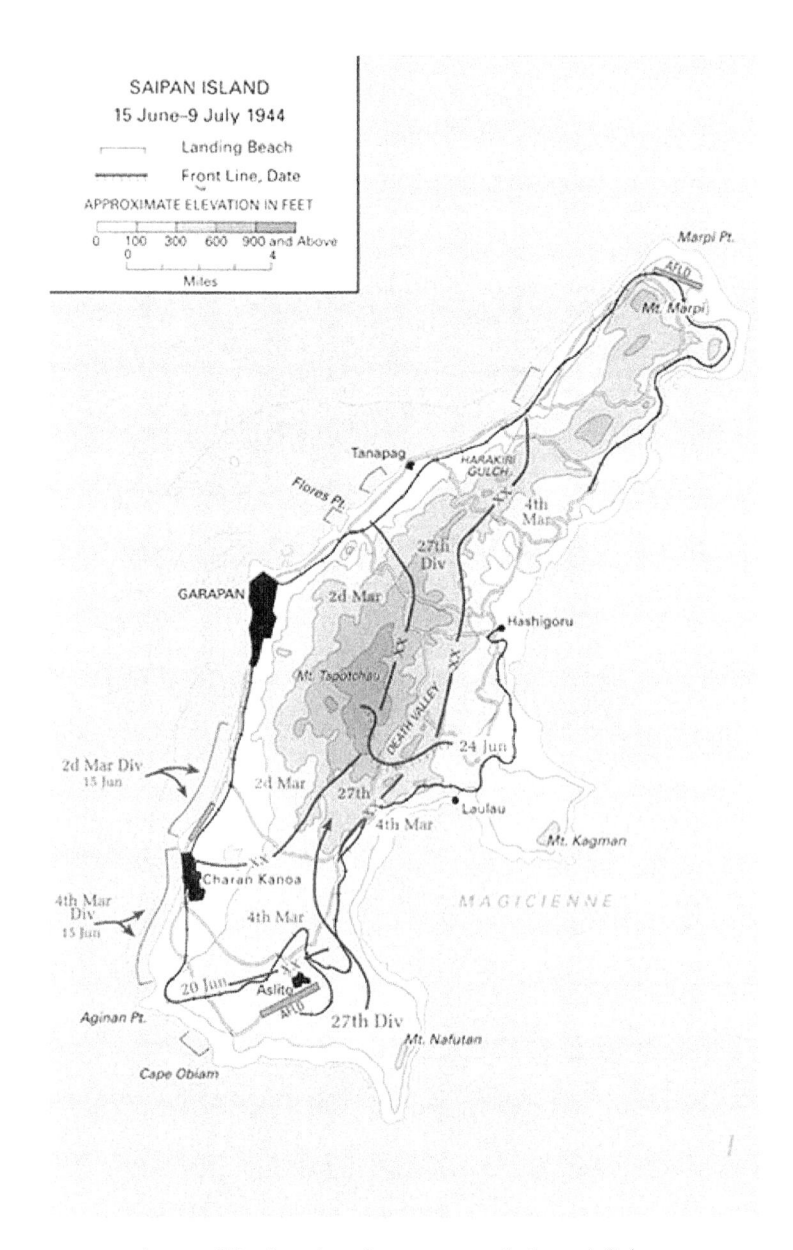

A map of the Americans' progress north through Saipan

While the Americans gathered their forces for a northward push on June 22nd, General Saito deployed his forces to hold the rugged high ground stretching across Saipan's midsection from Garapan in the west to the north end of Magicienne Bay in the east. Mount Tapochau stood at the center of this line, providing commanding views.

The Japanese had lost most of their tanks and a sizable portion of their artillery. Nevertheless, they retained the defiant samurai spirit as the diary of tanker Tokuno Matsuya described: "The fierce attacks of the enemy only increase our hostility. Every man is waiting for the assault with all weapons for close quarters fighting in readiness. We are […] ready for the word to rush forward recklessly into the enemy ranks with our swords in our hands. The only thing that worries me is what will happen to Japan after we die." (Crowl, 1994, 167).

On June 22nd, with 18 battalions of artillery in support, the USMC 2nd Division attacked towards Mount Tapochau, while the 4th Division pushed north along Magicienne Bay. The Marines gained considerable ground on the first day, up to 2,000 yards in places, despite challenging terrain and moderate Japanese resistance. The two divisions moved apart as Saipan widened somewhat, and the 27th Infantry Division occupied the center.

Over the next two days, the Americans continued pushing forward, though more slowly due to extremely difficult landscapes, now including many cliffs. On June 24th, the 2nd Marine Division attacked Garapan and Mount Tapochau, while the 4th Marine Division on the far side of the island pushed into the Kagman Peninsula. The 27th Infantry Division, however, met ferocious Japanese resistance in Death Valley and Purple Heart Ridge. This last combat caused the infamous "Smith vs. Smith" conflict between Generals Howlin' Mad Smith and Ralph Smith.

In Death Valley, the Army men found themselves forced to attack over relatively low ground towards bluffs and cliffs riddled with caves. The Japanese occupied these caves in force, concealing their entrances with brush, and commanded the valley from multiple angles with mortars, machine guns, and 75mm mountain guns. As the Americans pushed forward towards their objective, Japanese on their flanks let them pass, then opened fire against their rear at the same time as a powerful fusillade greeted them in front.

Private John Munka described the typical conditions in Death Valley: "[D]espite our success against the Japanese tanks, our platoon was cut off in the valley and trapped for over three hours, and most of the platoon was wiped out. We were in an open bowl. We were sitting ducks in that bowl. We were pinned down. Finally everyone tried to get out of there and they were cut down. Most of them didn't make it out. Only four or five men of the original thirty-six were not casualties of this battle. We didn't stand a prayer." (Goldberg, 2007, 161-162).

Encountering stiff resistance in Garapan, the Marines leveled it on June 25th with artillery and naval gun fire. Unlike the tough German Fallschirmjager "Green Devils" in the ruins of Monte Cassino on the other side of the world, the Japanese made no attempt to defend the wreckage despite its high defensive value. Artillery and tanks dislodged the Japanese from Mount Tapochau on the same day, while in the east, the 4th Marine Division also overran the central Saipan defenses.

A picture of American soldiers marching through Garapan in early July 1944

"Howlin' Mad" Smith cashiered Ralph Smith for his alleged lack of aggression in Death Valley, replacing him with Major General Sanderford Jarman. Nevertheless, Death Valley and Purple Heart Ridge did not fall until June 30th after nearly a week of hard fighting, thanks to the excellence of the Japanese positions and the terrain obstacles. The tardiness and even cowardice with which Howlin' Mad reproached the Army soldiers actually represented real difficulties in defeating a numerous, fanatically determined enemy in superb defensive positions. Nevertheless, Holland Smith refused to back down from his position, generating immense hostility between the Marines and Army troops – and, indeed, soon added more baseless accusations to his initial attack.

With the American troops now seething with bitter resentment towards each other, the three divisions prepared to finish the job of crushing the Japanese in Saipan's north in early July. "Howlin' Mad" Smith gave the order that supporting artillery be used heavily in this final push, believing that high American casualties resulted from excessive reliance on small arms among his commanders.

When the advance began, the flanking Marine divisions found only scanty resistance, advancing thousands of yards in just a few days in spite of terrain difficulties. The 27th Infantry Division in the center once again met some of the stiffest opposition, but also pushed forward inexorably while the Japanese retreated.

The last organized fighting occurred near Tanapag Village, in areas that acquired the nicknames "Hara-Kiri Gulch" and "the Coconut Grove." General Saito, knowing his forces were doomed, called together as many as possible on July 6th in the so-called "Valley of Hell." The Japanese general, brought to bay and wounded by shrapnel, planned a final suicidal banzai attack against the Americans that night. He made a speech despite his enfeebled condition and had mimeographed copies distributed to every unit. The speech read in part, "Whether we attack or whether we stay where we are, there is only death. However, in death there is life. We must utilize this opportunity to exalt true Japanese manhood. I will advance with those who remain to deliver still another blow to the American Devils, and leave my bones on Saipan as a bulwark of the Pacific. […] Follow me." (Denfeld, 1997,88).

At this point, General Saito and another general, plus two Japanese admirals, committed suicide. No reliable description of their deaths survives, but te most common version states that each man made a small ceremonial cut in his stomach, shouted out a loyal slogan to the Emperor, then died as an adjutant standing behind him blew his brains out with a pistol shot.

Soon after, thousands of frenzied, suicidal Japanese soldiers, many armed only with samurai swords or bayonets tied to the end of poles to make spears, rushed forward towards a gap in the American lines at 4 AM on July 7th. Men from a mixture of infantry regiments, engineer regiments, mountain artillery regiments, and even the 43rd Field Hospital gathered in this essentially leaderless but purposeful swarm. Behind them staggered the patients from the Japanese hospitals, many on crutches, attempting to reach US lines to kill an American and die for the Emperor's glory.

The main weight of the Japanese attack fell upon the 1st and 2nd Battalions of the 105th Infantry. The Japanese flung themselves on the Americans in a flurry of stabbing, slashing, and point-blank gunfights that reduced the Army units to bloody ribbons. Two remaining Japanese tanks led the three-pronged horde. First Lieutenant George O'Donnell, whose G Company held high ground and managed to survive the attack largely undamaged, described the scene in a letter: "It had just finished pouring, and we were all soaked, with our teeth chattering. But, no sooner had we dropped our eyes on that mob, than we forgot all our discomforts! And then, from our right and below us, came thousands of Japs!!! For two hours they passed by, and came right at us! […] We had a hard struggle keeping them from overrunning us, and we had a field day, firing, firing." (O'Brien, 2003, 232-233).

Most of 1st and 2nd Battalions fell under the onslaught after hours of desperate combat, which broke down into clumps of American soldiers falling back towards the beach, fighting hard to stay alive and often failing to do so. The Japanese stabbed their opponents, shot them, literally blew them to pieces with point-blank bursts of heavy machine gun fire, or sliced off their heads or limbs with the blows of samurai swords.

Three light battalions of 27th Infantry Division artillery provided fire support in the form of a frantic bombardment, which rained 2,666 shells on the Japanese in just one hour, or 40 shots per minute. The Japanese burst into Tanapag Village at 8 AM, and a wild melee swayed back and forth through the streets for the next four hours. Finally, at noon, Sherman tanks put in an appearance, smashing the Japanese attack with HE shells and torrents of machine gun fire.

406 men of the 105th Infantry died in the attack, while 512 suffered wounds, including having hands or feet lopped off by katana blows. Once again, Howlin' Mad accused the Army troops of cowardice and incompetence, claiming that only a few hundred Japanese troops had attacked and defeated them, the rest of the bodies resulting from the preparatory bombardment weeks before. In answer to this poisonous canard, the 105th collected and counted the bodies, 4,311 in all. Major General George W. Griner, Jr. toured the battle site and examined around 1,000 Japanese corpses laid out in rows for counting. Griner noted that all the men he saw appeared freshly killed, rather than having decomposed for nearly a month in tropical heat as would be the case with casualties from the preparatory bombardment.

Pictures of Marines fighting on Saipan in July 1944

The main battle for Saipan ended on July 10th, when General Holland Smith declared the island taken. However, one more ghastly drama remained to be played out, this time with the Americans as helpless spectators. As the Americans overran the Japanese positions, they found partially constructed gun emplacements and bunkers, a discovery subsequently made also on Tinian and Guam. Pieces of artillery, usually still wrapped in the packing materials used while transporting them to the islands, stood beside these incomplete installations, providing mute testimony both to the effectiveness of American logistical interception and chaotic local command.

While the American soldiers provided Japanese civilians with water and – when they would accept it – food in the form of C-rations, and generally treated these people humanely, the Marines and Army soldiers abruptly found themselves confronted by the horror of mass suicide at the island's northern end immediately after Saipan fell. The Japanese soldiers frequently killed themselves with grenades, but the civilians also believed that US Marines' induction involved killing their own parents, and that they therefore could not surrender to such barbarous individuals.

The mass suicides took place near Marpi Point on July 10th, while the Americans attempted futilely to intervene. Hundreds of Japanese leaped to their deaths off either Banzai Cliff, 265 feet tall, or the lofty, 800-foot Suicide Cliff. While many struck the rocks rather than the ocean, at such heights the substance on which they landed was practically immaterial. The Golden Gate Bridge, America's favorite bridge for suicides in the early 21st Century, stands 220 feet above the water, but "jumpers" almost always die with their internal organs pulverized by hitting the sea from such a height. Needless to say, an 800-foot leap into water is as lethal as one onto granite.

Some men gathered their families around them in a circle, then detonated a grenade, mowing down the whole group. In one case, an American shot a Japanese man who was in the process of killing a group of children with a knife. The Americans positioned loudspeakers and brought Japanese-speaking soldiers and IJA prisoners alike to assure the Japanese civilians they could surrender with no fear of being harmed. However, for the most part, the chanting Japanese ignored them and continued their orgy of self-destruction. A USMC corpsman, Chester Szech, later reported, "There was not anything the Americans could do about this terrible situation. We had an LST in the water asking them not to jump. We were down below and just sat there and watched them. There were a lot of women and kids. They were Japanese nationals stationed on Saipan and they just committed suicide. They would throw the kids, then the wife would jump and then he would jump." (Goldberg, 2007, 202).

When some people appeared reluctant to jump, nearby Japanese soldiers would throw grenades among them, blowing them to pieces, then leap off the cliffs themselves. Some Japanese walked out into the sea until the water closed over their heads. The mass suicide left the cliff-tops strewn with human body parts, the cliffs themselves streaked with long swatches of blood, and the sea carpeted with bodies.

Some Japanese soldiers swam out to the barrier reefs to make their last stands on these half-submerged ridges of coral. The Americans once again showed willingness to accept their surrender, but, usually met with a defiant hail of rifle and machine-gun fire, fired back and killed the Japanese. On another occasion, as eyewitness Robert Sherrod described, Lieutenant Kenneth Hensley of the 2nd Battalion, 6th Marines encountered the suicidal defiance of the Japanese along those same reefs: "Some Jap soldiers had fled to the reef, several hundred yards offshore. Hensley had taken a detachment of amphibious tractors to fetch them. As the amphtracs approached, one of the Japs, apparently an officer, drew his sword. The six men with him knelt on the coral rocks and the officer started to methodically slice off their heads. Four heads had rolled into the sea before the amphtracs closed in. Then the officer, sword in hand, charged the amphtracs. Hensley's men turned their machine guns on him." (Sherrod, 1945, 148).

Nevertheless, the Americans took a remarkable number of prisoners by Pacific Theater standards, perhaps indicating a notable percentage of unwilling conscripts among the Japanese. 17 officers and 904 enlisted men yielded to the Americans during the initial liberation of Saipan, often in exchange for water. Thousands of civilians also surrendered, once again frequently after being given water.

A picture of a Marine trying to convince Japanese civilians to surrender

Thousands of other Japanese soldiers, however, chose to hold out to the last in caves or spider-holes, sniping at the Marines and Army troops until killed with grenades or flamethrowers, or simply shot.

The Japanese unwillingness to surrender and determination to die made Saipan and the other islands perilous even after the Americans technically conquered them. A few days after the liberation of Saipan, 2nd Lieutenant Joseph Meighan of the 105th led a squad of men along a narrow trail traversing the Kagman Peninsula, sweeping the area for hidden Japanese: "A comrade and I were talking. […] just as he was about to turn his head to respond, a purple hole appeared in the center of his forehead. His eyes glazed in death before his body collapsed to the ground. About ten yards to our front center was a patch of camouflage. We […] fired into the camouflage and it yielded two Japs." (O'Brien, 2003, 315).

The 27th Infantry Division remained on Saipan from July 10th to October 4th. During that time they killed 2,000 Japanese soldiers and took 3,000 more civilians alive. The replacement unit, the 24th Infantry Division, continued rooting out Japanese through the end of the war, capturing or killing some 700 more. On Mount Tapotchau, 350 soldiers under Captain Oba Sakai held out until December 1945, when Oba and his last 46 men laid down their arms at the urging of Japanese officers brought to Saipan for that purpose.

While the battle for Saipan raged, Vice Admiral Ozawa Jisaburo – who earlier commanded Japanese forces during the abortive Aleutian Islands Campaign, when Americans and Japanese fought desperately for the bitterly cold islands off Alaska's coast – sallied with a fleet of 90 warships to try to destroy the American transports and other vital ships. Such a blow might have delayed the conquest of the Marianas by months, and could have resulted in the deaths of tens of thousands of Marines and Army troops, if it was not aggressively countered.

Ozawa

Admiral Raymond A. Spruance led the USN Fifth Fleet to intercept Ozawa's armada, mustering 129 ships against the Japanese 90. The resulting carrier battle took place on June 19th and 20th, with most of the action consisting of aerial combat and airstrikes on ships, while no actual ship-to-ship naval gunfire occurred.

American submarines sank two of the Japanese carriers in the thick of the action, at the same time that the capital ships sent out aircraft to attack the American fleet. USS *Albacore*, a *Gato*-class submarine skippered by James Blanchard, managed to hit the huge, new Japanese aircraft carrier *Taiho* with one torpedo out of a spread of six. Though the damage seemed initially light, the Japanese bungled damage control efforts profoundly, leading to the loss of the carrier, which also happened to be Ozawa's flagship.

The *Taiho*

The USS *Cavalla*, another *Gato*-class sub, torpedoed the veteran carrier *Shokaku*, leading to gasoline fume leakage which caused the carrier to detonate catastrophically. Grumman TBF Avengers managed to use aerial torpedoes to trigger a fatal explosion on board a third carrier, the *Hiyo*, before returning to the USS *Belleau Wood*.

The *Cavalla*

Besides these losses, the tough, deadly Grumman F6F Hellcats swept the sky of Japanese aircraft, destroying them by the hundred for relatively light losses. Hellcat ace Lieutenant Alexander Vraciu described some of the action, referring to a Japanese plane as a "meatball" due to its round, red recognition symbol: "The enemy planes had been pretty well chopped down, but a substantial number remained. […] The sky appeared full of smoke and pieces of planes, and we were trying to ride herd on the remainder to keep them from scattering. Another meatball broke formation ahead, and I slid onto his tail […] I gave him a short burst, but it was enough […] the burning plane twisted crazily out of control." (Tillman, 1994, 21).

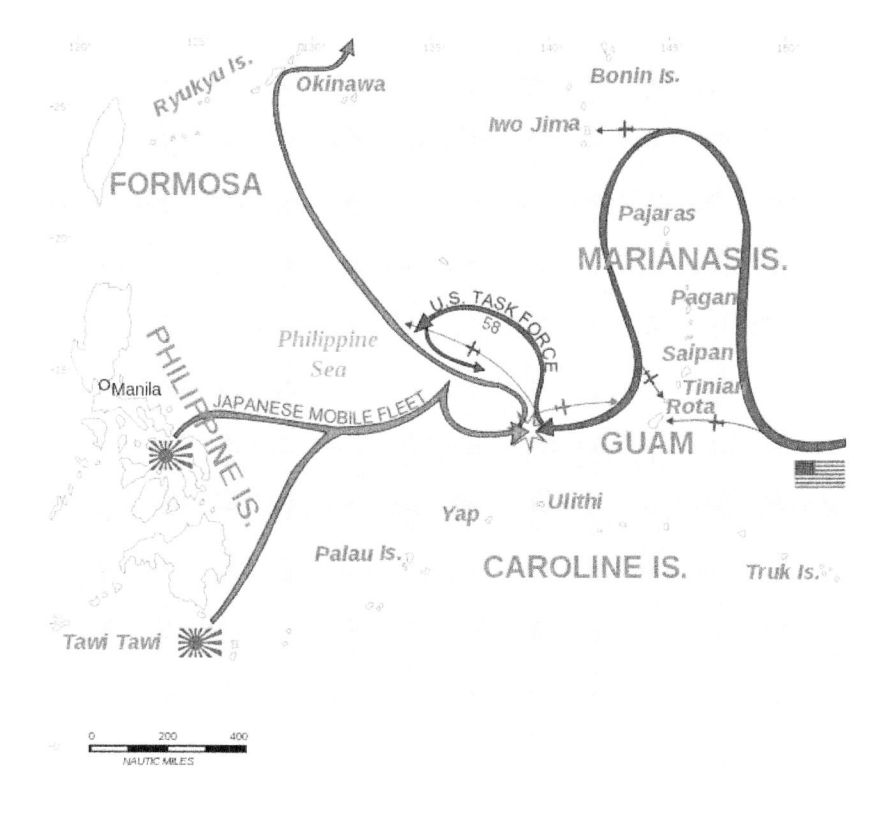

A map of the battle

With three of their carriers sunk and their aircraft swept relentlessly from the sky by the Hellcat pilots, the Japanese eventually retreated. Ozawa fell back under cover of darkness, allowing him to break off relatively cleanly despite American pursuit.

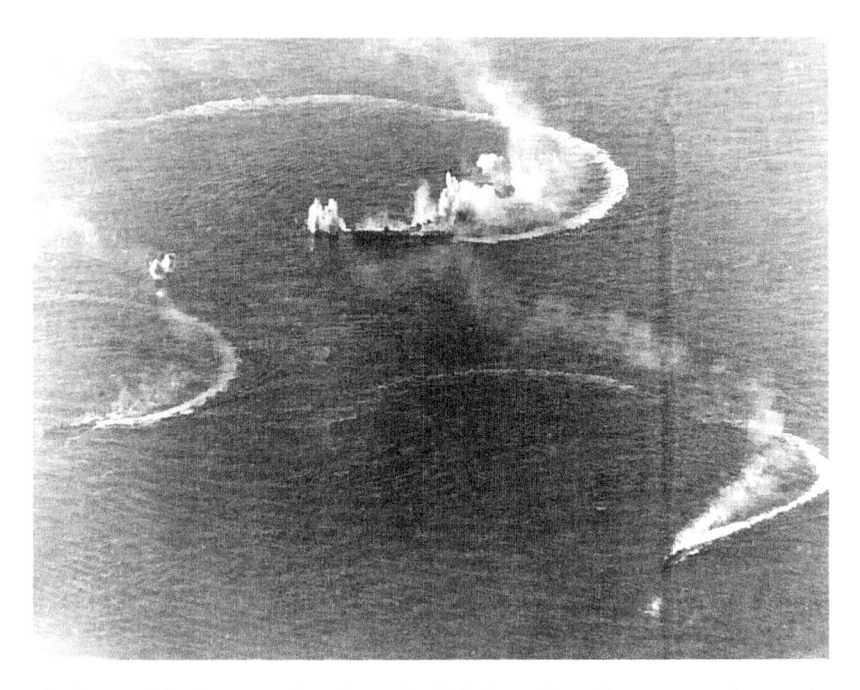

A picture of the Japanese aircraft carrier *Zuikaku* and two destroyers under attack during the battle

The Battle of the Philippine Sea gained its memorable historical nickname of the Great Marianas Turkey Shoot thanks to Lieutenant (junior grade) Zeigel "Ziggy" Neff, a farmer's son from Missouri. Upon returning to the USS *Lexington* after shooting down four Japanese aircraft, Ziggy told the debriefing officer that the battle resembled "an old-time turkey shoot" (Tillman, 1994, 28). His phrase traveled up the chain of command and eventually entered the history books.

Picture of a Grumman F6F-3 fighter landing aboard the *Lexington*

Nicknames aside, the Battle of the Philippine Sea not only ensured that the landings on Saipan went unopposed by the Imperial Japanese Navy (IJN) but also proved a decisive factor in the later stages of the war. The Americans sank three of Japan's irreplaceable fleet carriers, two by submarine action and one via aircraft attacks. Even worse, from a Japanese point of view, they lost between 550 and 645 aircraft, most of them taking their veteran pilots to their deaths, during the "Turkey Shoot" phase of the battle. This eliminated 92% of the fleet's carrier aircraft and 72% of its floatplanes, while the battle also wiped out most of Guam's air strength. For the rest of the war, the Japanese relied ever more heavily upon green pilots with very little training, increasing the frequency of kamikaze attacks and giving the Americans, with their highly skilled, trained pilots and excellent aircraft, decisive air superiority. American combat losses at the Great Marianas Turkey Shoot numbered 42 aircraft.

A picture of Marines coming ashore on Tinian

With Saipan taken and the Japanese fleet defeated once again at the Great Marianas Turkey Shoot, the Americans turned next to the liberation of Tinian, the second of the Mariana Islands on their agenda. Tinian lies just three miles south of Saipan, enabling M1 155mm Long Tom field artillery pieces in southern Saipan to batter Japanese positions on Tinian, using their 13-mile range.

Originally set with stunning optimism for June 18th, J-Day (the invasion date for Tinian) soon moved to the more realistic July 24th. Furthermore, despite having sustained 1,363 KIA and 10,419 wounded on Saipan and other recent assaults, the 2nd and 4th Marine Divisions found themselves earmarked for the Tinian invasion also. Each of the battle-weary divisions received approximately 850 replacement troops on July 11th, leaving the average battalion at roughly 60% strength. The 4th Division, intended to go ashore first on Tinian, received an extremely large vehicle complement to offset their reduced personnel complement, including seven battalions of amphibious tractors (one battalion armored), 68 amphibious tanks, 150 DUKWs, and assorted artillery.

Choosing the attack site on Tinian proved somewhat difficult at first due to its topography.

Though the island possesses a mostly flat surface, at the time it was covered with enormous fields of sugar cane, and cliffs fringe the majority of the coastline. These lava and coral cliffs range from 3-10 feet in the north to 150 feet high in the south. Two eminences loomed over the landscape – Mount Lasso, 500 feet tall, and a nameless ridge that was 580 feet high.

To add to the difficulty, beaches existed at only three points on the island. The largest beaches fronted on the capital of Tinian Town in the southwest, in Sunharon Bay. Though topographically the best choice for landings, the Japanese had set up large quantities of heavy artillery to sweep these beaches. The Marines landing there would even face ordnance as heavy as captured British 6-inch guns capable of annihilating most landing craft with a single hit, and 23 pillboxes defended the 400-yard wide Asiga Bay on the island's east coast. The Japanese also mined the approaches and strung barbed wire obstacles on the beach. This left only two very narrow beaches, White 1 and 2, in the northwest – 60 and 160 yards wide respectively.

Command remained dubious of the utility of these beaches until Captain Merwin Silverthorn and the men of Company A, Amphibious Reconnaissance Battalion checked the beaches on July 11th. The commanders expressed continued skepticism at Silverthorn's debriefing, leading to the peppery captain barking, "They were as flat as a billiard table!" (Meyers, 2004, 9). This convinced Admirals Raymond Spruance and Richmond "Terrible" Turner to approve use of the two beaches.

Turner

    Beginning at 5:57 AM on J-Day, the 2nd Marine Division made a series of threatening demonstrations against Tinian Town itself, prompting the Japanese to move reinforcements to repel a possible attack in Sunharon Bay. This unit, known as the Demonstration Group, launched two assault waves of LVTs, which made a show of advancing on the shore before turning back as though frightened off by Japanese firepower.

    The Japanese guns did not, in fact, hit the LVTs, but they did score a number of hits on the supporting USN ships, starting fires and killing men. In some cases, only the personal heroism of ordinary sailors aboard the ships averted potential disaster from these hits. On board the USS *Colorado*, Gunners' mate 2/C Albert Daniel Stredney eventually received the Navy cross for "fearlessly and unhesitatingly assisting in tearing open blazing ammunition ready boxes fired by enemy shelling. Stredney aided in extinguishing the flames, thereby preventing a serious explosion which undoubtedly would have killed many men and damaged his ship. Prompt and decisive in his actions and courageous while under enemy fire, Stredney contributed materially to the safety of his ship and to her successful participation in the assault." (Prefer, 2012, 70).

The 2nd Division kept up this pretense for four and a quarter hours before finally pulling back, at which point Tinian's defenders sent a triumphant message to Tokyo that they had defeated an American attack. Simultaneously, the 155mm Long Tom batteries in southern Saipan fired smoke shells at Mount Lasso, wrapping the peak in gray-white billows of smoke. Blinded by this smoke, Japanese observers did not see the LVTs full of Marines deploy from their LSTs and move inshore towards White Beaches 1 and 2, under cover of naval gunfire.

When the Marines reached the shore, the first battalions encountered a skeleton guard force of Japanese, but no serious resistance. They also found some mines, but the Japanese had neglected these and deterioration had rendered them inert. LVT(2) amtracs laid seven cliff ramps on the low cliffs flanking the White Beaches, effectively widening the practicable frontage of each – a plan devised by USN Captain and Seabee Paul Halloran. These ramps considerably quickened the exit of men and machines from the beaches.

Within 40 minutes, the Marines had a battalion ashore at each White Beach. The initial wave of "leathernecks" at White 2 bypassed a pair of Japanese pillboxes, which following troops rooted out swiftly and efficiently. Moving ashore with well-oiled professionalism, and facing only weak Japanese resistance, the Marines managed to land 15,614 men on Tinian by nightfall on J-Day, plus artillery. The total cost stood at just 15 men killed and 224 more wounded. With only feeble Japanese resistance, the Marines carved out a mile-deep beachhead on the first day, which they reinforced with barbed wire before waiting the inevitable night attacks.

Colonel Ogata Takashi, by now well aware of the actual American landing site, planned his counterstroke more carefully than had often been the case on Saipan. The Tinian defenders carefully probed the Marine lines with reconnaissance parties, building a clear picture of the defense for Ogata. The Japanese leader planned attacks from three directions, north (by IJN personnel from Ushi Airfield), east (at the junction between the 24th and 25th Marine Regiments), and south up the coastal road, with a force led by 5 tanks.

The Marines thwarted Ogata's plan through alertness and vigorous application of firepower. The 600 men working their way along the north coast met a powerful fusillade of weapons fire as soon as an alert Marine spotted them flitting through the night. Though they pressed the attack, the Japanese naval personnel finally fled, leaving 476 KIA behind, when the Americans counterattacked at dawn with Sherman tanks.

Marine observation posts detected the center attack grouping up two hours before its advance, ensuring the Americans could prepare thoroughly for the Japanese. Nevertheless, approximately 200 Japanese rushed through a gap in the line and ran amok in the rear briefly. Half of these infiltrators died attacking Marines defending the unit's howitzers, while Marine riflemen hunted down the rest.

The final group, attacking from the south, placed the five tanks in the lead, half of the armored vehicles available to Ogata. As the attacking column approached, star shells from the USN ships offshore burst overhead, brilliantly illuminating the men and machines. A sharp battle ensued in which USMC halftracks armed with 75mm guns engaged the Japanese tanks before bazooka teams closed to finish them off.

The Americans shredded Ogata's counterattacks despite the frenzied bravery of the Japanese soldiers. The Marines coolly stood their ground and contained every assault, losing just 100 wounded or killed against the 1,241 Japanese KIA. The action destroyed several Japanese units entirely, demoralizing the IJA men and bolstering the mood of the Marines.

A picture of Marines checking out a disabled Japanese tank

On July 25th, the amtracs carrying the Marine 2nd Division rolled ashore in waves, vastly reinforcing the American units on Tinian. Japanese artillery fire proved too inaccurate to knock out even a single amtrac. The "leathernecks" advanced east and south, encountering a Japanese delaying force in the caves and ravines of Mount Maga, slightly more than a mile from the White Beaches. Scarcely pausing in their advance, the Marines saturated Mount Maga with every type of ordnance available, from naval gunfire to tank guns firing HE shells, mortars, and strafing by carrier aircraft. With endless lethal blasts rippling over the eminence, the Japanese swiftly abandoned the position to flee south. One captured Japanese soldier remarked ruefully, "You couldn't drop a stick without bringing down artillery." (Crowl, 1994, 299).

Ogata, displaying the sudden fatalism that often overtook Japanese commanders after their first reverse, ordered two key positions abandoned. The Japanese left Ushi Airfield essentially undamaged, providing the Americans with the installation from which the Enola Gay and Bockscar would rise into the sky to drop nuclear bombs on Hiroshima and Nagasaki. He also ordered his men to abandon Mount Lasso, despite its superb defensive characteristics, including numerous caves with a commanding view of the American approach.

Throughout late July the Americans moved swiftly and steadily south, expertly breaking pockets of Japanese resistance. The defense collapsed as the remaining Japanese crowded the 580 foot ridge in Tinian's south, occupying its many caves and gullies. The Marines launched a land-side attack on Tinian Town on July 30th. A few Japanese gun crews had moved their anti-ship artillery to face inland and fired at the approaching Americans, but Sherman tanks moved up to blow the guns and their crews to pieces.

A picture of Marines conducting mop up operations

The Marines opened their assault on Ogata's ridge and plateau stronghold on July 31st. Though Shermans managed to knock out the Japanese antitank guns and mow their crews down with machine gun fire, the Japanese successfully threw back the first Marine attempts to scale the cliffs and assault Ogata's natural fortress. However, late in the day, a company of 8th Marines managed to establish a position on top of the plateau.

Ogata hurled his men at this foothold twice during the night, each time expecting his banzai attackers to overwhelm and butcher the Marines. However, both times, illumination proved key to holding the position. PFC Richard Watkins described how the use of mortar-fired flares deprived the Japanese effectively of the cover of darkness: "Late in the night, one of the light machine guns on our left flank opened up with a throaty roar. We could not see what they were firing at […] [A]long about three in the morning we could hear some enemy activity to our front and to the right of our position. The corporal called for a flare. The mortar platoon responded with a flare deep in enemy territory. In the silhouette we could see enemy troops." (Prefer, 2012, 149). The Marines, holding steady against the rushes of their more numerous opponents, cut down the majority of both attack forces with rifle, machine gun, and 37mm canister rounds.

The Marines expanded their presence on the plateau on August 1st, 2nd, and 3rd. Their presence prevented organized Japanese resistance, isolating individuals and squads in their caves. Two night attacks occurred on the nights of August 1st-2nd and 2nd-3rd, the latter involving 150 men. According to Japanese prisoners, Colonel Ogata died in the second banzai attack, shot down by a machine gun and left folded over a coil of barbed wire. The Americans never identified his body, a burial party placing him anonymously in a mass grave after the onslaught. Meanwhile, many Japanese holdouts remained in caves riddling the nameless ridge at Tinian's southern end. The Americans deployed Jeeps with loudspeakers, rather amusingly resembling gigantic versions of a gramophone horn, to broadcast the message in Japanese that those who surrendered would not be harmed.

Large numbers of civilians emerged from their shelters to surrender, and a few soldiers joined them, but the rest of the remaining soldiers chose to kill themselves, often by leaping over the cliffs into the sea or hiding in their caves until the Americans dynamited the entrances shut. Almost a thousand more eluded immediate capture, continuing to snipe at the American occupation troops for months. Over half of these Japanese holdouts died until the rest eventually surrendered.

The Americans' rapid conquest of Tinian cost them 389 men killed and 1,816 wounded. The Japanese, by contrast, lost 652 prisoners and approximately 8,000 killed. General Holland "Howlin' Mad" Smith declared himself pleased at the results, but the battle was still raging on Guam, with an additional week of fighting before the southern Marianas fell completely into American hands.

The large island of Guam, lying approximately 100 miles south of Saipan, appeared even more formidable. Measuring 210 square miles in extent, the island features similar fringing reefs and a more tropical climate, leading to extremely dense, lush jungle vegetation in areas not under cultivation. Additionally, the topography provided only 15 miles of western coastline, centered on Orote Peninsula, suitable for amphibious landings. 600 foot cliffs towered out of the sea at the island's northern end, while heavy surf battered the lower cliffs in the south and east, making landings there fatally dangerous.

With no equivalent to the poorly guarded "White Beach 1 and 2" on Tinian, both the Americans and Japanese knew the general location where the invading army would come ashore. With W-Day changed to July 21st, the Guam operation occurred simultaneously with the Tinian invasion and therefore involved different American units. The 3rd Marine Division and the attached 1st Marine Provisional Brigade, selected to spearhead the invasion of Guam, underwent remarkable hardships due to the postponement of W-Day. The men lived aboard their transports for 52 days, where, as an official historian remarked, "The tropical sun beating down on the steel decks turned the troop compartments into infernos. Sleeping proved difficult if not impossible, and a much sought after privilege was bedding "topside" under the night sky. Heat rash prevailed but the opportunity to eat good food, including fresh meat offset the discomfort caused by the skin irritation." (Gailey, 1997, 77).

Major General Roy Geiger commanded the 3rd Marine Division and other Marine units attached to it, while Major General Andrew Bruce led the 77th Infantry Division, intended to come ashore on the heels of the 3rd to help secure Guam. Opposing them, General Takashina Takeshi and General Obata Hideyoshi headed the defensive force of 18,657 men, soon to be matched against the Americans' 59,401 soldiers.

Geiger

Takeshi

Obata

With fairly good intelligence about Japanese dispositions on Guam both from aerial photography and from documents captured on Saipan, the Americans began a systematic bombardment of the island starting on July 8th. The constant hammering by airstrikes, bombing, and naval bombardment went on day and night, fraying the nerves of even the resolute Japanese. Most exposed gun positions suffered annihilation, though camouflaged positions such as pillboxes and cave batteries mostly survived.

A picture of American ships bombarding Guam

However, in order to survive, these guns had to hold their fire until the moment the invading force came ashore. The Japanese erected fake guns with wooden barrels in an effort to divert American fire away from actual emplacements. The weeks of attacks only killed approximately 100 men, making materiel losses much higher than personnel.

Despite the bombardment, some of the Japanese eagerly awaited the opportunity to test their mettle against the hated Americans, as in the case of Lieutenant Imanishi, whose diary stated, "We think that at last the enemy will land tonight, and so we will observe strict alert all night. We were issued hand grenades and are now waiting for the enemy to come. [...] If the enemy is coming, let him come. The spirit to fight to the death is high. We are anxiously waiting but nothing unusual has happened so far as dawn breaks." (Crowl, 1994, 321).

In the days immediately prior to the invasion, the Underwater Demolition Team (UDT) frogmen worked tirelessly to prepare the way to the two planned landing beaches, Asan Beach and Agat Beach. These dedicated teams began their work on July 14th, first thoroughly reconnoitering and mapping the approaches for three days.

Beginning on the 17th, under cover of smoke screens laid by the bombarding ships, the frogmen blasted holes in the coral reefs at key points and set about clearing Japanese obstacles. The UDT men destroyed approximately 1,000 obstacles, which took the form of either large palm log enclosures filled with coral or square wire cages packed with coral and cement. Remarkably, the teams lost only one man killed in these operations.

The American invasion force moved into place on the night of July 20th-21st, with a massive preparatory shore bombardment at 5:30 AM on the morning of the 21st. The outpouring of naval gunfire, rockets, and bombing dwarfed anything the Japanese had yet experienced, sending them rushing to their shelters to wait out the torrents of ordnance pounding the shore.

Finally, the bombardment lifted at 8 AM as the LSTs released swarms of LVT amtracs full of marines and DUKWs carrying artillery pieces, ammunition, fresh water, and supplies. These surged towards the shore under increasingly heavy Japanese fire. Shells plowed into LVTs, smashing the vehicles and setting them alight, while surviving Marines leaped off into the water to swim or wade to shore. Soon burning hulks dotted the coral reefs under the cloudless sky, but the main force pressed on.

A picture of Marines coming ashore

The LVTs disgorged their Marines onto the beaches at 8:30 AM. The heaviest weight of the attack landed on the northern Red, Green, and Blue Beaches – the Asan area, north of the Orote Peninsula. The 1st Marine Provisional Brigade landed here, as did the 3rd, 21st, and 9th Marine regiments. To the south of the Orote Peninsula, the 4th and 22nd Marines landed on the beaches named Yellow 1, Yellow 2, White 1, and White 2, all located in the Agat area.

When the first Marines rushed up the beach to take shelter and return the defenders' fire, they made an unusual discovery. The UDT frogmen who prepared the way for the attack reminded the Marines of their role by slipping ashore and nailing a large sign to a prominently located tree. The sign survived the bombardment and greeted the Marines with the message "Welcome Marines! USO that way." (Gailey, 1997, 88).

Working quickly and professionally, the Marine landing craft got the first tanks ashore by 9:10 AM, and almost the entire complement by an hour later. The DUKWs also landed almost all the divisional 75mm pack howitzers and 105mm howitzers before noon, following up with supplies of ammunition, food, fresh water (an important item in the disease-ridden tropics), and light vehicles such as Jeeps and halftracks.

A picture of Marines erecting a flag shortly after coming ashore

Enfiladed from the flanking points and peninsulas, the Marines nevertheless pushed forward to take the first ridge behind the beaches, assisted by tank support. A grueling fight through the thick vegetation brought the Marines to the crest of these ridges, where they established a perimeter for the coming night. They knew from long experience that the Japanese would almost certainly try a heavy counterattack under cover of darkness.

Particularly galling fire came from Chonito Cliff, a formation riddled with caves, each bristling with Japanese light artillery, machine guns, and riflemen. Suffering heavy losses in the process, two companies of the 3rd Marines scaled the cliff, supported by fire from tanks of the 3rd Tank Battalion. The Marines cleared the caves one after another with hand grenades and blasts of flaming liquid from their M1A1 flamethrowers, securing the cliff by noon.

In the south, the Marines smashed their way forward through Japanese strongpoints to the Harman road, then took several small, heavily defended hills swarming with Japanese machine gunners. A Japanese mortar crew scored a direct hit on the Agat area aid station, killing all medics and assistants with one shell, ensuring no more medics came ashore until later in the afternoon.

Brigadier General Lemuel Shepherd, Jr., commanding the Agat force, organized as much of a defense in depth as he could as night approached, also knowing that the Japanese would try infiltration attacks. The heaviest weight of the inevitable nighttime counterattacks fell on Shepherd's men, with only light skirmishing occurring in the north. Colonel Suenaga Tsunetaro led the attack personally, deploying two battalions of the Japanese 38th Infantry Regiment along with a number of tanks. One group evicted the Marines from the low knoll known as Hill 40, then retreated in turn as the Americans launched a determined counterattack. The two sides exchanged control of Hill 40 repeatedly that night, in a seesaw struggle which finally left the Marines in possession of the corpse-strewn eminence at dawn.

Shepherd

Simultaneously, another force struck along the Harmon road towards Agat village. However, these men encountered a Marine roadblock. Sherman tanks and bazooka teams quickly annihilated the poorly armored Japanese tanks, and, after a brisk firefight, the Japanese fell back. Colonel Suenaga himself suffered a wound in the thigh but pressed forward until a Marine rifleman shot him in the chest, killing him outright.

The Japanese showed no tactical finesse, instead attempting to show off their bravery with bizarre, even sophomoric – if lethal – antics, as one Marine described: "Just before the opening of a Banzai attack this Nip jumped to the crest of a ridge above the Marines. 'One, two, three, you can't catch me,' he shouted. Two dozen .30 caliber bullets promptly proved him wrong." (Gailey, 1997, 105).

On July 22nd and 23rd, the Marines consolidated their positions, bringing more men and materiel ashore despite Japanese artillery and mortar fire. The Marines also expanded the area they held against surprisingly light Japanese resistance, taking the commanding heights of Mount

Alifan with barely a shot fired. The Marines who reached the summit found no signs the Japanese had ever been there, despite its superb qualities as an observation point and possibly for defensive artillery.

The 22nd Marines, however, met furious Japanese resistance when they tried to overrun the Orote Peninsula, which still directed enfilading fire against both the northern and southern beaches. Sherman tanks quickly demolished the Japanese light and medium tanks holding a roadblock at the base of the Peninsula, but beyond, Japanese resistance quickly rose to a crescendo. The Japanese mauled the first battalion so badly that Shepherd withdrew it and replaced it with fresh men.

The 77th Infantry Division came ashore on July 22nd and 23rd also, adding to the forces available for operations on July 24th. On the 22nd through the 25th, the Marines and Army troops continued to expand their foothold and carry out the difficult reduction of Japanese defenses on Orote Peninsula. They did not realize that General Takashina busied himself at the same time preparing his last, doomed effort to rout the Americans.

The massive Japanese counterattack on the night of July 25th-26th assumed a bizarre character, as vividly described by Major O.R. Lodge of the USMC. The Japanese prepared for the fight by consuming large quantities of *sake* and beer, making themselves highly intoxicated. This, of course, largely countered the main advantage of a night attack – surprise – and gave the Marines ample time to prepare a fatal welcome: "Marines in the front lines could hear screaming, yelling, laughter, and the breaking of bottles as the Japanese made final arrangements. At times so much clamor could be heard that reports reached the command post that the assault had started. Afterwards someone aptly said that the confusion 'sounded like New Year's Eve in the Zoo.'" (Lodge, 1954, 78).

If not for the drunken uproar, the night would have offered a golden opportunity for genuine surprise. A dense cloud cover lay a few hundred feet above the treetops, pouring down heavy rain for hours and draping Guam in a cloak of utter blackness. The rushing roar of the rain on leaves would have covered the sounds of men moving forward if they had observed even the most basic tenets of stealthy movement.

Nonetheless, just a few minutes before midnight, the Japanese, utterly drunk, poured out of the mangroves of a swamp and surged towards the Marine positions. The Marines subjected the attacking force to a dense curtain of fire, including machine guns, rifles, mortars, 37mm guns firing canister shot, and heavier pieces. Once again, Lodge described the surreal charge: "Led by flag-waving, sword-swinging officers, the enlisted men stumbled forward, carrying everything conceivable. Unsteady hands clutched pitchforks, sticks, ballbats, and pieces of broken bottles, together with the normal infantry weapons. [...] At one time officers brought the fire of the Pack Howitzer Battalion, 22d Marines, to within 35 yards of 3/22's front lines in an attempt to stop the swarming horde. One weapons company lieutenant reported: 'Arms and legs flew like snowflakes. Japs ran amuck. They screamed in terror until they died.'" (Lodge, 1954, 78). Eventually, the survivors of the attack recoiled, fleeing back into the swamps while being pursued by American artillery fire.

   Elsewhere, more Japanese flung themselves at American lines. In one area, the Japanese troops rushed forward shouting in English, "Wake up, American, and die!" The Marines obligingly awakened, though in the main they were not the men who died.

   In some sectors, the Japanese approached so recklessly that the Americans mowed them down without sustaining any casualties of their own. In one place, however, a group of 400 Japanese burst through the lines. Major Lodge described the grotesque scene that followed: "At its height, flares revealed an out-of-this-world picture of Nipponese drunks reeling about in our forward positions, falling into foxholes, tossing aimless grenades here and there, yelling such English phrases as they had managed to pick up, and laughing crazily, to be exterminated in savage close-in fighting." (Lodge, 1954, 78).

   Naturally, this surreal counterattack proved an utter fiasco for the Japanese. Though they inflicted 166 killed and 645 wounded upon the Marines, they lost at least 3,500 men and possibly more, since the pack howitzer shells blew men into jumbled piles of flesh, bones, and severed limbs that made accurate body counts difficult. The suicidal, drunken banzai attack resulted in the erasure of 95% of the sector's commissioned officers, including a general, making organized resistance in the area almost impossible after the incident.

   Following the defeat of the Japanese counterstroke, the Americans began a relentless advance to sweep the island clear of their enemies. Due to the large land area of the island, General Takashina failed to establish any significant defensive lines in the manner of Saipan's defenders. The Americans not only enjoyed numerical superiority but exhibited flexibility, resourcefulness, and determination that the mid-20th century Japanese military mind – varying between hidebound, fatalistic protocol and wild, chaotic, self-destructive aggression – found extremely difficult to counter.

   Following the drunken night attack, the Marines worked their way forward eastward over the next several days, moving cautiously through the thick jungle. Japanese snipers harassed them constantly, and every outcropping seemed to hold Japanese soldiers in caves, where they refused to surrender and continued firing until blasted out with demolition charges, grenades, and flamethrowers.

   Most of the surviving Japanese appeared concentrated in the north of Guam – some 10,000 men, in fact. However, General Geiger worried that his men might be taken in the rear by Japanese lurking in the forested hills of the island's southern third. Accordingly, the 77th Infantry Division sent out five 5-man patrols on July 28th, each accompanied by a local Guamanian guide. The men set out cautiously into the thickly forested hinterlands, but soon realized that very few

Japanese occupied the south of the island.

Guamanian natives encountered during the patrol confirmed that the Japanese had all moved north; only a few stragglers remained to the east or south of the Americans. The Japanese had abandoned most of Guam without a fight. Geiger sent the 1st Marine Provisional Battalion to conduct mop-up operations in the south. By this point the Americans had suffered 513 killed and nearly 10 times as many wounded, but approximately 8,000 Japanese lay dead.

On July 31st, the 77th Infantry Division advanced all the way to the east coast through nearly impassible jungle hills and ridges, slick with mud in heavy tropical rains. This feat won commendation even from "Howlin' Mad" Smith and placed the 77th in position to advance north up Guam's east coast in the sweep just then beginning in earnest.

The Americans encountered numerous emaciated Guamanians as they pushed north, and they shared their rations with them whenever possible. During the first stages of the advance land mines presented a greater danger than the scattered Japanese resistance. Undeterred, the painstaking northward advance began on August 2nd. Both Marines and Army troops pushed forward through extremely dense foliage, tormented by dengue fever carrying mosquitoes and drenched by periodic rains. On August 3rd, the Americans took Barrigada Well, providing them with a much-needed forward source of fresh water, and Mount Barrigada, while encountering little resistance beyond occasional snipers.

On August 5th, the Americans entered some of the densest jungle they had yet encountered as they pushed towards the final Japanese positions around Mount Saint Rosa. On this day, the Army troops also experienced the first real Japanese counterattack seen for some time, which, for once, proved partly successful. Company A of the 1st Battalion, 307th Infantry Regiment had dug in for the evening when they heard the sound of approaching tanks. Since Shermans reportedly operated in the area, the men assumed American tanks produced the engine and track noises drawing closer through the forest. However, two Japanese tanks burst out of the woodland instead, supported by a platoon of infantry with machine guns.

Company A quickly mowed down the Japanese infantry, but the tanks burst through their perimeter and ran amok, spraying machine gun fire and HE shells in all directions. As panicking US infantry ran in all directions, the bazooka crews moved up, but in their excitement forgot to remove the safety pins from the rounds before firing. The bazooka shots rang harmlessly off the Japanese hulls, effectively rendered duds by crew error, and the Japanese tankers replied with bursts of machine gun fire. After a few minutes, the two tanks retreated at high speed, though the Americans shot and killed a lone Japanese infantryman clinging to one of their hulls. The vehicles left 15 Americans KIA and 46 more wounded in their wake, making this one of the most successful counterattacks since the drunken charge of July 26th.

In the succeeding few days, the Americans encountered more Japanese tanks. Though extremely few in number, these vehicles exhibited skilled handling by their crews, inflicting losses on the advancing Marines and Army troops. The narrow tracks with impenetrably thick rainforest vegetation on either side provided excellent positions for the tanks to meet the Americans with defilading fire, and the tankers fired HE shells into the treetops, where the branches deflected the shrapnel downward in a lethal shower.

Nevertheless, the American troops pushed forward, while naval gunfire and a mix of P-47s and B-26s hammered Japanese positions on Mount Saint Rosa. The 77th Infantry Division took the mountain on August 8th, with a loss of only 30 men killed. During the advance, the Americans had seen hundreds of Japanese who appeared to have committed suicide in various ways, while the main Saint Rosa defense force had retreated.

General Obata dispatched his final transmission to Imperial HQ as the Americans closed in, though circumstances denied him his planned banzai charge. He declared himself "overwhelmed with shame... most of the island has been lost and we are without weapons, ammunition, or food. The achievement of the original mission is now hopeless. I do not know how to express my apology. I will, with the remaining officers and men, engage the enemy in the last battle tomorrow, the 11th." (Denfeld, 1997,204).

On August 10-11, the main action on Guam ended when the Americans destroyed the caves of Mount Mataguac, killing the Japanese with machine gun fire or white phosphorous grenades, or simply collapsing the entrances with TNT. These caves housed the elaborate underground headquarters of General Obata. Denied the chance of a last banzai charge, the general and some 60 other men committed suicide, even as the Americans remained unaware of the general's presence at the time.

The US troops killed approximately 11,000 Japanese by the time General Geiger announced the island's pacification, leaving roughly 7,000 more still at large in small bands throughout the jungle. The conquest came at the price of 1,744 American lives, most of them men from Marine units, and 5,970 men wounded.

Once again, by an overwhelming majority, the Japanese preferred death to surrender. In one instance, the Marines took a man prisoner whose clever answer almost added a note of humor to the grim proceedings, as Marine machine gunner Robert Leckie recounted: "He was a forlorn scrimp of a man, small even for his race, and his tattered blouse and breeches were much too large. But there was an easiness about him that puzzled the Marines […] A Marine interpreter spoke to him. 'Why did you surrender?' 'My commanding officer told us to fight to the last man.' The Marine's eyebrows rose. 'Well?' The Japanese soldier's eyebrows also rose – in wounded innocence – and he exclaimed: 'I am the last man.'" (Leckie, 1990, 380).

Only a few hundred out of the 18,000 men originally garrisoning the island surrendered. Of the thousands still at large once the Americans took Guam, many simply starved to death or committed suicide. Others vindictively killed Guamanians until the Americans found and killed them. The last three holdouts did not return to civilization until the 1970s, when Guamanians found the men at various times and brought them to the authorities for repatriation.

Following the successful seizure of the three largest of the southern Mariana Islands, the Americans went on to take the nearby island of Palau, which, though not part of the island chain, provided strategic security for the new acquisitions.

The Americans established refugee camps where they could house and feed the native population, particularly on Guam, where the Japanese occupation had reduced Guamanians to the utmost extremity of misery. The Guamanians had, in fact, made a secret anthem during the years of Japanese dominance. Those who the Americans liberated often greeted them by singing the Marine Hymn as well as their own song in English, which ran in part:

Our lives are in danger –

You better come,

And kill all the Japanese

Right here on Guam.

Oh Mr. Sam, Sam, my dear Uncle Sam,

I want you please come back to Guam. (Leckie, 1990, 381).

Much more crucially to the war effort, the Americans immediately set about building massive airfields on all three islands, with all necessary supporting facilities. The US constructed five airfields in all, including Isely Field on Saipan, North Field and West Field on Tinian, and North Field and Northwest Field on Guam. The Americans worked with frenzied determination, to the extent that the first B-29 bombers launched from Saipan in late October and all fields were operational by late November.

A 1945 picture of Isely Field, filled with B-29 bombers, on Saipan

These B-29 raids hammered the Japanese home islands. Japanese fighter ace Sakai Saburo noted the effective immunity of the new B-29 aircraft to available Japanese interceptors, due to both their operational ceiling and speed: "[O]ur fighters did not have the rate of climb which would allow them to reach more than 30,000 feet in the few minutes available between the time the alarm was received and the time the bombers departed." (Prefer, 2012, 163).

As a result, besides the damage and proof to the ordinary Japanese that the Empire was clearly crumbling all around them, the Japanese moved their industry into remote locations. They split up factories and rebuilt them in caves and remote valleys, away from the frequently bombed urban centers. Though this allowed some factories to survive, it also cut production to the merest trickle; manufacturing a few parts here and there, then shipping them to another location for assembly, prevented mass production, particularly given the era's technology.

The Japanese remained defiant, however, and began massive preparations for a fanatical defense of the home islands. Faced with realistically calculated combat losses of anywhere from 500,000 to several million casualties, President Harry S. Truman eventually authorized use of the atomic bombs against Japan in 1945. That August, the two nuclear-equipped Silverplate B-29 bombers, *Enola Gay* and *Bockscar*, took off from North Field on Tinian for their missions to Hiroshima and Nagasaki.

The Philippines and Leyte Gulf

By March 1944, the Joint Chiefs instructed MacArthur to prepare his men to move into the southern Philippines by the end of the year, and then into Luzon by early 1945. They also ordered Admiral Chester Nimitz to prepare for an assault on Formosa for early 1945.

Nimitz

Meanwhile, between March and June of 1944, American intelligence had learned that Japan was in the process of reinforcing areas under their control in the western Pacific, especially

Formosa. This meant that the longer it took for the Americans to begin their attack on the island, the better-prepared Japanese forces would be to defend it. For the Joint Chiefs, this meant that in order to attack Formosa, they would have to move up their timetable to the fall of 1944 if they wanted to carry out an assault on the island.

Another complicating factor was the belief by American strategists that the Chinese resistance was in danger of collapsing against Japanese pressure. This would nullify one of the major reasons for privileging Formosa over the Philippines (aiding in the supply of Chinese forces on the mainland). By this time, both MacArthur and Nimitz were advocating the need to take the Philippines to secure air bases from which the Allies could launch further operations across the Pacific. In July 1944, Roosevelt sailed to Pearl Harbor to discuss strategy. Although often cited as the key event in the lead up to the invasion of the Philippines, the truth is that the meeting was indecisive. It was not until September 1944 that President Roosevelt, the Joint Chiefs, MacArthur and Nimitz were all committed to the plan of invading the Philippines before engaging in further attacks on Japan. This made sense mostly in terms of aircraft ranges and the imperative to keep ground forces under the umbrella of short range fighters, but as MacArthur was soon to discover, the carriers were not up to the job on their own.

Once military leaders settled on the Philippines-first plan, they began to prepare for the upcoming campaign. The Allied strategy would comprise of four phases. First, naval and ground units would establish a foothold on southeastern Mindanao, where they could establish airfields that would support further operations. Next, Allied units would move into the central Philippines at Leyte, where MacArthur would set up air and supply bases for the attack on Luzon. The third phase involved taking Luzon, and then the fourth phase would involve dislodging Japanese troops from the minor Philippines islands that had been bypassed during the first three phases.

Ultimately, in September 1944, MacArthur revised the plan and eliminated the first phase at Mindanao, instead collapsing the plan into a three-phased assault that would begin at Leyte. Admiral William "Bull" Halsey, in command of the U.S. 7th Fleet and directly subordinate to MacArthur, was a keen advocate of an attack on Leyte, a large island to the southeast of the Philippine archipelago. General Walter Krueger, commander of MacArthur's 8th army, was less enthusiastic. Buttressed by upbeat intelligence reports, MacArthur opted for Halsey's plan.

Halsey

Krueger

A problem the Allied forces encountered as they prepared for the Philippines invasion was Japanese reinforcements. Since Japanese military leaders were constantly moving troops and planes around, it became difficult for the Americans to estimate Japanese ground and aerial strength. For example, American leaders estimated that the Japanese had 400-500 planes in the Philippines, but that an additional 300-400 planes might be moved from Formosa, along with carrier-based planes that could be sent to the region to contest the American attack.

A map of the Philippines

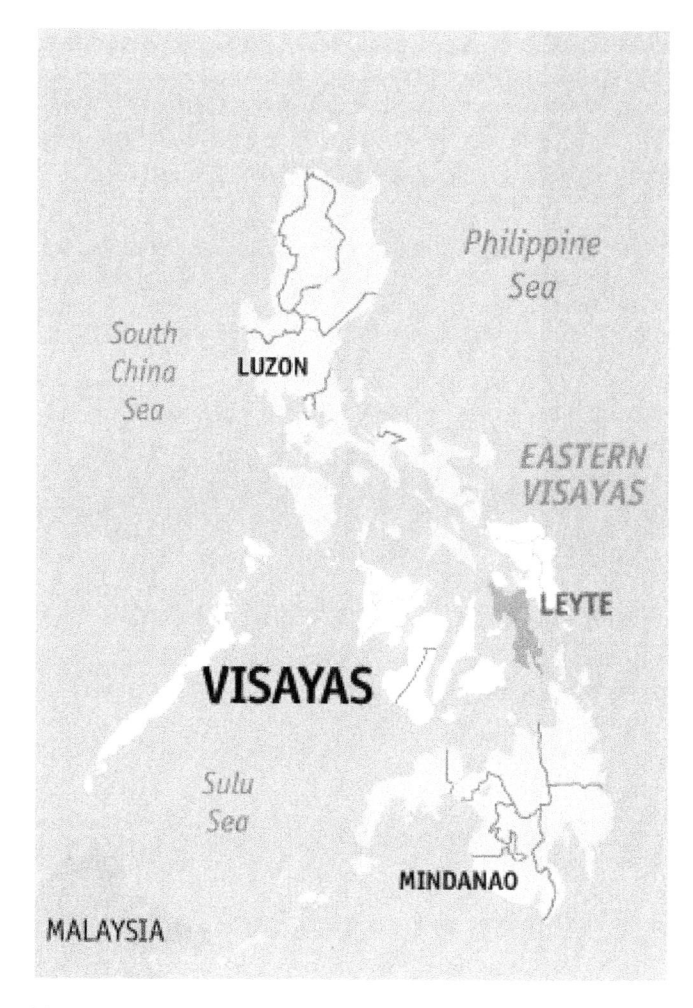

Magal Haes' map of Leyte and Luzon highlighted in the Philippines

Protecting the American landings at Leyte Gulf, two main forces of American vessels flanked the position to north and south. Vice Admiral Thomas Kinkaid watched the southern approach at Surigao Strait with a force of battleships, cruisers, destroyers, and torpedo boats (PT boats, or "patrol/torpedo"). This guarded the approaches from the Sulu Sea and the Mindinao Sea.

In the north, Halsey commanded the massive Task Force 38, containing a powerful grouping of

Essex-class aircraft carriers, plus fast modern battleships, heavy cruisers, and destroyers. Halsey undertook to guard the San Bernardino Strait to the north of Leyte Gulf, protecting the approaches from the Sibuyan Sea. On the Philippine Sea, three groups of 6 American *Casablanca*-class light carriers apiece, also known as escort carriers or jeep carriers (due to their small size rather than any onboard jeeps), provided air support to the American landings.

For their part, the Japanese planned a three-pronged attack against the American deployment. In the north, Vice Admiral Ozawa Jisaburo led the Northern Force, consisting of a single large aircraft carrier and three light carriers, plus supporting battleships, cruisers, and destroyers. The carriers lacked all but a handful of aircraft. The final remnant of Japan's once mighty carrier fleet, these craft would feint against the Americans' northern flank, hopefully drawing away the defenders of San Bernardino and Surigao Straits.

Ozawa

In the meantime, Center Force under Kurita Takeo, a massive flotilla centered around the two super-battleships *Yamato* and *Musashi*, would penetrate San Bernardino Strait via the Sibuyan Sea. A third task group, Force C, would cross the Sulu Sea and Mindinao Sea to force a passage through Surigao Strait. Coming from the north and south, these forces – if successful – would unite to sink the American *Essex*-class carriers if possible and wipe out the landing fleet in Leyte Gulf.

Kurita

The *Musashi*

A picture of Kurita's fleet anchored

Much of the plan depended on Northern Force's ability to lure the protective American warships away. The Japanese commanders later stated they believed they had a "50-50" chance of success, but with the Americans rolling ever closer to Japan, they believed the gamble worth the risk.

The first action of the battle occurred on October 23rd as Kurita's Center Force steamed across into the Palawan Passage, the western gateway to the Sibuyan Sea. However, danger lurked in the waters ahead, and the Japanese had no hint before it struck.

The American submarines *Dace* and *Darter*, commanded respectively by Bladen Claggett and David McLintock, patrolled the Passage on the early morning of the 23rd. At 1:16 AM, the two submarines, working in tandem, made contact with the Japanese force and reported its immense size and apparent heading to Task Force 38. Admiral Halsey heard the news approximately five hours later, after the message passed through the normal circuitous channels to his flagship.

Kurita's electronic warfare experts picked up the submarine radio signal, but Kurita – even more careless than Halsey – neglected to throw out a picket line of destroyers in advance of his force, moving through the Palawan Passage in three columns.

The two prowling submarines, unable to believe their good fortune, closed to attack at first light. Both fired a spread of torpedoes at Kurita's flagship, the heavy cruiser *Atago,* smashing its prow completely. Engulfed in black smoke shot through with bright orange flames, the cruiser sank rapidly by the bow almost immediately. Kurita leaped over the side along with the rest of his surviving crew, forced to tread water until the destroyer *Kishinama* came to his rescue and that of the other survivors.

The dawn attack continued with the torpedoing of the heavy cruiser *Takao,* which suffered so much damage its captain turned back to Brunei. The Americans completed their hit and run attack by firing a spread of six torpedoes into the cruiser *Maya,* one of which punched through its hull into the No. 7 boiler room. Almost instantly, internal explosions ripped the *Maya* apart, and the ship sank in 5 minutes. Ugaki reported that the cruiser simply "exploded, and after the spray and smoke had disappeared nothing remained of her to be seen" (Morison, 2002, 172).

The two *Gato*-class submarines, built at the same shipyard in Groton, Connecticut, shadowed the Japanese force for hours, trying to get in position for another attack. However, due to a navigational error, *Darter* ran aground on Bombay Shoal. After failed attempts to refloat the submarine and then failed attempts to sink it, the Americans finally transferred the crew to *Dace*. The overcrowded submarine set off for the Fremantle submarine base in Australia, enjoying what the crew described as a "pleasant voyage" despite running out of all food except mushroom soup and peanut butter sandwiches.

The two American submarines sank three of Kurita's heavy cruisers, but their most significant contribution perhaps consisted of the warning issued to Task Force 38. On the 24th, Center Force remained under American scrutiny as first the submarine USS *Guitarro*, then a reconnaissance aircraft, detected and reported its position.

The American carriers in the Philippine Sea launched strike after strike against Kurita's armada, with *Lexington, Essex, Intrepid, Franklin, Enterprise,* and *Cabot* contributing to the 259 sorties. The first squadrons arrived at 10:26 AM, formally beginning the Battle of the Sibuyan Sea. The Japanese ships put up heavy curtains of flak and, driven to desperation by their total lack of air cover, even fired their main guns at the flitting shapes of Hellcats, Avengers, and Helldivers as they swooped to deploy their ordnance, including both bombs and torpedoes, against the surface ships.

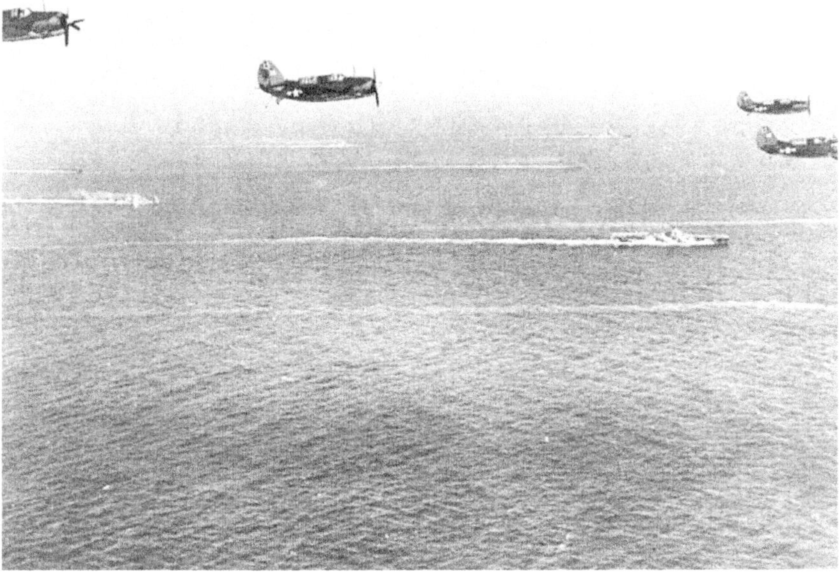

Pictures of Helldivers from Taskforce 38 during the battle

Picture of an Avenger during the battle

The Japanese only succeeded in destroying 18 aircraft in total, leading Vice Admiral Ugaki Matome, a profuse diarist who later flew a solo kamikaze mission rather than surrender, to remark, "The small number of enemy planes shot down is regrettable." (Morison, 2002, 184). Kurita requested air support time and again, but Vice Admiral Fukudome Shigeru deliberately ignored him, believing it better to deploy the aircraft directly against the American carriers once located.

The American aircraft damaged several battleships and cruisers, but the main feather in their cap consisted of the sinking of the super-battleship *Musashi*. This imposing *Yamato*-class vessel, armed with 18 inch guns, absorbed dozens of bomb hits and torpedo strikes over the course of several hours of air attacks.

Though doomed to never fire a shot in anger against another surface ship, the *Musashi* served some purpose at Sibuyan simply by being the main target. The Americans concentrated most of their wrath on the huge ship, which stubbornly refused to go down. The tremendous hull armor and resilient structure of the battleship came apart only very slowly under the impact of repeated strikes. No single hit sank the *Musashi* directly. Instead, it suffered a slow loss of power and hull integrity, which finally led to its sinking, with the loss of approximately half of its 2,400 man crew.

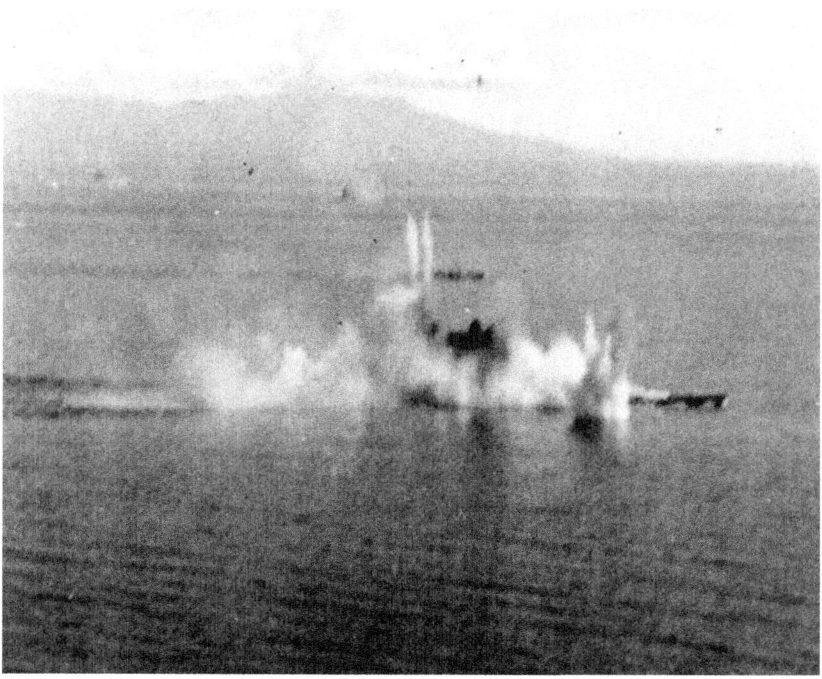

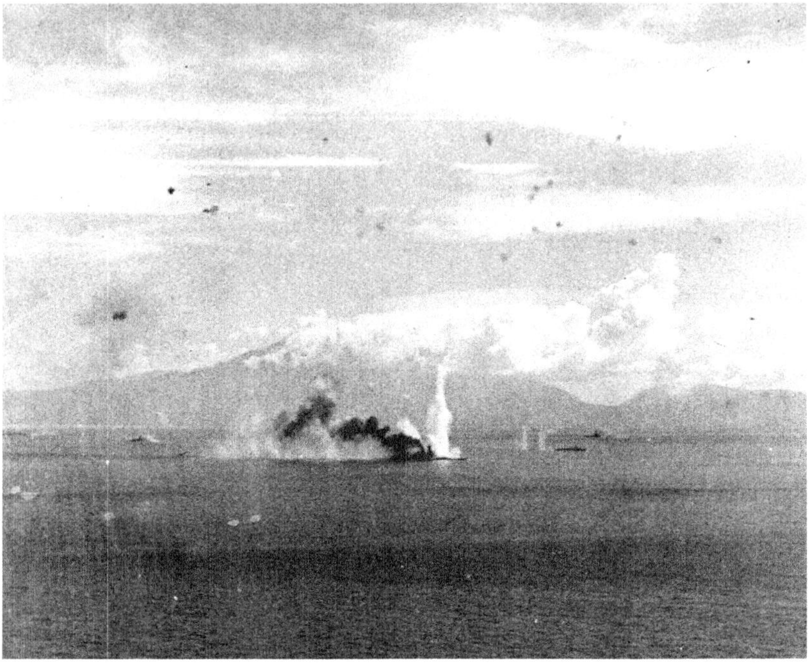

Pictures of the *Musashi* being attacked

In the face of the air attacks, the Japanese armada turned back and steamed the way it came. Kurita sent a report to Admiral Toyoda Teijiro, overall commander of the Japanese operation, explaining his situation and decisions: "As a result of five aerial attacks from 6:30 until 3:30 our damages are not light. The frequency and numerical strength of these enemy attacks is increasing. If we continue our present course our losses will increase incalculably, with little hope of success for our mission. Therefore, I have decided to withdraw outside the range of enemy air attack for the time being." (Hoyt, 1993, 147).

Halsey, who had assumed command from Vice Admiral Marc Mitscher – the actual commander of the American carrier force – ordered a halt to the airstrikes when his airmen reported the Japanese course reversal. Ironically, when Kurita took note of the cessation of air attacks, he was encouraged by this, so he reversed course again to make for San Bernardino Strait on the evening of the 24th.

In the meantime, Ozawa's Northern Force made its demonstration as noisily as possible, generating vast quantities of radio chatter to suggest a major carrier force moving to attack with full complements of strike aircraft. Halsey's scouts spotted the force at 3:40 PM, which led the impetuous "Bull" to charge off in search of a stunning naval victory. His own explanatory message to Chester Nimitz later stated, "Searches by my carrier planes revealed the presence of the Northern carrier force […] which completed the picture of all enemy naval forces. As it seemed childish to me to guard statically San Bernardino Strait, I concentrated TF 38 during the night and steamed north […] I believed that the Center Force had been so heavily damaged in the Sibuyan Sea that it could no longer be considered a serious menace." (Morison, 2002, 193).

In fact, Halsey took Ozawa's bait with a fervor even the Japanese could scarcely have hoped for. Gathering all his carriers, battleships, cruisers, and destroyers, he swept away northward in hot pursuit of what he believed represented a massive Japanese carrier fleet. In his wake, he left San Bernardino Strait unguarded by so much as a single PT boat, and he neglected to inform any of the other American commanders of his decision.

Not surprisingly, this would have a profound effect on the way the remainder of the fighting played out.

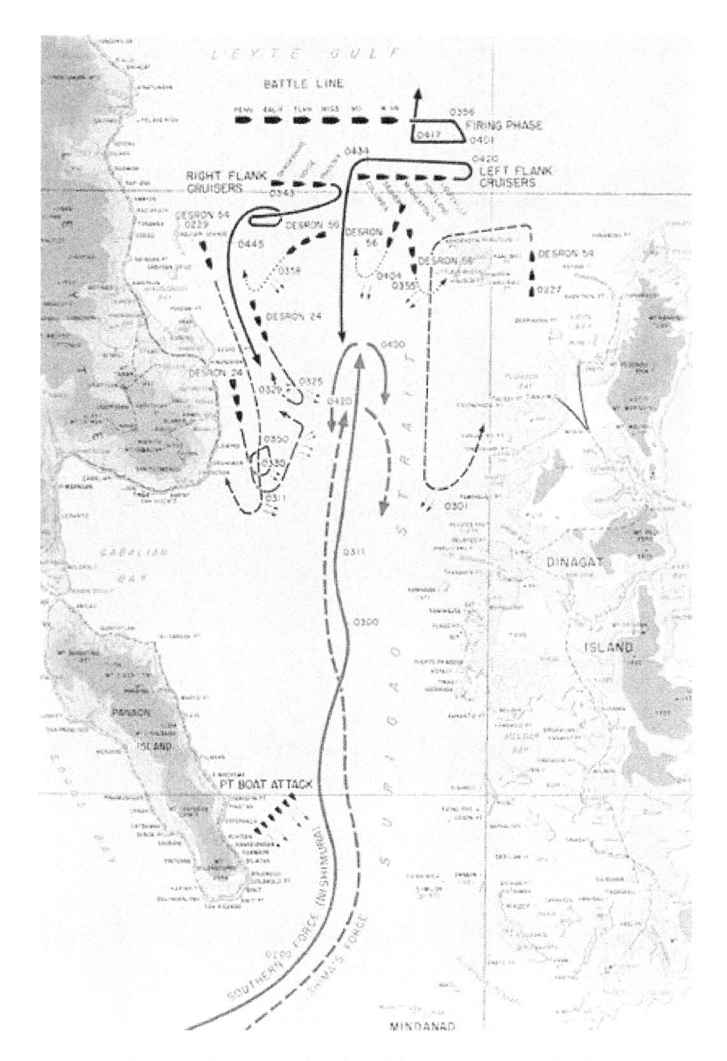

A map of the two sides' positions at Surigao Strait

While the Japanese northern pincer sailed unopposed through San Bernardino Strait, rashly left unguarded by "Bull" Halsey as he pursued the adroitly flourished red cape of a Japanese decoy, Force C – the southern pincer – approached Surigao Strait. Beyond the narrows between Leyte's coast on the west and Hibuson Island and the north cape of Mindinao to the east lay a bounty of transport ships, anchored and apparently ripe for sinking in Leyte Gulf.

The feebleness of Nishimura Shoji's thrust through Surigao Strait during the early morning hours of October 25th all but guaranteed its defeat if it met determined resistance. Four destroyers led the way in a loose wedge formation. Behind these followed two battleships, *Yamashiro* and *Fuso*, with the heavy cruiser *Mogami* bringing up the rear. The second half of the southern pincer, consisting of two heavy cruisers and one light cruiser plus four destroyers under Vice Admiral Shima Kiyohide, had fallen 25 miles behind.

The Japanese sent reconnaissance aircraft up Surigao Strait during October 24th, but the pilots somehow missed any sign of the American surface forces gathering to meet Nishimura. The scouts returned with encouraging reports that no destroyers, cruisers, battleships, or aircraft carriers sailed in Surigao. Some even insisted on an absence of warships even in Leyte Gulf. Nishimura, heartened, decided on a fast passage into Leyte Gulf, where his ships could run amok among nearly defenseless transports.

On October 24th, American aircraft located and attacked a trailing group of vessels attempting to link up to Shima's force. They attacked, after which they claimed several sinkings, but in fact they had inflicted trivial damage. Other aircraft attacked Nishimura's ships, claiming hits on the *Fuso* which did not in fact occur. Though causing no damage, the air attacks gave the Americans invaluable intelligence of the position and heading of the southern pincer.

Japanese fleet doctrine called for using night attacks. At Guadalcanal a few years earlier, the IJN employed this tactic to devastating effect against American and Australian warships defending the landing areas, and avoidance of a repeat disaster ranked very high among the concerns of American commanders at Leyte Gulf. Vice Admiral Thomas Kinkaid commanded the southern flank of U.S. forces at the Battle of Leyte Gulf from his flagship on the USS *Wasatch*. Kinkaid received a message from Halsey at 8:45 PM on the 24th, informing him of the move to the north against Matsuda's carriers. Kincaid, however, assumed that Halsey left a strong force to guard San Bernardino Strait, and therefore had no idea that only chance prevented the Japanese northern pincer from falling on his unprotected rear.

Kinkaid

   Kinkaid ordered Rear Admiral Jesse Oldendorf to deploy a powerful force of destroyers, battleships, and 39 patrol/torpedo boats (PT boats) in the 14 mile wide Surigao Strait to intercept Force C. Oldendorf, commanding the 7th Fleet Support Force, set about preparing what amounted to a massive naval ambush with skill and gusto.

Oldendorf

Starting at 2:45 PM on October 24th, Oldendorf began moving his ships into position. Though he believed he was facing a larger force than the one that actually approached, Oldendorf expected his plan to work, remarking grimly, "Never give a sucker a chance." (Woodward, 1947, 90). Nishimura, thanks to faulty intelligence that reported Surigao Strait void of large American surface ships, provided the perfect "sucker," as the diary of Ugaki corroborated: "The enemy fleet in Leyte Gulf had moved out and there were no large ships in the gulf […] On the basis of the situation reports of the previous day, (Oct 24), that the enemy battleship force had sortied eastward and that no powerful force remained in Leyte Gulf, the Third Section carried out its penetration in a headlong rush." (Tully, 2009, 133).

The 39 PT boats, grouped into 13 tactical sections of three boats each, formed the forward picket line, dotted across the expanse of the southern Surigao Strait. The Japanese advance would trigger this line, providing ample warning to the rest of Oldendorf's force. Experienced, tough, confident, and aggressive, the PT boat crews also expressed readiness to launch the first attacks on the much larger Japanese ships. These 72-foot wooden hulled boats often sported colorful nicknames such as *Termite's Delight, Geisha-Gooser,* or *Ramblin' Wreck,* among many other humorous, ribald, or defiant appellations.

Darkness lay over the waters of Surigao Strait as the American crews waited tensely, eyes and radar probing southward for signs of the Japanese. Periodically, sprays of tracers erupted into the dark sky as jumpy anti-aircraft gunners fired at aerial phantoms.

Early in the night, stars glittered overhead and a brilliant moon rode in the sky, but as the early morning of October 25th arrived, a tropical thunderstorm approached from the south. Howard Sauer, an officer aboard the USS *Maryland*, reported the meteorological conditions at the northern extremity of Surigao Strait: "Squalls were reported in the area, but for us it was an increasingly overcast, black night, strangely still. The sea was smooth, the visibility good. Since we had no secondary battery radar, we practiced more than most on the development of night vision. You don't look directly at the object you wish to see. Using that technique, we could make out the looming darker shapes of the nearby vessels." (Sauer, 1999, 115-116).

A three-boat PT section near Bohol Island made first contact with the IJN task force before midnight and immediately went on the attack despite the lethal fragility of their completely unarmored craft. This group consisted of PT 131, *Tarfu* (i.e. Things Are Really F****d Up), under Ensign Peter R. Gadd; PT 130, *New Guinea Crud*, commanded by Lt. Ian Malcom; and PT 152, *Lack-a-Nookie*, skippered by Lt. Joseph Eddins.

Gadd's radarman picked out the approaching ships at 10:50 PM, and the three irreverently named craft immediately went into action, deploying towards the Japanese at full speed. However, the IJN lookouts, showing their usual professional acumen, spotted the distant bow waves and moving shapes of the PT boats almost immediately, even in the darkness under the storm-clouds.

That darkness did not last long. The destroyer *Shigure* fired two starshells, glaringly illuminating the trio of boats at a range of 3 miles, too far away for the short-range American torpedoes. With these targets available, the *Shigure* opened fire, soon joined by the guns of the battleship *Yamashiro*. Bracketed by well-aimed shells, the PT boats had no choice but to flee.

Shigure, however, turned to pursue, hounding the small vessels for a desperate 23 minutes. A shell struck Eddins' *Lack-a-Nookie*, destroying the bow 37mm gun, mortally wounding the gunner Charlie Midgett, and setting the PT boat afire. A near miss from a massive shell put the fire out with its splash, but the Japanese followed the tiny boat with a searchlight. Eddins' crew fired their 40mm gun at the searchlight, while PT 130, *New Guinea Crud*, laid smoke.

After a desperate, weaving chase, the searchlight finally blinked out, and the *Shigure* rejoined its formation. Despite coming very close to annihilation, the morale of the PT boat crews remained high, and they tried to catch up to the rapidly northbound Japanese force to exact revenge with their torpedoes, like chihuahuas harrying a herd of elephants: "Pullen and Eddins had no intention of calling it a day – or a night. *Lack-a-Nookie* roared off in pursuit of the withdrawing Nipponese DDs with the intention of launching a torpedo attack. The enemy warships were making at least twenty-two knots and had a big lead, so, after trying an hour to catch up, Pullen and Eddins had to call off the chase." (Breuer, 1995, 186).

In their excitement, the PT boat crews made a serious error in not radioing their contact to the fleet. During the chase, Japanese fire destroyed the radios on all three craft, rendering them unable to communicate once Force C resumed its northward course. Eventually, Malcolm's *New Guinea Crud* found PT boat Section 2 near Camiguin Island. Ensign Dudley Johnson of PT 127 finally informed Oldendorf's flagship of the Japanese presence at 12:26 AM on October 25th.

In the meantime, Shima's force began catching up to Nishimura's. This gave the admiral greater confidence and even the beginning of hope that he might successfully penetrate the Surigao Strait after all. Nevertheless, the Japanese remained on high alert, expecting the ambush that did in fact await them.

Over the next several hours, the PT boats continued their brave but futile attacks on the Japanese. Japanese jamming and the deteriorating weather both interfered with their radio signals, but enough transmissions leaked through to keep Oldendorf and his captains apprised of IJN progress northward. Despite launching many torpedoes, the PT boats inflicted no damage, in part due to the poor firing conditions caused by constant salvos of Japanese shells and other ordnance.

By now, a storm front had developed, and the Japanese used it skillfully to mask their progress. In fact, despite hours of PT boat attacks, Force C managed to take at least one section of torpedo craft completely by surprise. At around 2 AM on the 25th, the men in PTs 490, 491, and 493 saw the first squall line rolling towards them across the sea, blurred with rain underneath and shot through with lightning. As the violent storm rushed closer, the glowing blue barbs of St. Elmo's Fire formed eerily around the machine guns and radio equipment aboard many of the boats, a weather phenomenon well understood by 20th century seamen.

However, what was unbeknownst to the men waiting tensely on the wooden decks of the three boats was that Nishimura's force sailed just behind the rain front, screened from long-range visual contact and partially from radar by the torrential downpour. PT 491 (nicknamed *Devil's Daughter*) under Harley Thronson made contact with the Japanese force as the storm rushed over them, though different crew members recalled the scene differently, as Thronson's recollection and executive officer Terry Chambers' narrative both indicate: "Terry remembered the Japanese ships coming in right behind the squall line. 'I saw a lightning flash, and there they were in column.' Boat 491's skipper Harley Thronson's recollection had a different flavor. 'The weather was miserable – really poor visibility. Suddenly we were in the middle of the Japanese formation. They turned on searchlights and opened fire.'" (Sears, 2005, 115-116).

In addition to radio signals, the men aboard the lurking American warships now received visual confirmation of the Japanese approach. Gazing south, they suddenly perceived searchlights strobing wildly across the southern horizon, accompanied by the flashes of gunfire. The time to spring Oldendorf's trap had nearly arrived.

Moving behind the storm curtain, the Japanese force nosed into the narrowest point of Surigao Strait, the passage between Sumilon and Panaon Islands. *Devil's Daughter* and its two accompanying PT boats attacked the Japanese within moments, despite their crews' initial shock, and PT 134, *Eight Ball*, joined the attack alone. While the Japanese evaded all the torpedo wakes, which were clearly visible on the dark ocean surface, they lost headway in doing so.

Terry Chambers once again described the close-quarters action: "Somehow, we'd gotten inside their destroyer screen […] We were facing big ships and all we could do was aim our guns at the lights and the ships' bridges – like sticking our fingers in their eyes. We'd knock one light out and another went on." (Sears, 2005, 125).

During the exchange of fire, a shell crashed into PT 490, *Little Butch,* Lt. John McElfresh commanding. The shell wounded a number of men and started a serious leak, only slowed when Engineer Albert Brunelle, formerly dismissed as a "sissy" but about to win the respect of his fellow crewmen, stuffed his lifejacket into the hole. The *Little Butch* limped away, eventually sinking near Panaon Island, but another boat rescued its crew.

The PT boat attacks ceased at around 2:25 AM, and darkness and deep silence fell as the Japanese ships sailed forward against the strong Surigao Strait current. In fact, the order had come through from Oldendorf's flagship ordering the torpedo craft to break off so they would not be sunk by friendly fire during the imminent destroyer ambush.

A PT boat after the battle

Nishimura, however, interpreted the American retreat as the end of the attempt to bar his ships from passing the Strait. Despite restrained protests from some of his captains, he ordered Force C forward at full speed without even waiting to resume battle formation. He wanted to make up for lost time and pounce on his Leyte Gulf quarry within a few hours, with Shima's armada joining in upon arrival.

At 3 AM, a Japanese searchlight swept over the sea surface and illuminated the five destroyers of Captain Jesse Coward's DesRon 54. Revealed suddenly to the presumably surprised Japanese, the American destroyers immediately sped forward, releasing their torpedoes, and then swerved away, generating smokescreens as they did so. The combination of rapid maneuvering and smoke kept them well clear of the retaliatory salvos launched by the Japanese.

Over the next 20 minutes, the destroyers used the same tactic, firing their torpedoes and then getting away to avoid Japanese gunfire. Japanese shells rushed overhead with a "freight train" sound, sometimes exploding beyond the destroyers and back-lighting them, providing a momentary target for the IJN gunners.

Many of the torpedoes missed, but one struck the massive battleship *Fuso* amidships. A tower of spray erupted from beside the mighty vessel's flank as the torpedo warhead detonated, punching through the armored hull. Two more strikes followed in quick succession. The force of the explosions sent a thunderous sound pulsating through the hull and threw the ship over almost on its side, before it rolled heavily upright again.

A picture of the wounded *Fuso*

The cruiser *Mogami*, following closely, swerved abruptly to avoid *Fuso*, already halted by the destruction of its boilers. The *Mogami* – named for a river in Japan frequently cited in *haiku* and other poems – passed the stricken vessel and fell into place astern of Nishimura's flagship, the *Yamashiro*. Nishimura glanced back, saw the *Mogami*, and assumed it to be the *Fuso*, failing to realize that one of his two battleships had suffered fatal damage in the first seconds of the engagement.

The *Yamashiro*

Like the caracoling pistol cavalry of an earlier age, the destroyers of DesRon 54 swooped away into the darkness, letting a second DesRon – DesRon 24 – move in. Consisting of 5 American destroyers and 1 Australian destroyer, the HMAS *Arunta*, the ships found a scene of devastation already unfolding. Just half an hour after the first shots of the ambush, Nishimura's force was almost finished.

The Japanese found themselves under attack by enemies they could barely discern in the stormy blackness. As a surviving Japanese lookout later explained, "It was very dark and the sky was heavily clouded, not to mention a fine haze [...] Suddenly, two or three torpedo wakes appeared at almost a direct angle from the direction of the island, racing toward the force. Their phosphorescent wakes became well visible, almost as if someone had suddenly turned the lights on. Nevertheless, neither the flashes from their launching nor the attacking DDs could be seen in the darkness." (Tully, 2009, 156-157).

Nishimura ordered his ships to turn to starboard to meet the threat, since most of the torpedoes raced out of the darkness from that direction. Shortly thereafter, however, he ordered a course change back to due north, putting the Japanese back in line astern. The Admiral's fatal choice hastened the inevitable, putting his ships broadside to the attacking swarms of American destroyers.

Nishimura's error in believing the *Fuso* was still present emboldened him to continue. The illusion strengthened due to radio chatter using the crippled battleship's name as Japanese vessels in Force C mistook one another for the missing vessel. *Fuso* itself had lost all radio communication permanently at the moment of the torpedo strikes.

The destroyer torpedoes took a massive toll from the understrength Japanese armada as it advanced. First to perish after the *Fuso*'s fatal wounding was the destroyer *Yamagumo*, captained by Shiro Ono, after it sustained a minimum of two torpedo strikes at 3:20 AM. These torpedoes, fired by the destroyer USS *McDermut*, tore through the large destroyer's hull and caused it to detonate immediately in a spectacular fireball which lit the sea, as one American observer described, like the "Fourth of July." All of the destroyer's torpedo tubes, loaded and ready to fire back at the Americans, exploded onboard instead, spreading the blast to the magazines and torpedo storage instantly.

The 230 men aboard died almost to a man at the moment of detonation. Pieces of debris, smashed human bodies, and severed limbs pattered down on the nearby Japanese ships, spaced at 600 yard intervals. Within a matter of minutes, the *Yamagumo* slipped under the waters, a gutted, fire-blackened husk smeared with the pulverized flesh and bone of most of the vessel's crew. Still heated by the blast, the sinking ship made a powerful hissing sound like a massive forging being quenched.

Almost simultaneously, an American torpedo hit the destroyer *Asagumo* in the bow, causing the forecastle to crumple in on itself due to a design flaw present in most classes of Japanese destroyers. Just one minute later, the destroyer *Michishio* took two hits, with one collapsing the forecastle and the second annihilating the port engine room, leaving the ship dead in the water with no power. Water rushed in through the hull breach as men struggled to escape in the pitch blackness inside the damaged vessel.

At this point, only the destroyer *Shigure*, the heavy cruiser *Mogami*, and the battleship *Yamashiro* remained in fighting trim. Nishimura, still improbably optimistic and believing his force intact – in part due to *Mogami*'s radio chatter with the nonexistent *Fuso* (which was actually mistakenly directed at his own ship) - continued the advance into the trap, towards the six battleships and flanking cruisers waiting in the darkness ahead.

The *Mogami*

In the meantime, *Fuso* suffered a lonely death in the wake of the other vessels. Its captain, Rear Admiral Ban Masami, turned the ship west, possibly trying to escape, or at least reach shallow coastal waters where his crew could more easily abandon ship. Hovering torpedo boats, headed by PT 495, *Miss Fury*, observed the battleship for some time, but decided not to attack due to earlier orders to stay out of the fight.

The *Fuso* turned southward after a time and continued underway for some time. While American after-action reports and numerous history books reported that a magazine fire blew the battleship in half, with the two halves floating separately for a time before sinking, this appears to have resulted from an error. The destroyers spotted two large fires on the sea surface following the torpedo strikes on *Fuso* and interpreted these as halves of the vessel. However, these likely represented no more than a pair of burning slicks created by oil leaking from the bunkers of the fleeing, damaged battleship.

Instead, the *Fuso* leaned more and more to starboard as it limped away under the storm-wrack, seawater welling up to overwhelm deck after deck. Soon, the ship's prow was running underwater, forcing the crew to crowd the after deck as they evacuated the deeper parts of the ship and the gun turrets.

The increasingly panicky men jostled and surged in a pitch-black night so dark that men standing next to them appeared as no more than anonymous shadows. They could see white water combing over the foredeck, however, creeping aft towards them as the sea began to swallow the *Fuso*. Only at this point did Ban order the "abandon ship." A strident bugle-call sliced through the near-silence, and men began pouring over the rails.

At that moment, the *Fuso* suddenly toppled over on its starboard side, throwing men into the sea. Then the ship writhed, its prow sinking while its stern rose into the air. One of the bare handful of survivors – 10 men out of a complement of 1,900 – named Ogawa Hideo, later reported the battleship's final moments: "In the darkness, the huge black hull of our ship stood high above the water, and the forward bridge was about to fall down sideways. [...] Soon the bridge disappeared into the water. The stern, about 60 meters long aft of No. 6 turret, was above water at an angle of about 50 degrees, stood still, which showed an awkward figure in the night sky. The screws [...] were running in the air hopelessly." (Tully, 2009, 177).

As Ogawa and other survivors swam, giant masses of stinking fuel oil suddenly bubbled up to the surface. Ogawa fought his way clear of the clinging petroleum slime, but behind him, the oil caught fire with a deafening sizzling sound. The agonized screams of hundreds of men burning alive in the liquid flame echoed over the water, prompting the survivors outside the inferno to swim faster. A pair of deep shocks through the water indicated the magazines might have exploded far below the surface.

The cruiser *Nachi* sped past the survivors, its crew hearing their desperate cries for help but ignoring them. Many surviving men swam to Leyte's shores, but the Filipinos, enraged by years of Japanese atrocities, slaughtered most of them as they lay exhausted on the beach or killed them with machetes or rifles in the coastal waters. PT boats picked up two or three Japanese they found swimming, while the rest of the *Fuso*'s remaining survivors were captured by the Filipinos, who brought them as prisoners to American intelligence officers. The Americans repatriated all 10 to Japan following the war.

These men found themselves in an internment camp with survivors from the other sunken ships. Speaking freely for the first time in years, they worked out a rough reconstruction of the battle for their own edification. Their account actually jibed remarkably well with the true development of the battle, though they believed the PT boats, rather than destroyers, inflicted the lethal defeat on Force C. With their habits of suicidal submission and obedience to authority broken by disaster and captivity, they also placed blame for the catastrophe squarely on Admiral Nishimura, Some expressed satisfaction at Nishimura's presumed death.

The final action at Surigao Strait unfolded to the north at the same time as *Fuso* endured its death throes. However, new players entered the scene at about this time also. Shima's force of ships, including the heavy cruisers *Nachi* (Shima's flagship) and *Ashigara*, the light cruiser *Abukuma*, plus the destroyers *Shiranuhi, Kasumi, Ushio,* and *Akebono*, steamed rapidly up the Strait towards the action.

The PT boats, obeying orders to stay clear of the main engagement by lurking in the darkness, quickly took note of this new selection of targets hastening past them. With predictable aggressiveness, some of the 72-foot boats shadowed the newcomers, waiting for the opportunity to launch attacks on Shima's much larger, but unprepared, vessels.

Furious rain squalls and swaths of sea-mist obscured the way, and Shima's force almost came to grief in a startling fashion due to the poor visibility. The navigators failed to account for the powerful southbound current rushing through the Surigao Strait, which distorted their course. With no visible landmarks, the error went unnoticed until *Abukuma* broke clear of a bank of sea-mist and observed the white tumult of breakers just ahead, with a mountain looming out of the clouds miles beyond; Shima's force was in danger of running aground en masse on the coast of Palaon Island. The ships turned desperately, only just managing to avoid a humiliating end on the rocks and beaches.

As *Abukuma* labored in the water, slowed to a crawl and highly vulnerable, the swift shapes of American PT boats materialized out of the night. PT 137, *The Dutchess*, led the attack. The Japanese cruiser, trapped with nowhere to maneuver, sustained several torpedo hits, one barely missing the magazine. 37 men died instantly and more suffered wounds. With gaping holes in the ship's side, the *Abukuma* fell out of formation. Though the crew immediately began work on emergency repairs, Captain Kimura Masatomi knew he would probably remain unable to join the battle in the north before it reached a decision, a fact which frustrated him immensely.

With course corrections now properly in place, Shima's force moved north to support Nishimura. The flashes of gunfire and torpedo explosions, augmented by the glare of burning ships, showed clearly that a fierce battle continued to the north. The reinforcements pushed their ships' engines as hard as they could, achieving a speed of 28 knots as they charged north to their comrades' aid at 3:38 AM.

As it turned out, Shima arrived too late to alter the doom of Nishimura's Force C. As the *Yamashiro* continued to steam directly ahead, it came within range of the massive guns of the line of six battleships blocking the strait ahead. The four remaining Japanese ships – *Yamashiro*, *Mogami*, *Shigure*, and the half-crippled but still bravely advancing *Asagumo* – now all had deck fires from the 5-inch shells of the destroyers' guns, making them visible for miles on the darkened sea.

Nishimura, with incredible optimism, seemed to believe victory lay within his grasp nevertheless. His ships' radar had informed him shortly before of the battleship line ahead, yet the incorrigibly positive Admiral believed he had "caught" the Americans totally unprepared and could sink the battleships before moving on to Leyte Gulf. Accordingly, he issued a radio order for the ships to slow and reassume an attack formation.

Nishimura issued this order at 3:50 AM. At 3:51 AM, Oldendorf gave the order to the battleship line to open fire. The IJN ships therefore slowed at precisely the moment the Americans chose to fire on them, making themselves immobile targets for the eager American gunners sitting in their sweltering turrets to the north.

The cruisers on the right flank opened fire first, pouring a total of 3,100 shells onto the burning ships, and soon the "bulldogs" – the battleships forming the main line – joined in. The whole line of ships erupted time and time again in blinding flashes of discharge, while the thunder of the cannons nearly deafened the men on board and shook ill-secured items loose throughout the vessels. The force of each salvo, indeed, caused the ships to "shunt" across the water tens of yards in the opposite direction.

A picture of the cruisers opening fire in the pitch black

American destroyer captain Roland Smoot, standing on the fragile bridge of his craft, admired the aesthetics of the lethal pyrotechnic display: "The devastating accuracy of this gunfire was the most beautiful sight I have ever witnessed. The arched line of tracers in the darkness looked like a continual stream of lighted railroad cars going over a hill. No target could be observed at first; then shortly there would be fires and explosions, and another ship would be accounted for." (Hornfischer, 2004, 98).

While Smoot admired the accuracy of the gunfire, friendly fire claimed at least one notable victim. The destroyers continued their runs against the Japanese despite the appalling risk, and USS *Grant* paid the price. Stricken by Japanese shells, but even more frequently by American shells from the cruisers and "bulldogs," the ship came to a sudden halt, racked by internal explosions. Bursting shells killed dozens of men and wounded many more, smashing boilers that boiled men to death or left them appallingly injured and shattering the ship's weaponry and decks. A frantic radio call brought a temporary halt in the American ships' firing, after which the destroyers *Newcomb* and *Richard P. Leary* hastened to the maimed vessel's aid.

Despite the pyrotechnics, the Japanese on the receiving end of the bombardment could not even see the distant muzzle flashes of the battleships pounding them to pieces. The tracers appeared out of the darkness with no apparent source, and the shells arrived with a whistling shriek that ended in great fountains of spray or the fiery thunder of a direct hit on the slowly-disintegrating vessels.

The Americans concentrated first on *Yamashiro*, pounding the battleship until pieces of dead men strewed its decks and fires burned across nearly every part of the ship. Some of the ships then switched fire to *Mogami*, inflicting heavy damage on the cruiser and starting several fires. Soon, the fires turned into a roaring tower rising from much of ship's superstructure, illuminating the sea around the wounded vessel. Aboard the *USS West Virginia*, men later reported a gunnery officer laughing triumphantly every time fresh explosions rocked the distant targets.

The *West Virginia*

Independently, the *Yamashiro* and the *Mogami* finally turned in an attempt to flee. The *Shigure* continued forward briefly, hoping to acquire torpedo targets. However, as dozens of shells landed in the water all around it, the immense shocks smashed every instrument on the bridge, including the radar. *Shigure's* captain decided that escaping would be preferable to firing blindly at targets miles away, hidden by darkness. "At 0413 or 0415, being unsuccessful in finding the enemy, and determining that the rest of our force had been annihilated, I decided to withdraw without receiving orders from anyone." (Woodward, 1947, 116).

For its part, the *Yamashiro* did not die without a fight. While turning, the huge battleship raked the American lines with gunfire, which, while it inflicted little damage (except on *USS Grant*) impressed the USN officers and men with its relative accuracy. When the American battleships ceased fire to enable the rescue of *Grant*, the Japanese flagship turned south and fled at long last.

The *Yamashiro*

The *Yamashiro* did not get far, however. According to the few survivors later fished from the Surigao Strait, the battleship abruptly listed to port. Its towering "pagoda bridge" – an unmistakable feature of Japanese World War II warships – leaned towards the ocean, adding its weight to the rotational forces already in play. The captain issued an "abandon ship" order. However, just two minutes later, the battleship rolled over completely, pointing its keel towards the sky. Three minutes after that, it settled under the waves, sucking most of its officers and men down with it. Between 100 and 300 men managed to swim clear and reach Leyte. Here, again, they found vengeful Filipinos waiting, and only 10 men ultimately returned to Japan.

Shima's flotilla began reaching the scene of the action around 4:20 AM. The *Nachi* first passed the sinking *Fuso*, ignoring the men in the water who shouted for rescue. It then encountered the *Shigure*, partly on fire, listing, and laying down a smokescreen desperately as it steamed south. Seeking news from the fleeing ship, Shima received in answer only a terse message informing him that the *Shigure* was experiencing rudder trouble.

After these ominous sightings, the *Nachi* next encountered the burning *Mogami*. With remarkably bad luck, Shima decided *Mogami* must be dead in the water and ordered his ship to pass immediately in front of the cruiser's bow. Instead, *Mogami* was steaming south at the greatest speed it could muster. Unable to turn in time, the cruiser slammed into *Nachi*'s port flank, punching an enormous hole in the other cruiser. This accident rendered *Nachi* half-crippled and thus useless in a fight.

After sending his four destroyers north in a vain search for a parting shot, Shima ordered his ships to turn about and retreat southward also, trying to escape the deadly waters of Surigao Strait. The Americans, however, decided to pursue and finish off the Japanese remnants. When morning came, some destroyers crisscrossed the strait, attempting to rescue the numerous Japanese in the water. A few accepted help, but most ignored ropes thrown to them by the Americans. Many would not even look at the American ships trying to save their lives, instead floating silently in the waves waiting to die.

Even when a Japanese sailor allowed himself to be rescued, risks continued, as Tom Tenner aboard PT 127 reported, "I threw the guy a line and told him to climb up. He was small and soaking wet—if he weighed one hundred pounds that was a lot. He spoke a little English and told us the war was lost as far as he was concerned. We gave him a life jacket to wear [...] Then somebody said, 'We better search him.' We found he still had four hand grenades strapped to him. It showed what a bunch of bozos we were." (Sears, 2005. 169).

American destroyers, cruisers, and carrier aircraft hunted the surviving ships on the morning of the 25th, and they succeeded in sinking the *Asagumo*, the *Mogami*, and the *Abukumo*. Out of Nishimura's seven leading ships, only one, the *Shigure*, managed to escape, suffering 2 deaths on board. The rest sank, taking approximately 5,000 Japanese to their deaths.

Oldendorf, aboard the USS *Louisville*, toured the strait shortly after the sun came up, and the admiral appeared greatly pleased at the outcome, as well he should have been; his plan had worked, sinking a number of Japanese ships and forcing the rest to flee at minimal loss to his own forces. He received a congratulatory message from 7th Fleet at 7:28 AM.

Just 10 minutes later, however, his mood suffered a shattering blow. A desperate radio call came in at 7:38 sharp, informing Oldendorf that a second Japanese force was in his rear. Somehow, the Japanese had penetrated San Bernardino Strait, which Oldendorf and Kinkaid believed Halsey had left forces to guard. As a result, while Nishimura's last vessels fled south, the powerful ships of the northern pincer were about to surprise the fragile, nearly undefended

USN escort carriers in the ocean off Samar.

At the same time Nishimura was beginning his suicidal run into the teeth of Oldendorf's ambush far away in the south, Admiral Kurita Takao's Center Force moved cautiously into the San Bernardino Strait, north of Leyte Gulf, in the early morning of the 25th. Kurita had no way to know for certain if the decoy fleet to the north would lure Halsey away entirely or if the Americans would leave powerful ships to guard the key passage.

Kurita commanded an extremely powerful striking force, albeit one based on what was becoming a nearly obsolescent concept of naval combat. The Battle of Midway, a turning point in the Pacific, had been a battle between naval forces that never even sighted each other, and in many ways the Battle of Leyte Gulf would be the last major naval battle in which battleships fired at other surface ships rather than at targets onshore. Kurita had no choice, however, because he had no carriers, so he had to rely on land-based aircraft support, including the first dedicated kamikaze pilots to see action.

The centerpiece of his fleet, the super-battleship *Yamato*, represented one of the two mightiest cannon-armed ships to sail the seas, but the other, the *Musashi*, already resided on the floor of the Sibuyan Sea that morning. His force also included three regular battleships, the *Nagato*, *Kongo*, and *Haruna*; six heavy cruisers, the *Suzuya*, *Tone*, *Chikuma*, *Haguro*, *Kumano*, and *Chokai*; two light cruisers, the *Yahagi* and *Noshiro*; and 11 destroyers. In all, Kurita mustered 23 formidable fighting ships.

The Japanese ships moved eastward through the San Bernardino Strait in a stately column under clear moonlight at 3 AM on the 25th, debouching into the Philippine Sea. Despite keeping a tense watch, the IJN crews saw no signs of American surface ship activity. While the Americans sent carrier aircraft to patrol the Strait, and a trio of Catalina flying boats crisscrossed it, accidents of timing prevented them from spotting Kurita's powerful armada.

As a result, thanks to two strokes of luck – Halsey's impetuous decision to leave the Strait unguarded, and the failure of the American scouting aircraft and their Japanese targets to ever be at the same place simultaneously – Kurita achieved complete surprise. At 5 AM, shortly before sunrise, Kurita learned via radio chatter of the probable destruction of Force C in Surigao Strait, but undeterred, he formed up his ships and turned south around Samar, on course for Leyte Gulf and the American invasion fleet.

Ahead, three groups of tiny *Casablanca*-class US "jeep" carriers floated on the long, gentle swell of the tropical morning. These groups, designated Taffy I, Taffy II, and Taffy III, expected no surface ship attack, believing themselves protected by Oldendorf to the south and "Bull" Halsey to the north. Each "Taffy" detachment contained six carriers plus shepherding destroyers and destroyer escorts.

On the morning of the 25th, their crews busied themselves launching aircraft missions, mostly in support of the Surigao mop-up. Vice Admiral Fitzhugh Lee, aboard the Taffy III jeep carrier USS *Manila Bay*, described the situation in the brief dawn calm prior to the start of the Samar battle: "We just sent off planes engaged in close air support for the Army troops that were going ashore in routine unopposed amphibious landings. [...] we were in three circular carrier formations in a north-south line, with about 7 or 8 miles, maybe 10 miles, between groups. We could just see the group to the north of us, and we could not even see the third group, which was even farther north over the horizon." (Wooldridge, 1993, 206).

Taffy III consisted of six jeep carriers, including USS *Fanshaw Bay, Saint Lo, White Plains, Kalinin Bay, Kitkun Bay,* and *Gambier Bay*; three destroyers, *Hoel, Heermann,* and *Johnston;* and three tiny destroyer escorts, *Dennis, John C. Butler, Raymond,* and *Samuel B. Roberts*. None of the men aboard, including the overall commander Rear Admiral Clifton "Ziggy" Sprague, guessed they would soon enter the annals of U.S. naval history thanks to a desperately courageous last stand action.

The *Samuel B. Roberts*

The *Saint Lo* launched a six-airplane submarine recon detachment as a standard precaution that morning. Four Grumman TBF Avenger torpedo bombers and two Grumman F4F Wildcats left the deck and fanned out across the ocean in search of submarines running on the surface or other signs of enemy activity. One of the Avengers, piloted by William Brooks, flew northwest towards San Bernardino Strait.

Tom Van Brunt, an Avenger pilot scouting northeast, later reported the events that unfolded at 6:43 AM: "We hadn't been airborne more than fifteen minutes when Bill [Brooks] came on the net using our call sign. 'Derby Base, Derby Base, contact, contact. I have the Japanese navy in sight.' There was a pause and then a skeptical voice came back. 'How do you know they're Japanese?' Bill's response was slow, exasperated: 'I can see the biggest damn red meatball flag flying from the biggest pagoda mast I ever saw! They're shooting at me!'" (Sears, 2005, 127).

Brooks' astonishment at encountering a massive and instantly hostile Japanese fleet was matched by the surprise of the Japanese at encountering American aircraft and carriers on the Philippine Sea, not in Leyte Gulf. The flak batteries opened fire on the lone Avenger at the same time that lookouts spotted Taffy III to the southeast. The Americans floated in a loose defensive formation, the jeep carriers in the center, and the destroyers and destroyer escorts forming a ring around them to intercept submarines.

Brooks dropped his four depth charges in a futile effort to damage one of the cruisers, braving a whirlwind of flak to do so, then headed away south just 50 feet above the ocean surface, jinking unpredictably right and left. This maneuver, copied from the game birds he liked to hunt in the U.S., permitted his escape. He then set a course towards Taffy II to try to get a torpedo fitted to his Avenger.

On board the Japanese fleet, reactions ranged from dismay to jubilation. Kurita himself believed a stunning victory lay within his grasp. With the age-old tendency of human beings to see and hear what they wish to rather than what is actually in front of them, the Japanese officers identified the small *Casablanca*-class escort carriers as full-sized *Essex* carriers, the heart of the American naval juggernaut. With the jeep carriers inflated in their minds to the looming *Essex*-class, the Japanese also magnified the destroyers into battleships and the destroyer escorts into heavy cruisers in their imaginations. Kurita thought he had the chance to smash six carriers, three battleships, and four cruisers, perhaps enough on its own to bring the Americans to the negotiating table. The Admiral sent an exultant radio message back to Japan: "We are engaging enemy in gun battle […] By heaven-sent opportunity we are dashing to attack the enemy carriers." (Hornfischer, 2004, 137).

Ranging shells began falling near Taffy III at extreme range. Looking northwest, the Americans could see the ominous towers of Imperial pagoda bridges looming darkly out of a rain squall as the gigantic force advanced to smash them. The main Japanese force headed straight towards Taffy III, while Vice Admiral Shiraishi Kazutaka led the six heavy cruisers eastward to outflank the Americans.

Unsettled weather prevailed during the action. Though the morning sun flashed and glistened at times on the tropical sea, cumulus clouds covered approximately 30% of the sky. Hazy conditions prevailed, with occasional rain showers under some of the cumulus clouds. As the morning warmed, periodic squalls developed over the Philippine Sea.

Moreover, the battle off Samar witnessed the first deployment of a weapons system soon to achieve permanent notoriety. One of the most fascinating aspects of World War II was Japan's use of suicide pilots, known around the globe as kamikazes, though the Japanese referred to them as Tokubetsu kōgekitai ("Special Attack Units"). Translated as "God Wind," "Divine Wind" and "God Spirit," kamikazes would sink 47 Allied vessels and damage over 300 by the end of the war, but the rise in the use of kamikaze attacks was evidence of the loss of Japan's air superiority and its waning industrial might. This method of fighting would become more common by the time Iwo Jima was fought over in early 1945, and it was especially prevalent during the invasion of Okinawa in April 1945.

The "privilege" of being selected as a kamikaze pilot played directly into the deep-seated Japanese mindset of "death before defeat." The pilot training manual assured each kamikaze candidate that when they eliminated all thoughts of life and death, fear of losing the earthly life can be easily overcome. Still, not all cases of those chosen to be kamikazes were equally noble. Recruits were trained with torturous regimens or corporal punishment, and stories of mental impairment caused by drugs or saki abound. Some were described as "tottering" and dazed, being carried to their planes by maintenance officers, and forcibly pushed in if they backed down. Pilots who could not find their targets were told to turn around and spare their own lives for another day, but if a pilot returned nine times, he was to be shot. At the moment of collision, he was instructed to keep his eyes open at all times, and to shout "Hissatsu" ("clear kill").

Altogether, nearly 4,000 kamikaze pilots died in combat between October 1944 and August 1945, and about one in seven managed to hit his target. At their peak, they did far more damage to the American navy than did conventional air attacks, and they undoubtedly placed a significant new obstacle in the path of the American forces slowly encircling the Japanese home islands. However, the widespread use of kamikaze tactics darkened and hardened attitudes toward Japan within the American military and helped to set the stage for the total war on Japanese civilians that the American military waged in the closing months of the war. *The Marine Corps Gazette* noted, "The ruthless atrocities by the Japanese throughout the war had already brought on an altered behavior (deemed so by traditional standards) by many Americans resulting in the desecration of Japanese remains, but the Japanese tactic of using the Okinawan people as human shields brought about a new aspect of terror and torment to the psychological capacity of the Americans." As one sailor aboard the USS *Miami* recalled about kamikaze attacks at Okinawa, "They came in swarms from all directions. The barrels of our ship's guns got so hot we had to use firehoses to cool them down."

The kamikazes were the most effective weapon the Japanese had in terms of sinking ships, but they only appeared in the final year of the war. The fact that Japan's military leadership concluded it was both necessary and justified to establish special units of pilots trained to sacrifice their own lives by crashing their planes into enemy vessels was a mark of their own desperation. In the heat of battle, individual soldiers occasionally risked certain or near-certain death to protect their comrades or advance their mission, but organized unites devoted to suicide tactics were virtually unknown before 1944. They appeared only once the course of the war had turned decidedly against the Japanese.

The concept in its modern form developed in the 1920s, with a history dating back to the deep thirst for self-destruction often shown by the samurai. One pilot, Shimamura Ataru, attempted to put the mood of the kamikaze pilots into words prior to leaving on his own fatal mission: "I shall fall, smiling and singing songs. Please visit and worship at Yasukuni Shrine this spring. There I shall be a cherry blossom, smiling, with many other colleagues. I died smiling, so please smile. Please do not cry. Make my death meaningful." (Rielly, 2010, 36).

Having lost the vast majority of its experienced flyers, and with demand for pilots higher than ever before, the Japanese Navy had no choice but to rush new recruits through highly abbreviated training programs. By 1944, American pilots received two years of training, including at least 300 hours of flight-time, before entering combat, but new Japanese pilots typically received 40 hours of in-flight training or less, and instead of learning navigation, they were simply instructed to tail their group leaders. Looking back, a flight instructor of the time wrote, "Everything was urgent. We were told to rush men through. We abandoned refinements, just tried to teach them how to fly and shoot. One after another, singly, in twos and threes, training planes smashed into the ground, gyrated wildly through the air. For long, tedious months, I tried to create fighter pilots. It was a hopeless task. Our resources were too meagre, the demand too great." (Sakai, 213).

As the U.S. forces steadily moved closer to Japan, the Japanese had neither the aircraft nor the trained pilots needed to mount carrier-based operations. Facing this dilemma, and called upon to stage a last-ditch defense of Japan's empire against the oncoming American advance, the Naval Air Service sought out a radical change in tactics. In fact, the desperate situation of Japanese aviators on and around the Philippines had already driven several to adopt haphazard kamikaze attacks. There were two unsuccessful attempts at suicide attacks on September 13, 1944, and another on October 15. On October 21, the same day that the first organized *Tokubetsu kōgekitai* strike took off from Luzon, a single Japanese aircraft, likely either an Aichi D3A dive-bomber or a Mitsubishi Ki-51, seemed to crash deliberately into the *HMAS Australia*, an Australian heavy cruiser, killing 30, wounding 64, and causing major damage. The unknown pilot apparently acted on his own initiative, and his attack was not part of an organized kamikaze strike.

If any officer in the Japanese Navy was qualified to oversee a radical departure in tactics, it was Vice Admiral Ōnishi Takijirō. He had served as a junior officer to Admiral Yamamoto Isoroku, architect of the Pearl Harbor attack, and like Yamamoto, Ōnishi had a forceful creative personality, a powerful bond with his men, and a reputation among his superiors as a maverick. He had a firm grasp of the practical details of naval aviation thanks to the fact that he had personally flown every type of Japanese aircraft, and he was courageous to the point of endangering himself without thinking about it. He was even the first officer in the Imperial Navy to practice parachuting.

Vice Admiral Ōnishi Takijirō

In October 1944, Ōnishi arrived in Manila to take command of the First Naval Air Fleet and was determined to keep the Philippines out of American hands. The islands had been an American territory since the 1898 Spanish-American War, and in 1935, the United States granted the Philippines commonwealth status and began preparations for full independence, but these plans were swept away in the weeks following the attack on Pearl Harbor. A Japanese invasion force landed on northern Luzon on December 10, 1945, and quickly advanced south, forcing General Douglas MacArthur, Commander of the United States Armed Forces in the Far East, into a humiliating and costly retreat. By late 1944, however, the Japanese occupiers were caught between a growing guerilla resistance movement and a looming American invasion. Ōnishi, his officers, and superiors all understood the importance of holding the islands, which served as a key midpoint in the transport of vital raw materials from Japan's new southeast Asian territories to the home islands.

The Philippines were crucial to Japan's war effort, and within days of his arrival, Ōnishi was promoting organized kamikaze tactics. As he told an October 19 meeting of officers at Mabalacat, headquarters of the 201st Air Group, "In my opinion, there is only one way of assuring that our meagre strength will be effective to a maximum degree. That is to organize attack units composed of Zero fighters armed with two-hundred-fifty kilogram bombs, with each place to crash-dive into an enemy carrier…What do you think?" (Inoguchi and Nakajima, 463). Ōnishi argued that suicide tactics could help to equalize the growing imbalance of forces, and by taking advantage of the unique spirit of discipline and self-sacrifice that he and other officers attributed to the Japanese military, relatively untrained pilots could deliver 500 pound bombs to their targets with far greater accuracy than conventional bombers. Furthermore, since the missions would be one-way by design, they could effectively double the ranges of their aircraft.

Despite the obviously radical nature of his suggestion, Ōnishi's fellow officers were largely open to the idea, which was indicative of their increasing desperation and their willingness to adopt any new tactic that might improve the odds. In fact, it was Captain Inoguchi Ren'ya who was responsible for their name. Officially, the group would be known as the *Tokubetsu kōgekitai*, "Special Attack Units," or *Tokkōtai*, but Captain Inoguchi suggested a more evocative title: *shinpū*. The name was a combination of two Chinese characters: *shin* (meaning "gods," "spirits," or "divine") and *fū* (meaning "wind"). Read in the classical Chinese fashion, the *on'yomi*, they yielded the compound *shinpū*, but when read in the native Japanese style, the *kun'yomi*, the same characters form the name *kamikaze*.

By 1945, the Naval Air Service would run short of volunteers for kamikaze missions, and of the nearly 4,000 kamikaze pilots who perished during the war, a considerable majority were conscripts who enrolled in the program under varying degrees of compulsion. At this early stage, however, Ōnishi's call for volunteers met with considerable enthusiasm among Japanese naval pilots in the Philippines. At a base in Cebu, all but two pilots on staff volunteered for kamikaze missions, and those two holdouts were laid up in the sick bay. One ardent volunteer, Lieutenant Seki Yukio of the 201st Air Group, was a newlywed who had been married for just three months to a woman he had been courting through the mail. "I'm doing this for my beloved wife," he explained to a war correspondent before departing on his final mission. Similarly, before his own final mission on October 28, 1944, Petty Officer Isao Matsuo addressed a letter to his father and mother: "Dear Parents, please congratulate me. I have been given a splendid opportunity to die. This is my last day."

Moreover, as the tide of the war turned decisively against Japan, and as casualty counts grew more and more lopsided, the distinction between suicide and conventional missions was not as clear as one might think. Japanese pilots were outnumbered, outgunned, undertrained, and underequipped, so they faced increasingly bleak odds when they flew into combat. For example, the second Japanese air strike of the Battle of the Philippine Sea (June 1944) was comprised of 107 attacking aircraft, and despite being a conventional operation, only 10 survived.

High casualties were not unusual for the Japanese in the latter stages of the war either. Of about 77,000 Japanese servicemen defending Okinawa between April and June of 1945, only about 7,000 survived. Increasingly, service in the Japanese military had itself become a sort of "suicide" mission. With the specter of death already hanging so closely over them, battle-weary Japanese pilots may not have regarded adoption of kamikaze tactics as the profound existential leap it appears to people today.

The first official *Tokkōtai* unit set off on its inaugural mission on October 21, and the night before the mission, Ōnishi addressed his men: "Japan is in grave danger. The salvation of our country is now beyond the power of the ministers of state, the general staff, and humble commanders like myself. It can come only from spirited young men like you. Thus, on behalf of your hundred million countrymen, I ask this sacrifice of you and pray for your success." (Ito, 37–38).However, this first mission ended in failure because the group was unable to locate a target and instead returned to base.

Ready for another attempt, two units of freshly minted kamikazes set out from Japanese airbases on the morning of the 25th to support Kurita's attack. The Americans had heard occasional rumors of suicide pilots, but they truly witnessed a sustained kamikaze attack for the first time at Samar.

This photograph shows the men of the first kamikaze unit. The men are being offered a ceremonial toast of water as a farewell. Yukio Seki, the leader of the first kamikaze unit, is shown with a cup in his hands, and Vice Admiral Ōnishi is in the middle of the photo facing the five men of the unit.

As the splashes of gunfire stalked towards them over the sea – brightly colored by the dye placed in Japanese shells so that observers could identify and correct the salvos of specific vessels – the escort carriers turned east into the light wind. This facing helped the aircraft still on their decks to take off, and explained why Vice Admiral Shiraishi's cruisers tried to move east of the American formation.

All the Grumman Avengers, F4F Wildcats, and other aircraft still aboard the jeep carriers launched with desperate speed. The American airmen gathered in squadrons and steered towards the pursuing Japanese fleet. The top speed for the American *Casablanca* carriers stood at 18 knots due to their engines, originally built for ore carriers on the Great Lakes hauling taconite iron ore from the "Twin Ports" of Duluth, Minnesota and Superior, Wisconsin. Conversely, many of Kurita's ships traveled at 35 knots, which meant that with about 15 miles still between them, every 5 minutes of sailing brought the Japanese a mile closer.

The mixed force of Avengers and F4Fs flew northwest to engage the Japanese. The pilots found motivation both in the ordinary aggression of fighting men and in sheer survival, since if the IJN forces sank the carriers, the airplanes might have nowhere to land, forcing them to ditch in the sea and most likely condemning their occupants to a lonely death in the waves.

Many of the aircraft had no ordnance loads but attempted to strafe the gigantic ships cleaving through the sea below them. Others carried bombs or torpedoes and managed to score hits on their targets. Tom Van Brunt dropped depth bombs on the cruiser *Suzuya*. Whether from his unorthodox depth charge attack or the unrecorded efforts of another plane, the cruiser suffered heavy damage, dropping out of formation and sinking hours later, though Van Brunt knew nothing of this until after the war: "I climbed and dived, but when I got through the cloud I realized I'd come in too shallow. I had to climb again and make a steeper dive […] When I finally dropped the depth bombs and began to pull up I almost blacked out. […] My gunner John South and my radioman Lester Frederickson told me two of the bombs straddled the cruiser. They saw explosions but couldn't give any damage assessment." (Sears, 2005, 147).

At approximately the same time that the American Avengers and F4Fs made their attack runs on Kurita's fleet, six kamikazes of the "Morning Sun" and "Floating Chrysanthemum" squadrons under First Flying Petty Officers Ueno Keeichi and Kato Toyobumi reached Taffy I from their base at Davao.

The Taffy I ships had just sent most of their remaining aircraft to aid Taffy III, leaving them with no effective air cover. In fact, live ordnance strewed the decks of the jeep carriers as the crews worked to rearm Avengers and other aircraft coming in singly after bombing the Japanese fleet.

The first kamikaze plunged into the deck of the USS *Santee*, a moment captured in an eerie photograph showing the air full of shrapnel and two American seamen crouching for cover behind a gun. 16 men died along with the kamikaze pilot, and dozens more were injured. The aircraft punched a hole in the deck and missed a pile of 1,000 lb bombs by a hairsbreadth.

A second kamikaze swooped at the USS *Sangamon* but a single impeccably aimed shot from the *Suwannee's* 5-inch gun smashed it out of the air just short of the *Sangamon's* bow, though the debris killed one man and wounded two others on the deck. The flak guns on the USS *Petrof Bay* downed a third attacker.

The fourth kamikaze appeared hesitant to die now that the moment had actually arrived. He dodged through the clouds and squalls for nearly half an hour, moving back and forth over the ships, apparently unable to force himself to take his final plunge. However, an F6F Hellcat finally made the decision for him. When the American aircraft damaged the kamikaze's plane, he finally dived at the USS *Suwannee* at 8:04 AM and punched through the deck. Nevertheless, despite leaving a 20-foot hole in his wake, the kamikaze only slightly delayed the *Suwannee's* continued launching of aircraft. As a terse report to Taffy I's commander from the jeep carrier stated, "All we found of the Jap are bits of his flesh. We're ready for battle again." (Y'Blood, 1987, 296). The relative failure of the kamikazes lulled the Americans into a false sense of their ineffectuality, which would soon be dispelled by bitter subsequent experiences.

The USS *Suwannee* in the distance shortly after being hit by a kamikaze

Taffy III, in the meantime, enjoyed a brief piece of good fortune in the shape of a heavy rain squall that swept over them. The escort carriers plunged into the blinding gray curtains of rain, which sluiced in glistening rivers over their decks and pounded on their islands and catwalks in a frantic dance of exploding, silvery drops. Sprague ordered an immediate turn to the south, and the Japanese salvos began missing as the shadowy shapes of the CVEs blended into the squall.

For 15 minutes, the rain played havoc with the Japanese aim, then tailed off. Kurita, uttering an IJN aphorism – "A sighted enemy is the equivalent of a dead enemy" – ordered the pursuit to continue. As the rain swept away over the sea, leaving Taffy III relatively exposed to its enemies except for the volumes of smoke produced by the destroyers (DDs) and destroyer escorts (DEs),

Sprague ordered the seven small escorts to attack the Japanese with their torpedoes.

Smoke coming from some of Taffy III's destroyers

Commander William Dow Thomas on the USS *Hoel* quickly organized the desperate attack against the vastly superior force of Japanese cruisers, battleships, and destroyers. The three destroyers would spearhead the charge, while the four lighter destroyer escorts would follow up, moving forward through the smoke laid by the destroyers during their attack run. Lieutenant Commander Robert Copeland of the Samuel B. Roberts used his megaphone to tell his crew they faced "a fight against overwhelming odds from which survival could not be expected." (Woodward, 1947, 175).

With courage equaling any Japanese banzai charge, the crews of the three destroyers *Hoel*, *Heermann*, and *Johnston* accelerated to flank speed and plowed through the seas straight towards the mighty Japanese armada, centered on the super-battleship *Yamato*. As they charged out of their own smokescreen, the IJN vessels opened fire. The air filled with the roar of incoming shells and the sea erupted into columns and curtains of varicolored spray as the dye-laden explosives tore into its surface.

Even as the first shells crashed through their structure, the plucky destroyers launched spreads of torpedoes and loosed salvos from their 5-inch guns, then wheeled away, back into the billows of white and black smoke lingering in the humid air. Aboard the *Johnston,* the captain of Turret Four, Robert Hollenbaugh, witnessed a devastating hit from a Japanese gun: "After the torpedo attack we made a sharp turn [...] Hauling ass, I mean we were going! [...] all of a sudden I heard this big 'Thump.' It was a shell hitting on the port side, just forward of mount four. It pierced the deck [...] and knocked out one of our engines. The stern just came up out of the water and slammed back down. [...] I heard Bobby Chastain, the trainer, and Sam Moody, the pointer, saying, 'Boats, we got no power.'" (Sears, 2005, 151).

The thin skins of the American destroyers, earning them their nickname of "tin cans," failed to set off the impact fuses of the Japanese shells, which passed through and detonated only when they struck the sea beyond. Nevertheless, the kinetic energy of the huge missiles still punched large holes in the destroyers, destroyed their equipment, and killed men or wounded them terribly.

The *Johnston* sat briefly, motionless and exposed to IJN fire, but almost immediately, a torrential rain squall swept over the vessel. This gave the crew time to start the engines again, make a few hasty repairs, and offer some treatment to the wounded. When the squall cleared, the *Johnston* could manage 17 knots again, returning to the attack.

"Stormed at with shot and shell," as the British had been on another October 25th long before at Balaclava, the seven small ships darted and wove, laying smoke, launching torpedoes, and firing at the Japanese ships with their 5-inch cannons and 40mm guns. As they did, the Japanese slowly shot them to pieces, reducing the upper works of the ships to torn rags of steel and butchering the crews. Headless bodies strewed the decks amid rivulets of blood, pieces of limbs and intestines, and pitifully wounded men.

However, the attack of the DD and DE squadron seriously hampered the Japanese. Many of the ships in Kurita's force found themselves compelled to turn and turn again, avoiding incoming torpedo wakes. Even the mighty *Yamato* made a lumbering turn to narrowly avoid a lethal spread of torpedoes, taking Kurita out of the center of the fight. The Japanese formation turned to a chaotic jumble, its advance greatly slowed, and Taffy III's few remaining aircraft continued to pound the IJN ships as well.

Inevitably, the American destroyers began to drop out of the fight. The *Hoel* sank first, with two-thirds of its crew slaughtered by the lethal fire. *Samuel B. Roberts* succumbed next, its hull blown open by a pair of massive 14 inch shells. Copeland ordered "abandon ship" at 9 AM. Men, many of them wounded or mangled, scrambled over the side to an emergency raft with boarding nets attached to its sides. As the skipper, medic, and other personnel swept the ship from stem to stern for survivors – with shells still plowing into the vessel, killing some of the men – they found Gunner's Mate Third Class Paul H. Carr fatally wounded by the rear 5-inch gun. Carr, dying from a huge wound in the guts, still held a 5-inch shell in his hands – the last of 325, the other 324 having already been fired. Carr asked the men to help him load and fire the shell. When they left for a moment to fetch the medic, Copeland and his group returned to find Carr unsteadily on his feet, trying feebly to push the shell into the gun's smashed breech in order to fire it. The men administered first aid to Carr, but he soon died, and the remaining sailors abandoned ship immediately before it sank.

The ship's mascot, a black-furred 15-lb mixed breed dog named Sammy, swam to the raft and sat on it briefly. After a minute or two, however, he slipped into the water and swam back to the *Roberts* immediately before it sank. The men interpreted his action as a desire to "go down with the ship," though a more likely explanation is that Sammy held a strong attachment for one of the crew, and, finding the man absent from the raft, returned to the doomed ship to look for him.

With *Hoel* and *Roberts* gone, a ring of Japanese destroyers formed around *Johnston*, firing their guns unceasingly into the disintegrating American DD. Soon, the crew found themselves forced to abandon ship. As the destroyer sank prow-first, one of the IJN destroyers approached, slowing as it did. The burned, wounded, battered men floating in the sea watched nervously. Then they saw that the Japanese captain stood at the rail in his impeccable uniform, rigidly at attention, saluting the American destroyer and its crew.

Clint Carter noticed that most of the Japanese crew followed the example of their leader: "It appeared to me that every man on her deck was standing at attention, like a muster, giving us one big salute." (Hornfischer, 2005, 276). One man, however, thumbed his nose at the Americans, a gesture probably learned from the cinema. Another threw them a bulky can of tomatoes whose faded label still bore the legend "Product of Arkansas." Then the Japanese destroyer slid away in pursuit of Taffy III.

Despite the valor of the destroyermen, the escort carriers did not all escape. The Japanese cruisers shot *USS Gambier Bay,* sailing at the eastern end of the formation, to pieces during the course of the running battle. Finally holed below the waterline and devastated by internal explosions, the jeep carrier capsized and sank. Around 60 men died during the shelling and sinking; 800 lived to abandon ship, only to have sharks kill a number of them prior to rescue on October 27th.

Between them, however, the seven escorts (four of whom survived despite damage) and the small, mixed force of USN aircraft managed to sink four of Kurita's ships, all heavy cruisers – *Suzuya, Chokai, Chikuma,* and *Kumano.* Some historians of the battle think Kurita's *Yamato* was too far north to watch events, causing the admiral to temporarily recall his ships to re-form them. However, one of the surviving photographs of the *Gambier Bay's* last moments shows what strongly resembles a *Yamato*-class battleship in the background, perhaps a mile distant. If the photo does indeed show the super-battleship, Kurita made his decision to break off while on the scene.

Regardless of his exact location, the Japanese admiral gave a withdrawal order around 9 AM. The Japanese ships sailed north for two hours, then to the west for an hour. At noon, Kurita turned south again as if to resume the attack, but then, 30 minutes later, changed his mind again and made the final decision to sail for San Bernardino Strait and escape. He later stated he did not believe the destroyers would attack so furiously without heavy ship support nearby, and that that the constant American radio chatter between various task forces made him fear being caught in a trap.

Thanks to that withdrawal, the attack of seven determined American destroyers and a handful of Avenger and F4F aircraft had effectively frightened off a 23-ship armada made up of battleships, heavy cruisers, and the exceptionally large, powerful destroyers of the Emperor's navy. he sacrificial courage of the destroyers and destroyer escorts had, to the amazement of the Americans, helped turn away Kurita's massed surface ships, and in at least one case won the grudging admiration of a Japanese captain. The final shots of the surface engagement ceased between 9:07 and 9:10 AM, as the USS *Heermann* and the IJN cruiser *Tone* hurled a few final, defiant parting shots at one another. Sprague heard a yell from one of his signalmen: "God damn it, boys, they're getting away!" (Hornfischer, 2004, 257). Whether that was yelled ironically or in actual frustration remains unclear.

Ziggy Sprague knew Taffy III remained in fatal danger, however, and took immediate steps to leave the area. Kurita's force could easily return, and other hazards might appear at any moment. At 9:17, Sprague issued the order to lay smoke on the port quarter of the escort carriers, raising a smoke screen between his ships and the retiring Japanese. Under cover of the artificial vapor, the American ships limped back into formation, then moved off to the south, increasing their distance from the enemy. Officers allowed many of the crewmen to leave their combat stations to eat quickly.

The carrier *Gambier Bay* laying a smokescreen

As it turned out, there was indeed another force bore down on the limping, battered escort carriers: the day's second detachment of kamikazes. The "Shikishima" kamikaze unit under Lieutenant Seki Yukio lifted off from the Mabalacat airfield at 7:25 AM, arriving near Taffy 3 at 10:30 AM. This unit consisted of five kamikazes, including Seki himself, plus four escort fighters. Seki spent around 15 minutes observing the American vessels, lurking in the rows and clusters of cumulus clouds knotted across the sky. At 10:49, he gave the attack signal by waggling his aircraft's wings, avoiding any telltale radio signal.

At 10:51, a sharp-eyed lookout on the USS *Raymond* spotted the aircraft and opened fire. This alerted the rest of the ships, which also poured torrents of flak upwards towards the diving Japanese. The first kamikaze, probably already dead at his controls, missed the *Kitkun Bay*'s island and instead tore away part of the port catwalk, killing one man, before plunging into the ocean. At the same time, the *Fanshaw Bay,* Ziggy Sprague's flagship, blew another kamikaze to pieces before the aircraft came anywhere near its target.

A sharp turn to port by *White Plains* made the kamikaze aiming for it smash into the ocean nearby, wounding 11 men with shrapnel thrown up by the water impact but causing no serious damage. At this moment, however, the attack took a fateful turn. A kamikaze approached *White Plains*, suffered a flak hit, and swerved abruptly to plunge towards *Saint Lo* instead. The pilot released his bomb to crash through the jeep carrier's flight deck, then plunged through himself somewhat farther on. Both explosions caused massive fires on the hangar deck, where several aircraft had just been refueled and rearmed with bombs and torpedoes. These aircraft caught fire and exploded.

Picture of a kamikaze attempting to hit the USS *White Plains*

Picture of the explosion on the *Saint Lo* after being hit by a kamikaze

The crew, responding quickly, could have put out the flames if not for a fatal design flaw present in the escort carriers, but not larger American carriers. The firefighting piping system used cast iron pipes, which fractured and leaked under the violent shock of the bomb and kamikaze impacts. Some of the sprinklers worked, while others failed, and the firefighting hoses lost pressure within a few minutes.

Captain Francis McKenna ordered the ship abandoned when it became clear no means for stopping the fire existed. The Captain himself left the ship last, half an hour after the kamikaze strike. Shortly after he slid down one of the prepared escape lines into the ocean, the *Saint Lo* suffered a catastrophic internal explosion that ripped its hull violently open. The remains of the ship sank quickly after the blast. 113 men died out of 889, with 30 more perishing from their injuries following rescue.

At this point, several additional kamikazes appeared, though their origin remains murky. They attacked the *Kitkun Bay* and *Kalinin Bay*, scoring several glancing hits on the latter that inflicted moderate damage. One pilot dived too steeply and, despite passing the flak unharmed, plunged straight into the sea rather than hitting his target.

As the kamikaze attacks ceased, Sprague ordered the retirement to the southeast to continue. He detached all of the four surviving escorts to pick up survivors from *Saint Lo*. Sprague, at the time and later also, expressed great bitterness at the failure of other help to materialize to rescue his men from the sea. Regarding the decision to use all his escorts to rescue *Saint Lo*'s crew, he remarked, "This desperate expedient which left the Task Unit without any screen for the next eight hours was made necessary by the absence of any rescue effort from other sources. [...] We had been through so much by then that it didn't seem to make any difference whether we had escorts with us or not." (Y'Blood, 1987, 307).

While Taffy III's remnants finally made their escape, dramatic events unfolded elsewhere in the American fleet in response to the battle off Samar. Sprague had broadcast a plain language appeal for help to Admiral Kinkaid in desperation at the height of the action. Learning of the apparent catastrophe unfolding in the Philippine Sea, and unable to understand how Kurita moved such a powerful armada through the San Bernardino Strait unopposed, Admiral Chester Nimitz sent a message to "Bull" Halsey at 10 AM. This message consisted of a single sentence betraying Nimitz's astonishment: "Where is, repeat, where is TF 34?"

However, the radioman on Halsey's flagship USS *New Jersey* left in the "padding" at the end of the message, intended to confuse Japanese codebreakers: "The world wonders." Halsey read the message – "Where is, repeat, where is TF 34? The world wonders" – and instantly flew into an aggrieved rage. He pulled the hat from his head and flung it to the deck, then began swearing and raving at a shout; some sources even suggest he sobbed in frustration. He interpreted the message as a piercing criticism from Nimitz, probably in part due to realization of how massively he had erred.

After Halsey's tantrum continued for several minutes, Rear Admiral Robert Carney barked at his superior, "Stop it! What the hell's the matter with you? Pull yourself together." (Hornfischer, 2004, 178). This had the effect of calming Halsey, though he dithered for over an hour before finally deciding to send the battleships back to aid Sprague at 11:15 AM. Their belated and ultimately futile race to help at Samar earned this maneuver the mocking title of "the Battle of Bull's Run," a clever pun playing off of Halsey's nickname and the first major land battle of the American Civil War.

Though Halsey later claimed ignorance of the situation to his south prior to receipt of the "world wonders" transmission, strong evidence suggests that he became aware of Taffy III's plight earlier and chose to ignore it. Admiral John S. "Slew" McCain, grandfather of 2008 presidential candidate John McCain, commanded Task Group 38.1, refueling at Ulithi on the morning of October 28th. At 7:25 AM, his radio operators intercepted a call from Kinkaid to Halsey describing the attack on Taffy 3 – which, unless Halsey failed to receive it, gave him almost real-time news of the potential disaster. "Slew" McCain immediately ordered an end to refueling and set Task Group 38.1 in motion towards Halsey's position, intending to support him against the Japanese carriers of the feint.

Then, at 9:40 AM, his radiomen picked up another Kincaid message, describing a massive Japanese fleet action against Taffy III. On his own initiative, McCain ordered Task Group 38.1

to alter course, sailing to the aid of Ziggy Sprague and his embattled flattops. At 10:30 AM, with a range of 330 miles still between his task group and Taffy III, McCain launched air attacks from his *Essex*-class carriers. Though the air groups failed to sink any more Japanese vessels, they achieved some bomb hits on Kurita's retiring forces, persuading them to continue on their way. As McCain later described the action, "The escort carriers put up a big fight, one of the biggest fights I've ever seen. I don't claim credit. […] I went down to Leyte at 10:30 the morning of the 25th, a half hour before the Jap fleet turned around. It turned around for at least two reasons. Our escort carriers fought so furiously the Japs assumed they were a larger force. Also because we sent in carrier groups to help out." (Gilbert, 2006, 153-154).

Airstrikes from McCain's ships would sink a further cruiser in Kurita's retiring force the following day, October 26th. Altogether, Task Group 38.1 lost 18 aircraft during the Battle of Leyte Gulf, most of them to Japanese anti-aircraft fire. The surviving aircraft of the jeep carriers also aided in harassing the Japanese retreat during the ensuing days.

Throughout this time, Sprague radioed Kinkaid and asked for help in rescuing the men from the Taffy III escorts sunk during the action. Kinkaid sent a scout aircraft to find the men, which it did successfully. Unfortunately, the pilot radioed drastically incorrect coordinates, so when the ships sent by Kinkaid arrived at the designated location, they found only empty waves. The men from the sunken destroyers thus faced several grisly days in the water prior to rescue. Clinging to rafts too small to support all of them at once, the men suffered incredible hardships as they floated in the tepid tropical seas. The badly wounded died first, though a few, incredibly, survived only to die within minutes of being rescued.

On top of that, even those who were lightly injured or able-bodied soon found themselves marked for death. Sharks approached the rafts within a few hours of the sinking. Initially driven off by the men's shouts and splashing, they soon returned to circle in the clear water below the rafts. Survivors later claimed that some of the sharks measured 10 to 12 feet in length, and they began to attack their nearly helpless prey, taking bites out of limbs and bodies.

Desperately, the survivors tried hauling the injured out of the water in an effort to save them, but many quickly bled to death. One man, with a large bite taken out of his guts, screamed and begged with his comrades to kill him for around an hour before another sailor, unable to bear the sight and sound of his agony any longer, first attempted to shoot him with a waterlogged pistol, then opened the vein in his neck with a clasp knife.

Scorched by the sun, tortured by thirst, and frazzled by shark attacks, many of the men slipped into delirium. In a perhaps more merciful death than others suffered, these men spoke of their hallucinations of fountains of fresh water, beer, lemonade, beautiful women, and other marvels before swimming away to drown or simply diving straight down. Even those who survived began to experience frequent hallucinations, brought on by thirst, the slow hypothermia of the lukewarm tropical sea, and drinking seawater.

Lieutenant Everett Roberts of the *Samuel B. Roberts* found himself just as vulnerable to these curious visions as his crew: "As the currents propelled the survivors westward through the night, Roberts discerned a point of land that was dotted with fine homes. A gala dinner party was in progress, tuxedoed men and gloriously begowned women enjoying a high time by the sea." (Hornfischer, 2004, 304).

Even as the men had to endure all of that, the sharks continued to harry the survivors, often attacking in the night. The sleeping and half-sleeping men would awaken to frantic screams and the sight of a man being dragged off the raft by a shark. Despite their efforts to beat off the predatory fish, the victim usually vanished under the surface in a swirl of blood, never to be seen again. Other men, utterly exhausted, drowned when they fell asleep; the mild water entering their noses and mouths failed to wake them, and they died without ever realizing they were drowning.

Many of those who survived did so because they lost the energy and interest needed for the tempting phantoms of their imagination to lure them into the effort required to leave the raft. A few men actually reached the Philippine shore, where the Filipino guerillas gave them a very different welcome than they extended to the Japanese. The destroyermen were fed, given water and whatever medical care the local people had to offer, and found themselves hidden and protected by bands of fighters armed with machetes and submachine guns. When they recovered sufficiently, the Filipinos took them to American intelligence outposts or the rapidly advancing American front lines.

Most, however, remained at sea until the 27th, when an LCI (Landing Craft Infantry) found the clusters of survivors and picked them up off their rafts. Most proved unable to eat, throwing up anything they consumed, but they drank large quantities of water. Crammed into any belowdecks spaces available, they slept for extended periods as the LCI took them to a location where a hospital ship awaited.

Ziggy Sprague eventually arranged for their return to the United States for recuperation aboard commandeered cruise ships, and the survivors of the desperate Samar destroyer charge found themselves returning "Stateside" in luxury suites and well-appointed cabins that accommodated tourists in more peaceful times. Sprague later offered his own interpretation of the Samar action and the remarkable survival of Taffy III when confronted by one of the most powerful concentrations of Japanese non-carrier warships ever assembled: "In summation, the failure of the enemy main body and encircling light forces to completely wipe out all vessels of this Task Unit can be attributed to our successful smoke screen, our torpedo counterattack, continuous harassment of enemy by bomb, torpedo, and strafing air attacks, timely maneuvers, and the definite partiality of Almighty God." (Hornfischer, 2004, 322).

The final major action of the Battle of Leyte Gulf occurred near Cape Engaño, where elements of Halsey's task force clashed with Vice Admiral Ozawa Jisaburo's decoy Northern Force. Ozawa, a gaunt figure 6 feet 7 inches tall, acquired the nickname "Onigawara" – roughly "ogre-gargoyle" – due to his combined height and supposed ugliness, but his intelligence, professionalism, and concern for his men's welfare won him considerable popularity among them.

The battle at Cape Engaño, one-sided from the beginning, could only end in disaster for Ozawa. His entire purpose consisted of serving as a sacrificial pawn drawing Halsey's force away from San Bernardino, in which he succeeded admirably. However, it remained necessary to persuade the Americans that the decoy force presented enough of a threat to prevent "Bull" from turning back too soon.

With just 108 aircraft available, Ozawa and his men prepared to fight, and Ozawa himself described this strategy following the war: "A decoy, that was our first primary mission, to act as a decoy. My fleet could not very well give direct protection to Kurita's force because we were very weak, so I tried to attack as many American carriers as possible [...] The main mission was all sacrifice. An attack with a very weak force of planes comes under the heading of sacrifice of planes and ships." (Woodward, 1947, 149).

The Northern Force sent 80 of its 108 aircraft to launch a strike on Halsey's task force to sting him into action. The other 28 aircraft provided a meager fighter cover to Ozawa's carrier, three light carriers, two hybrid battleship carriers, three light cruisers, and ten destroyers. Of these aircraft, approximately 40 survived to land on Luzon airfields.

On the night of the 25th, Halsey sped north around midnight and, as he approached Ozawa's slowly retiring force, formed his battleships, cruisers, and destroyers into Task Force 34. This surface fleet pushed out ahead of the carriers. Bull Halsey's plan consisted of devastating the IJN armada with airstrikes, at which time Task Force 34 would arrive to blow the survivors to pieces with direct gunfire.

Scouting aircraft kept Halsey apprised of his opponents' position in the ocean from 1 AM onward in the early morning of the 26th. Eventually, the Americans lost contact with the Japanese for a time. Regardless, the American carriers sent off their first strike groups at 6 AM, keeping them "orbiting" ahead of the fleet until scouts reestablished contact. The scouts continued probing north, but found nothing. Two junior lieutenants serving as part of the fleet's intelligence section, Lt. Byron White and Lt. Calvert Cheston, pored over charts and decided the Japanese fleet probably lay in an easterly direction. They argued passionately with their superiors, and the admirals eventually gave them permission to send a squadron of four fighters to the east.

At 7:35, under a brilliantly sunny sky, the fighter pilots bore out White's and Cheston's hunch by finding Ozawa's entire force northeast of Halsey's task forces. With this information in hand, Halsey released the full strength of Task Force 38's strike units against the Japanese.

The first massed formations brushed aside the tiny fighter umbrella of 28 aircraft, shooting down some and forcing the rest to retreat. The first raid sank one of the Japanese light carriers, the *Chiyoda,* and immobilized another, the *Chitose*. Though this represented a triumph, the American pilots concentrated on the already damaged ships rather than picking fresh targets. Rear Admiral Carney, soon to snap Halsey out of his rage with a well-chosen rebuke, ascribed this fact scathingly to "an inherent mammalian tendency to jump on cripples." (Woodward, 1947, 142).

During this attack, one of the bombs caused damage that may have accidentally saved Admiral Ozawa's life. This bomb struck the *Zuikaku,* Ozawa's only full-sized carrier and his flagship. The explosion completely destroyed the carrier's radio equipment. A modern commander without a radio is utterly useless, so Ozawa found himself compelled to move his headquarters to *Oyoda,* a nearby light cruiser.

American strikes continued through the day, and in all, 527 sorties pounded Ozawa's Northern Force. In the late morning, Kinkaid's and Nimitz's communications intervened, impelling Halsey to take his fast battleships and many other ships south to deal with Taffy III's critical situation. Perhaps characteristically, Halsey stripped Task Force 38 of most of its heavy ships, including all the battleships, leaving the carriers relatively vulnerable despite their screen of destroyers and heavy cruisers.

Vice Admiral Marc Mitscher commanded Task Force 38 following Halsey's exit, continuing the pressure on Ozawa's force. At 1:30 PM, under a light cover of cumulus clouds, the American aircraft, including Helldiver torpedo planes, located and attacked the carrier *Zuikaku* and the light carrier *Zuiho,* setting both afire. Repeated attacks continued, until the *Zuikaku* developed a heavy list. A surviving photograph from on board the famous carrier during its final moments shows a crowd of men standing on the violently canted deck, saluting the Japanese flag.

At 2:30 PM, the *Zuikaku* rolled over and sank, taking half of its crew to the bottom with it. At 3 PM, the *Zuiho* also sank as torpedo attacks and bombing continued. At this point, Mitscher loosed his cruisers and destroyers to finish off the Japanese ships, as well as search for downed pilots. Mitscher always showed great solicitude towards American airmen shot down in action, putting forth major efforts to locate and rescue them.

The cruisers attacked and sank the crippled light carrier *Chitose*, then looked for further targets. At the same time, Ozawa learned of the exposed position of these relatively light American warships and sent his two battleships south again, hoping to destroy some *Essex* carriers or at least a few destroyers and cruisers. Ultimately, the two forces missed each other on the vast expanses of the Philippine Sea. Airstrikes petered out during the late afternoon, and the surviving ships of Ozawa withdrew northward, having lost the remaining Japanese carriers plus a destroyer.

The final blow in the battle of Cape Engaño went to SS-368, the USS *Jallao*, a submarine of the tough *Balao*-class built in Manitowoc, Wisconsin. Captained by Lieutenant Commander Joseph Icenhower, the *Jallao* detected Ozawa's retreating ships and moved in, seeking a kill on its first combat patrol. As radarman Jack B. Weinstein, later a U.S. federal judge, described in an interview: "As we closed in, I noticed two pips on the radar. He asked what it was [...] I had never seen that phenomenon, but I said, 'Captain, it looks like a large destroyer or a small cruiser,' which was kind of nervy, I suppose. It turned out to be a small cruiser. [...] We made an attack, half-submerged with a spread of four torpedoes, as I recall, and the ship sunk immediately." (US Courts, 2014, online).

The *Jallao* sank the cruiser *Tama*, which broke in half when struck by the torpedoes with the loss of its full complement of 450 men. This event, at 11:10 PM, represented the final sinking during the main action at Leyte Gulf.

The American naval victory in Leyte Gulf allowed for an amphibious invasion of Leyte Island itself, and over the course of two months worth of fighting, the Allies eventually established themselves on the island and mostly wiped out the Japanese contingent, killing an estimated 50,000 Japanese. It was also at Leyte that the iconic picture of MacArthur wading ashore was taken, an image that has become closely associated with his return to the Philippines.

Picture of the amphibious invasion of Leyte

American soldiers fighting on Leyte

MacArthur walking ashore onto Leyte Island during the 1945 Philippines campaign

As MacArthur's campaign was progressing on Leyte, Allied forces began their attack on the Philippines with a landing at Mindoro, from which they planned to provide developed airfields that would allow them to give air cover to ships moving toward the Lingayen Gulf at Luzon. Secondarily, these airfields at Mindoro would give the Allies more options from which to contest Japanese air power in the region. American planners estimated the Japanese garrison on Mindoro to be roughly 1,000 men made up of a mix of the Japanese 8th Division and the 105th Division.

MacArthur assigned the American Sixth Army under General Krueger to carry out operations on Mindoro, and he would be supported by both air and naval units. Krueger delegated the task to Brigadier General William Dunckel, who utilized the 19th Regimental Combat Team of the 24th Division and the 503d Parachute RCT to carry out the mission. The ground forces began moving toward Mindoro on December 12, 1944 aboard the ships of Task Group 77.12. The Task Group moved unopposed through the Mindanao Sea until the next day, December 13, when they were spotted by Japanese surveillance. Japanese commanders held off attacking the Allied ships because they wanted to figure out the destination of the Task Group before engaging it, but by the middle of that afternoon, 10 Japanese plans, including three kamikaze planes, attacked the Task Group, with one kamikaze crashing into the flagship *Nashville*. With roughly 190 wounded sailors to deal with, some ships picked up survivors and returned to Leyte, while the command staff was transferred to the *Dashiell* to continue the mission.

Picture of a Japanese kamikaze plane during the campaign

Picture of an anti-aircraft crew on a Navy destroyer trying to cover Mindoro

By this time, the Japanese military believed the Task Group was headed toward either Panay, Cebu, or Negros, and in the course of searching for it near those areas, they wasted valuable time in which they could have continued their attacks. Meanwhile, on the morning of December 15, the Task Group reached Mindoro and began preparations for beach landings. As the landing units were disembarking, Japanese air operations attempted to aid ground troops in repelling the Allied forces. Although much of the Japanese air power was destroyed by Allied planes, kamikazes did manage to sink two landing ships, as well as the destroyer *Moale*. Japanese planes also damaged one other landing ship, the destroyer *Howorth*, and the CVE *Marcus Island*. In the air attacks, the Allies suffered 27 casualties, but aside from that, the troops of the 19th and 503d were able to land with little resistance, and this allowed some of the naval vessels of the Task Group to withdraw from the operation and move to support units in other locations.

As this was occurring, Allied planes attacked Luzon on December 16th, and the aircraft carriers designated for the Philippines campaign withdrew to the east for refueling before beginning a second series of attacks that took place on December 19th. Over the course of the next few days, naval and aerial engagements with Japanese aircraft destroyed an estimated 450 enemy planes, leaving the Allies with almost complete air superiority over the Philippines until the Japanese called in reinforcements from Formosa and the home islands.

By December 15th, the 19th and 503d had created a beachhead seven miles inland at Mindoro and had taken the airfield at the town of San Jose. Army engineers who had accompanied the landing parties then began building new airstrips roughly three miles south of the airfield at San Jose. The new airstrips, at a site they called Hill Drome, became operational on December 20th, and on that day American P-38s and P-61s began arriving from elsewhere in the Pacific. These airfields would be important in opposing a Japanese counterattack, which began on December 20th when 50 Japanese planes flew in to reinforce the existing 15 planes the Japanese Army Air Force had at Mindoro. Air attacks on December 21st destroyed two more landing craft, and ground units stationed on Mindoro were also attacked, causing roughly 70 casualties.

To counter the Allies, Japanese commanders ordered their Southwestern Area Fleet, which was comprised of two cruisers and six destroyers and was stationed at Manila, to Mindoro on a raiding mission to try to sink Allied ships off the coast. However, the Southwester Area Fleet was spotted in the South China Sea by Allied submarines, and 105 planes were sent from Mindoro to engage with the fleet. Although the Southwestern Fleet was attacked from the air, they managed to make their way to the beachhead, where they shelled the beach and airfields for roughly 40 minutes before withdrawing. In total, the Southwestern Area Fleet managed to destroy 26 planes and damage some Allied installations on Mindoro, while suffering the loss of one destroyer and sustaining damage to nearly all of the ships in the fleet.

On December 28th, Japanese air attacks resumed against Allied naval units near Mindoro, where they sunk three ships, along with a tanker and two landing vessels. Although these were heavy losses for the Allied naval presence at Mindoro, the Japanese lost 50 aircraft between December 28th and January 4th, and with no more reinforcements forthcoming, Japanese air power in the region was once again basically nullified.

Meanwhile, on Mindoro proper, Allied ground units began patrols on December 19th, where they searched for Japanese troops and guarded areas that might be landing spots for reinforcements for the Japanese garrisons on Luzon. Mindoro guerrillas also worked with Allied troops by helping to guide the patrols and engaging some of the remaining Japanese soldiers in mopping-up operations across the island. Reinforcing the 19th and 503d, General Krueger sent the 21st Division to Mindoro after the Southwestern Fleet Raid just in case a ground-based attack was being planned by Japan.

Army engineers continued building on Mindoro, and MacArthur sent additional bombers and fighters to the air bases there in preparation for later missions. He also had engineers build airfields for heavy bombers that would target areas in the southern Philippines and Formosa. Work on these heavy bomber airfields began on January 2nd, but they would not be ready for heavy bomber support in time for the invasion of Luzon. Nonetheless, by the middle of January, Allied Air Forces had three fighter groups, two medium bomber groups, two night fighter squadrons, three tactical reconnaissance squadrons, a photographic squadron, and an air-sea rescue squadron. With this air power mustered at Mindoro, the principal goal of the invasion of the island of Mindoro was complete, as the Allies now had their air bases in which to launch further air attacks. They now also had a base close to Luzon that put pressure on the Japanese to defend multiple possible entry points onto that island.

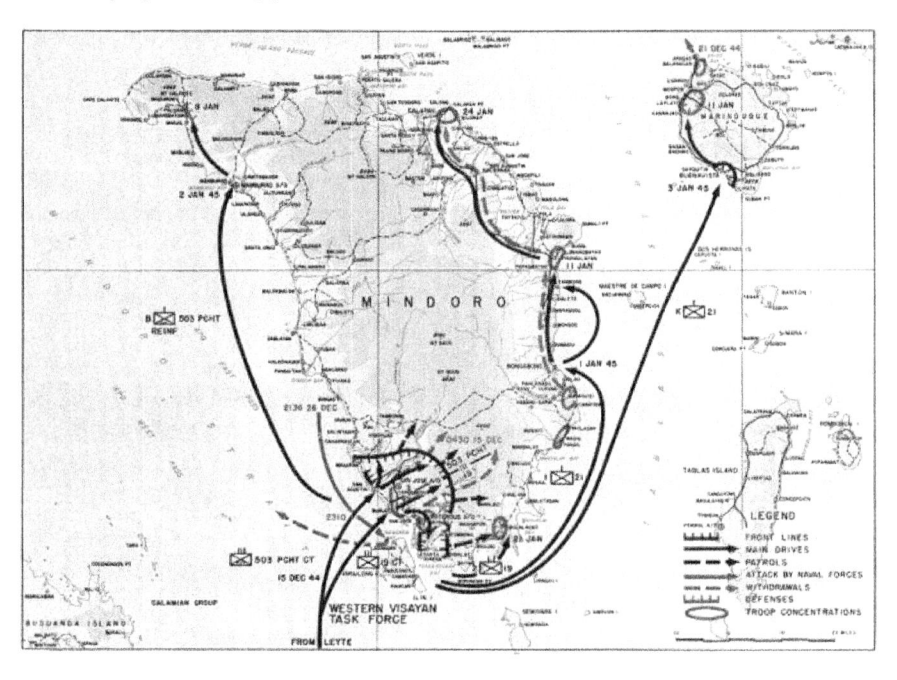

A map of action around Mindoro

With southern Mindoro under Allied control, MacArthur began a series of three feints to confuse Japanese forces on Luzon. First, he sent the Western Visayan Task Force to seize northeastern Mindoro and Marinduque Island, which he hoped would lead the Japanese to believe that the two areas would be bases from which the Allies would try to launch an invasion on southern Luzon. Then, naval units would begin fake maneuvers along the southern coast of Luzon, while guerrillas operating on Luzon would work with Allied forces in destroying infrastructure like railroads, bridges and communications lines in southern Luzon. Finally, Allied forces throughout the Pacific would maneuver to give the impression that Formosa, and not Luzon, was the next target for their operations.

On January 1st, the Western Visayan Task Force began its part of the operation by moving from its base in southern Mindoro toward northeastern Mindoro, which took them roughly 30 days to complete. As this was occurring, guerrilla operations in Mindoro had neutralized the remainder of the Japanese garrison on the island. These guerrillas killed 50 soldiers, and the remaining 300 stationed there fled into the interior.

However, the rest of the planned deception did not go as planned. The delays that the Western Visayan Task Force faced in moving to the north of the island meant that they did not arrive in time to put their part of the plan in place, but they did succeed in freeing groups of Filipinos on Mindoro. Nonetheless, Japanese commanders were well aware that Luzon was the next target of Allied operations, and that an attack would not occur in the southern region but instead would focus on the Lingayen Gulf, which was the same invasion point that the Japanese had used for its invasion back in 1941.

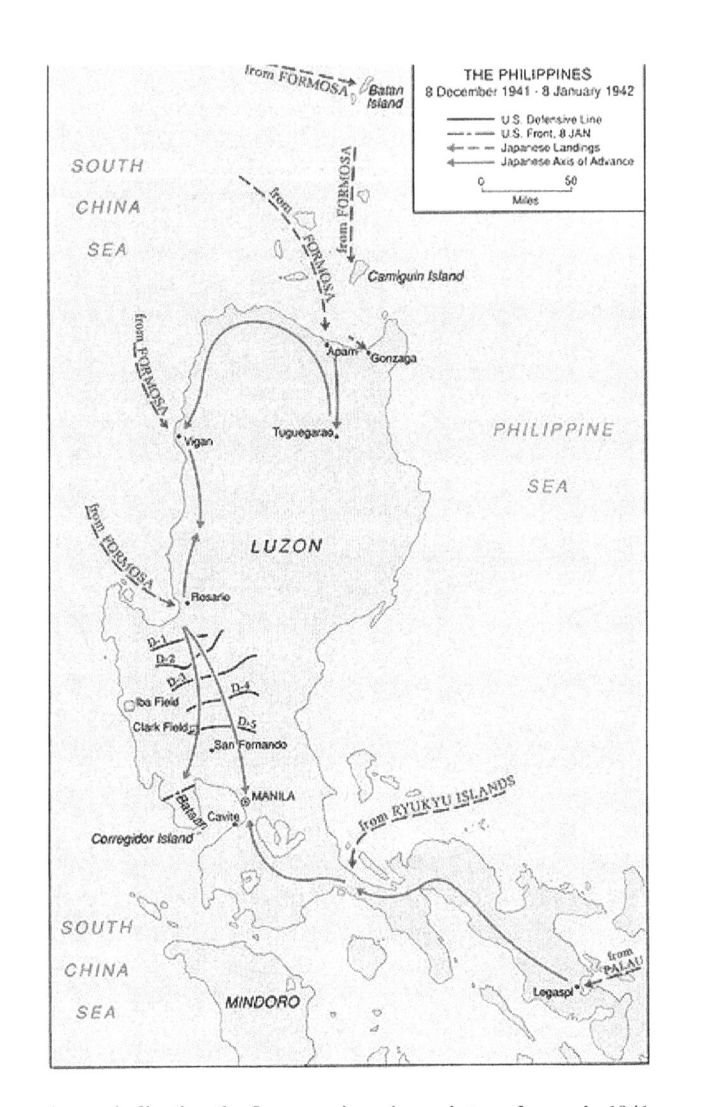

A map indicating the Japanese invasion points on Luzon in 1941

A picture of Filipino guerrillas on Mindoro

Allied aerial bombard of Luzon had begun in the fall of 1944, and they had already knocked out key military installations. Naval units also began to move on Luzon, with Admiral Halsey's carrier group and Admiral Kinkaid's surface forces nearing the Lingayen Gulf. In fact, during the beginning of the assault on Lingayen, military officials had problems coordinating staging activities between ground troops, naval vessels, and landing craft between the various launch and landing points. The initial landing at Lingayen Gulf involved two ground units, the XIV Corps and the I Corps. Along with these two ground units, the ships of the II and III Amphibious Force had the task of ferrying these units to their landing locations.

American battleships heading towards Lingayen Gulf

The landing units were designated the Luzon Attack Force, with the first group, consisting of screening and support ships, leaving from Leyte Gulf on January 2, 1945. Between January 4th and 5th, a second group left Leyte Gulf, this time consisting of three light cruisers, six destroyers, as well as smaller covering vessels. Finally, on January 6th, the ships carrying ground forces began making their way to the Lingayen Gulf.

To support this convoy of ships moving toward Lingayen Gulf, Mindoro-based planes began increasingly heavy attacks on Japanese targets in late December and early January. They especially targeted defensive installations at the Lingayen beaches, as well as Japanese transports bringing reinforcements to Luzon. The Third Fleet's fast carriers also moved into the region, and by January 3rd, they were in position to begin operations targeting Japanese air bases within range of Luzon: Formosa, the Ryukyu Islands, and the Pescadores. By January 6th, the fast carriers moved again, this time to the coast of Luzon, where they would provide cover over North Luzon (with Allied Air Force planes from Mindoro covering the Lingayen Gulf and Clark Field).

Picture of the Third Fleet moving towards the Philippines

In terms of the Japanese presence at Luzon by early January, 1945, when air attacks against island accelerated, they had only a minimal air presence remaining to contest the skies, so military leaders in Japan began to devote their resources to consolidating air power for the home islands rather than spreading out their remaining planes in an attempt to protect territories like the Philippines. The remaining Japanese planes at Luzon attempted a series of attacks on American naval units. They attacked a mine sweeping group off the coast of Mindoro and a kamikaze crashed into one ship, killing 95 men and wounding another 65. As these operations made clear, Japanese air tactics in their defense of the Philippines increasingly centered on the use of kamikazes, and on January 5th, planes attacked the Third Fleet, which was preparing for a new set of strikes on Luzon. Kamikaze planes hit two CVE, two heavy cruisers, three destroyers, a destroyer transport, and a mine sweeper, with total casualties for the day within the Third Fleet amounting to 65 dead and 195 wounded. On the other hand, the Japanese lost nearly all of the 45 planes that began the attacks, further depleting their already weak air forces.

At the same time, Japanese naval units also attempted to engage Allied forces. During the afternoon of January 5th, Allied ships spotted two Japanese destroyers that were attempting to attack a mine sweeper group near Manila Bay. A mixed group of two Australian frigates and an American destroyer attempted to intercept these ships, but when they were unable to get within firing range, they had to call off their attack plans and return to Manila Bay. Japanese submarines harassed other Allied naval vessels, with one group, which included the *Boise*, MacArthur's command ship, being fired upon by torpedoes. The torpedoes missed their marks, and one Japanese submarine was sunk by return fire.

At Lingayen Gulf, kamikaze planes were a major problem for Allied naval vessels. Admiral Jesse Oldendorf noted the problems he had in defending against kamikaze planes, as it only took one or two planes escaping away from Allied air cover to deal heavy damage to his ships. Anti-aircraft weapons were also problematic because their 5-inch antiaircraft weapons equipped with proximity fuses had problems tracking the erratic flight techniques of kamikaze pilots. Meanwhile, their 40 mm and 20 mm automatic batteries often did not deal enough damage to halt the heavily armored kamikaze planes. Fortunately, even though Allied forces had trouble dealing with kamikaze planes, the problem was lessened by the lack of aircraft that the Japanese on Luzon possessed. By January 6th, they had only a small number of operational planes remaining.

Oldendorf

A picture of the initial landings on Luzon

Allied soldiers advancing on Luzon

The plan for the Lingayen landings was to have 6th Army establish beachheads and then secure a base from which supplies and reinforcements could come ashore. They would then coordinate offensive maneuvers against the Japanese 14th Area Army. Thus, on January 9th, 1945, or S-day, the naval vessels positioned off the coast began their bombardment of potential Japanese positions at 0700. After half an hour, assault troops from the XIV Corps began coming ashore and were followed by the 37th Infantry Division, which landed to the XIV Corps' left, while the 40th Division landed on the right. The Japanese defenders did not contest the beaches here, and in fact, Filipino guerrillas began coming toward the American troops to help them.

By the evening of the 9th, some units had made their way as far as four miles into the interior of the island, but the next day, January 10th, saw some resistance from Japanese forces when a platoon of Japanese infantry attacked the 160th Division, which suffered 15 casualties, the most of any regiment in the first three days on Luzon. As they continued to move away from the beaches, with the 185th Infantry moving to the west and the 160th moving toward the south, a gap began to open between them. General Rapp Brush therefore moved the 108th Infantry to close this gap and stop a potential weak point in case of a Japanese counterattack.

Meanwhile, the 148th Infantry moved to the southeast, and with no resistance against it, quickly moved into its designated zone by the afternoon of January 10th. Nearby, the 129th Infantry made contact with Filipino guerrillas at the town of Malasiqui, and then later were attacked by Japanese units, forcing them to halt for the remainder of the day. Even with some slight delays, by January 11th, nearly all Allied assault units had reached their designated Army Beachhead Line zones, except on the right flank, where a series of hills and rough terrain made movement difficult.

The I Corps, which landed to the left of XIV Corps, was also able to complete their landings without any engagement by Japanese forces. The units that made up the I Corps included the 172nd Infantry, 1st and 3rd Battalions of the 43rd Division, and the 20th Infantry, along with the 6th Division being held in reserve, and they were able to move an average of three and a half miles in the first day. The 43rd Division of the I Corps had the most difficulty moving out from the beaches at Lingayen, as they had to travel over a series of hills whose compactness provided Japanese troops with natural cover from which to attack the Americans. As the 43rd Division's 169th Infantry moved to the southeast, they were attacked by Japanese mortar and artillery fire. The 169th Infantry was ordered to take Hill 470, one of the largest of the hill structure, but reconnaissance showed that the Japanese had strong defensive positions on that hill.

The 172nd Infantry also encountered artillery and mortar fire as it moved away from its landing location. Although harassed, they were able to quickly move away from the beaches and take their objective of Hill 247. On the next day, January 9th, the 103rd Infantry, was ordered to take Hill 200, a small cluster of hills on which the Japanese had built some defensive positions. Hill 200 was relatively geographically unimportant, but it blocked the most direct path to Route 3, a major north-south highway that led to Manila. The 103rd Infantry encountered sporadic attacks by small groups of Japanese troops that delayed their advance, and they were forced to halt for the night near the town of San Jacinto.

On January 10th, the 6th Division moved four miles inland, and by the time they stopped as night fell, they too had faced skirmishes with Japanese troops. Because of the harassment from Japanese units, these units within I Corps had fallen behind the scheduled pace, and now a gap appeared between XIV Corps and the I Corps. Another potential problem sprang up when the 103rd Infantry pursued and cleared nearby Japanese artillery pieces. This was an important task that neutralized their shelling of American troops in the area, but it opened another gap when the 103rd Infantry lost contact with the 6th Division on its right and the 169th Infantry, which was positioned to the left.

Also on the 10th, the 169th Infantry continued their attempt to take Hill 470, where they faced heavy resistance from Japanese units stationed there. The 169th battled their way forward and took the hill by the afternoon, and they were then ordered to take another area designated Hill 318, where they were pinned down by mortar and artillery fire. The 169th Infantry spent the rest of January 10th and January 11th dealing with the Japanese company that had dug in at Hill 318.

Another unit that was having problems advancing was the 172nd Infantry, also positioned on the left of the I Corps. Like the 169th, the 172nd had to face entrenched Japanese positions on hills that gave them the high ground on which to see American movements and position their artillery and mortars. While the Japanese soldiers did not directly engage the 172nd, they did target them with heavy shelling that made it difficult for the unit to progress. In fact, the 172nd Infantry was halted by Japanese shelling and had to be relieved by members of the Sixth Army Reserve on January 11th.

At MacArthur's headquarters, army commanders decided to commit the bulk of the Sixth Army Reserve to the I Corps, and to place them on the left flank, the only zone in which American troops were facing strong resistance from the Japanese. MacArthur came to believe that the Japanese had decided not to contest the beach landings and had withdrawn into the interior in an attempt to lure the Americans into a false sense of security and to overextend them, which would allow for a counterattack by Japanese units. He felt that on the left of I Corps, his troops had made contact with the forward Japanese defensive lines, and that they would have to be careful in advancing from this point on.

As MacArthur focused his attention on the left, he sent reconnaissance missions and made contact with Filipino guerrillas who provided information on Japanese troop movements. These sources painted a picture of the Japanese holding positions to the north and east of the I Corps landing sites, and the engagements that had occurred on January 10th and 11th were designed to slow the American drive to give Japanese forces from elsewhere on the island time to gather and prepare for a counterattack.

The Japanese 14th Area Army, under the command of General Tomoyuki Yamashita, was aware of the imminent American invasion, and that it would occur through Lingayen Gulf, but the Japanese did not expect it to occur as soon as it did. Japanese commanders had originally planned to make a decisive stand at Luzon, but when the Americans invaded Leyte, they decided to commit to a major engagement there. Leyte was a complete disaster for the Japanese, and the significant losses they faced there directly impacted their ability to defend Luzon later on in the war. Three divisions were diverted from Leyte in late fall of 1944 to aid in the defense of Luzon, but Allied air and naval attacks sunk transports that cost the Japanese nearly a third of their reinforcements and a large quantity of supplies. Yamashita had been planning to use his reinforcements to mount a counterattack shortly after the Americans landed, but with the losses that these divisions faced in transport to Luzon, he decided instead on drawing up defensive lines and holding out for as long as possible.

Yamashita

    Like the American defense of Luzon in 1941, Yamashita and the 14th Area Army faced shortages of food, ammunition and medical supplies that would greatly impact their ability to hold out. In fact, by mid-November 1944, even before the American landings, food shortages were so dire that many soldiers had their rations cut by one-third. Also mirroring the American defense of Luzon, Yamashita decided against defending Manila and instead moved supplies away from the city for a more decentralized defense of the island. Japanese troop strength was very poor, as divisions were hastily formed from garrison units, as well as sailors stationed on the island and even Japanese civilians. Regular units were also in poor condition and lacked equipment. This would play a heavy role in Yamashita's ability to defend Luzon in the face of the American advance.

    Unlike MacArthur in 1941-1942, Yamashita did not plan to withdraw into the Bataan peninsula, which he felt was too compact an area in which to mount a defense with the 275,000 soldiers that were available to him. Instead, he decided to leave the southern portion of the Lingayen Gulf undefended, where the terrain was too flat to mount a serious defense, so he gathered his troops to the north and east, where the hills and mountains that made up that zone would allow him to create strong defensive positions. For this, he created a special force called the Shobu Group, whose 152,000 troops were ordered to hold the hills and mountains in the area.

Yamashita also decided to defend a second area, a mountainous region near Clark Field in the Central Plains. His goal here was to stop Allied forces from being able to use the main airfield in Luzon for as long as possible. The soldiers sent to this area were called the Kembu Group, and numbered roughly 30,000 men, but were composed of a mix of army engineers, airplane ground crews, and antiaircraft units, in addition to experienced soldiers.

Yamashita set up a third major force called the Shimbu Group, which was ordered to defend the mountains to the north and east of Manila. The Shimbu Group was supposed to help facilitate the removal of supplies from Manila, and once this had been accomplished, they were ordered to destroy major roads and bridges surrounding the city. The Shimbu Group consisted of roughly 80,000 men.

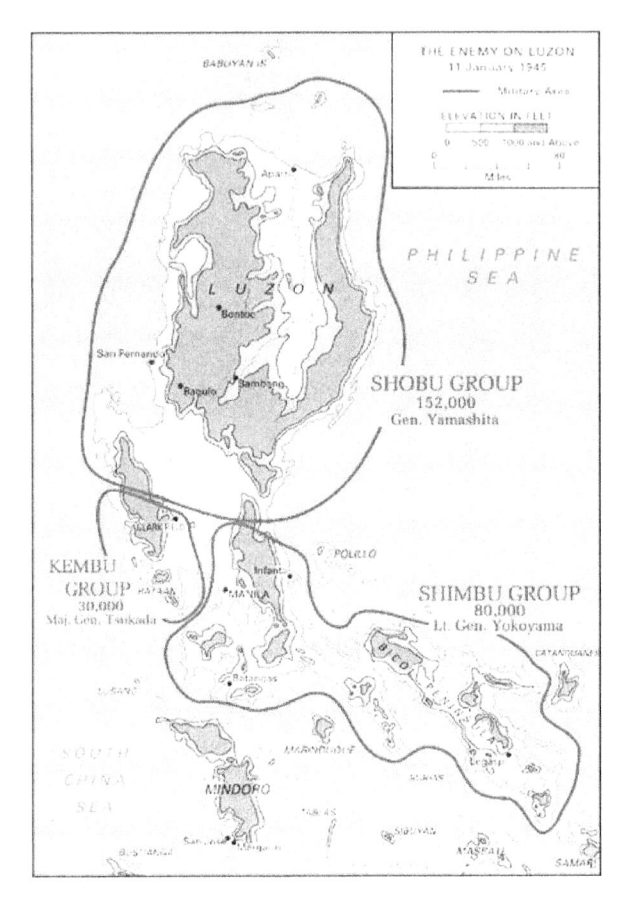

A map indicating the defense zones for different Japanese groups on Luzon

The Japanese soldiers who made contact with American troops after the Lingayen landings were members of the Shobu Group, and these soldiers had created a triangular defensive perimeter among the mountains of northern Luzon. Their goal was to hold the roads leading to the Cagayan Valley until the Japanese could move supplies out of the valley. Yamashita deployed reconnaissance units to patrol along the southern shores of the Lingayen Gulf with orders to withdraw if they encountered any resistance, but some units were caught out of position during the Allied landings, and these were the Japanese soldiers who the American I Corps first made contact with.

On January 11th, the I Corps began moving north hoping to capture the junction of Routes 3 and 11, which would secure the left flank and would allow the Sixth Army to begin its drive toward Manila without fear of counterattacks from this area. This important junction was defended by the Japanese 58th IMB, which had taken the high ground and had constructed a number of trenches and tunnels along the area's hills. There were 6,900 soldiers in the 58th IMB, and they also had 15 75 mm guns and 12 artillery pieces to help them in their defense. The American advance troops, composed of the 158th RCT with about 4,500 men, were tasked with making contact with the 58th IMB and would then have the help of nearby planes and ships, which would bombard the Japanese positions before a ground assault.

On January 12th, the 172nd Infantry began an attack on Hill 580, which was a Japanese advanced position located four miles away from the junction. Their first attempt on the hill was unsuccessful, and it would take until the next day before they were able to overcome the Japanese troops defending it. Once Hill 580 was captured, the 172nd continued forward with help from the 43rd Division's 103rd Field Artillery Battalion, and they captured Hill 565 before moving to within two and a half miles of the main Japanese position at the junction of Routes 3 and 11. A second operation involving the 63rd and 158th Infantry Regiments engaged nearby Japanese fortified positions, but problems with their artillery support delayed their movement, and the 63rd Infantry had problems linking up with the 158th Infantry at the designated point near Routes 3 and 11.

On January 14th, the 158th Infantry was surprised by the Japanese 58th IMB, allowing the Japanese to deal heavy damage with their artillery pieces. Japanese troops had also been able to hide from American patrols in the network of caves and tunnels they had dug, and since the Americans had no idea that this Japanese position stood in their way, they inflicted 85 more casualties. The next day, the 158th called in air and naval support, which allowed them to advance about 1,000 yards. At the same time, the 63rd Infantry, positioned to the east of the 158th, was also taking heavy fire from Japanese artillery positions.

By January 15th, American commanders realized that both the 158th and 63rd were facing much stronger Japanese positions than they had originally believed, and therefore General Leonard Wing redirected the 172nd Infantry to flank the Japanese by coming through the town of Rosario and then attacking Japanese artillery positions on the north of Route 3 from behind. He also sent some troops from the 169th Infantry to bolster these forces. However, even with the new troops moving into the area, Allied forces were unable to dislodge the Japanese from their strong defensive positions among the hills near the Route 3 and 11 junction, and a stalemate developed that halted all progress along the 43rd Division's left.

Along the right, the 103rd and 169th Infantry Regiments were driving eastward. By January 13th, they had reached the Japanese 23rd Division's outer defense perimeter, and they began operations to take two major points along this outer perimeter: Hill 319 and Hill 355. The 169th Infantry attacked the Japanese 64th Infantry, whose orders were to hold the western approaches to

Route 3. The 64th Infantry held the high ground on Hill 318, which allowed them to observe all activities by the Allied forces and utilize excellent artillery placement for their defense of the hill. The 169th Infantry was ordered to embark on a frontal assault of Hill 318, which they accomplished at the cost of 70 casualties. From the first few days on Luzon, American commanders realized that the time-consuming nature of assaults on dug-in Japanese hill-top positions meant that a rapid advance onto Route 3 was probably impossible, and so General Wing ordered the 169th Infantry to go around Hill 355 rather than attack it and instead move through the town of Palacpalac.

The 103rd Infantry was ordered to take a Japanese position south of the 169th's position called Hill 200. Hill 200 was another Japanese perimeter position in which they linked a series of hills by building tunnels and caves. As at other similar locations, aerial bombardment did little damage to these positions because Japanese troops could hide in the caves to avoid most bombs. This meant that the 103rd had to painstakingly clear Hill 200, beginning on January 12th. Hill 200 was only manned by 400 Japanese soldiers, but it took about four days to completely take the hill, and by the night of January 16th, the Americans had just concluded mopping up operations when they were attacked by a force of Japanese tanks moving in from the east. The Japanese counterattack was not a large-scale concerted effort to push out against Allied troops but merely consisted of a series of smaller counterattacks that Yamashita allowed his subordinates to engage in. Yamashita wanted to avoid the possibility of losing a large number of soldiers in one engagement, but he also wanted to delay the Allied advance.

In this series of counterattacks, the Japanese 71st Infantry attacked the rear of the Allied 172nd and 169th Infantry Regiments, while the Japanese 72nd Infantry attacked the rear of the Allied 169th and 103rd Infantry Regiments. As this was occurring, the 23rd Division sent a tank-infantry force to stop the advance of the Allied 103rd Infantry. Although the Japanese 71st and 72nd were able to get to the rear of the Allied positions, they were quickly pushed back.

At Palacpalac, 200 Japanese soldiers came into contact with the 1st Battalion of the 169th Infantry during the night of January 16th. Both groups were surprised by the attack, as the Japanese did not expect to see American soldiers at that location. The ensuing engagement lasted until the night of the 17th, and the 169th suffered 30 casualties in the fighting. The largest of the series of counterattacks occurred with the Shigemi Detachment attacking the 3rd Battalion of the 103rd Infantry. During nighttime on January 16th, Japanese tanks and infantry attacked an American position near the town of Potpot, and two Japanese tanks broke through the perimeter while a third was destroyed by antitank fire. The accompanying Japanese infantry then engaged in a two-hour battle with American soldiers before finally withdrawing. The two tanks that had broken through the line later returned in the early morning hours of January 17th, where they were engaged by American troops and destroyed. In this battle, the Americans suffered 12 casualties and lost one 37 mm antitank gun, a jeep, a scout car, and a tank. The Japanese lost 11 tanks in the engagement, as well as 50 soldiers killed.

By sunrise on January 17th, the Japanese counterattacks had ended and American commanders began reinforcing their forward positions (the 169th and 103rd Infantry Regiments). On the 17th, American forces held a 25 mile wide front that included some important Japanese perimeter defense positions, but even with these gains, the 43rd Division still had important work to do in its sector of the front. They needed to take the junction connecting Routes 3 and 11, and then they needed to push through to the southern portion of Route 3, which was an important road for Japanese movements of supplies and troops. Making things more difficult, as of January 17th, the 43rd Division had seen the bulk of fighting against the Japanese and had suffered roughly 800 casualties up to that point.

The 43rd Division, along with its reinforcements from the 158th and 63rd Infantry Regiments, began moving toward the Route 3 and 11 junction, which was being defended by the Japanese 58th IMB and 23rd Division, which held territory south of the junction. Japanese forces observed as American troops began moving toward their positions and did not engage as the Americans took control of the junction; instead, they allowed American forces to continue moving south of the junction to a defensive complex called Hill 35-Mt. Alava, which they had heavily fortified. The American 169th Infantry, meanwhile, probed the area for new approaches to Hill 355 and Mt. Alava while one battalion was posted near Hill 355 in order to keep Japanese units from counterattacking from that position.

The 169th Infantry spent January 17th and 18th preparing to attack Mt. Alava from the east and southeast. On the 18th the 2nd Battalion scouted new approaches to the Japanese position before moving past the town of Sison by midday, but in the late afternoon, Japanese forces began firing mortars and artillery at the 169th, pinning the American troops down near the town. On the 19th, some units of the Japanese 64th Infantry began withdrawing to Mt. Alava to attack the 169th Infantry's 2nd Battalion from the southwest, and by midday on the 19th, Japanese artillery and ground troops forced American troops to withdraw in the face of heavy fire. Since the Americans had to withdraw on flat land with no protection, they faced casualties of nearly half their troop strength (350 combat-ready men out of an initial force of 1,000), but they were eventually able to link up with the 716th Tank Battalion near Route 3, which forced the Japanese to call off their pursuit. The Japanese 64th Infantry at Mt. Alava also took heavy losses in the engagement, as they had compromised their defensive positions in the attack and roughly 400 of their men had been killed in the process of forcing an American retreat. Mt. Alava was now in a precarious position, and when the Americans launched an attack on Japanese defenses there on January 20th, they were able to overcome the small force still stationed there, taking the crest of the mountain by late afternoon and finishing up operations by the 21st.

Having taken one of the key points in the area, American forces now began preparations to take Hill 355, which they had initially isolated and bypassed. During January 22nd and 23rd, American troops engaged in a series of assaults on the hill against dogged resistance from Japanese soldiers, but by late on the 24th, American troops had finally taken most of Hill 355, killing 500 Japanese soldiers from the 64th Infantry in the process. Mopping up operations continued until January 28th as American units continued to engage the last remaining clusters of Japanese troops on Hill 355, killing 150 and capturing an assortment of artillery and antitank guns. By January 29th, after having wiped out Japanese troops at both Hill 355 and Mt. Alava, the 169th Infantry returned to join up with the other American forces in the area.

As the 169th Infantry was engaging Japanese troops on Mt. Alava and Hill 355, the 103rd Infantry began operations nearby at Pozorrubio. The 103rd began by attacking Hill 600, an elevated area between Pozorrubio and the Routes 3 and 11 junction. The 103rd attacked through frontal assaults on the Japanese positions, gaining some ground on the hill, but they were unable to overcome Japanese defenses. On January 22nd, after the attack had been ongoing for a few days, a group of officers was meeting at a forward area on Hill 600 when they were hit by Japanese artillery fire. The unit lost four company commanders and 2 other officers, as well as 7 enlisted men, with 33 other soldiers injured in the attack. This forced the 103rd Infantry to retreat from their positions on Hill 600, and American strategists decided to regroup and plan a new strategy against Hill 600 and other nearby hills.

General Wing began by deploying the 103rd Infantry to attack Hill 600 from the northwest before moving on to Hill 800. The 169th Infantry moved up to the north of the 103rd, where they would take Question Mark Hill, located near Hill 800. Finally, the 63rd Infantry, which had previously been held back as I Corps reserves, was deployed to take Benchmark Hill, located northwest of Question Mark Hill. The operation began on January 25th and continued until January 27th as American troops engaged in a series of frontal assaults on Japanese positions. The 3rd Battalion, 63rd Infantry attacked from the west side of Benchmark Hill and were able to secure it after taking 36 casualties. They then joined the rest of the 63rd Infantry to clear Hill 1500.

The 169th Infantry attacked Question Mark Hill and were able to take most of the hill, but they could not dislodge the Japanese soldiers fighting on the eastern side of the hill. On the 27th, they changed tactics and brought artillery and bombers to attack the remaining Japanese troops on that hill. The 103rd Infantry moved against Japanese positions on Hill 700 and Hill 600 on January 25th, but they were pushed back by intense Japanese fire against their attacks. Late in the afternoon, members of the 103rd found an undefended area connecting the two hills, and they were able to use this area to launch renewed attacks that surprised the Japanese defenders, allowing the Americans to take both hills.

As I Corps was pushing forward, XIV Corps was moving through the Central Plains, where up to January 18th they had suffered few casualties. General Oscar Griswold, XIV Corps commander planned to push his troops forward in a series of controlled advances to make sure they kept their supply line secured and did not outrun I Corps. Their continued lack of engagement with Japanese forces meant that the XIV Corps moved quickly through January 21st until its forward elements created a perimeter line south of the towns of Victoria and Tarlac. Tarlac especially had been an important railroad junction for the Japanese, who had stored a large quantity of supplies there, and Allied bombers had hit Tarlac heavily in the buildup to the landings, so when the forward units of the XIV Corps arrived, the Japanese garrison had withdrawn into the interior of Luzon and the town itself was badly damaged.

Griswold

Encountering no resistance from Japanese troops, the XIV Corps advanced past the Victoria-Tarlac line, and with the speed at which they were advancing, General Griswold was instructed to take Clark Air Field. Even though his troops had not faced significant Japanese opposition, Griswold was worried about the speed with which the XIV Corps was advancing. At one level, he believed he was stretching his supply lines thin, which would be a big problem if his troops later faced Japanese counterattacks, and he was also concerned that a gap had opened between the XIV Corps and the I Corps, which meant his left flank was exposed between the towns of Cuyapo and La Paz. Griswold had received vague reports of Japanese troops movements near Cabanatuan, 15 miles east of La Paz, and American patrols in the following days came into contact with Japanese troops at Moncada and La Paz. During the night of January 21-22, a platoon of Japanese infantry, in concert with one tank, attacked the 148th Infantry's perimeter one mile west of La Paz. The Japanese withdrew after destroying a bridge in the area.

American commanders decided to shore up the area between I Corps and XIV Corps by having the 37th Division and 40th Division move into the XIV Corps' left, where they would also float into the I Corps sector, thus filling the gap between the two forces. During the evening of January 22nd, the advanced elements of the 160th Infantry, along with the 40th Reconnaissance Troop, reached Capas, where they nearly came upon the Japanese garrison stationed there. The Japanese just managed to evade an attack, hurriedly escaping while leaving supplies behind. The next day, on the 40th Reconnaissance's left, the 108th Infantry came across some Japanese soldiers who had not retreated in time from the towns surrounding Capas and engaged them. On the right, the bulk of the 160th Infantry advanced unopposed to take Bamban Airfield, while one battalion of the 160th was tasked with securing the town of Bamban, where they fought with Japanese soldiers defending the town. It took them most of the day to secure the town, but once this was accomplished, they rejoined with the rest of the 160th and moved toward a network of ridges to the west of the town, where they were engaged by Japanese positions utilizing small arms fire and mortars.

This strong Japanese position surprised American commanders, who believed that the main Japanese defense of the area would be centered on Clark Field. After halting and gathering his forces, General Griswold had the 160th Infantry engage the Japanese defenses while the 40th Division probed for Japanese positions to the west and southwest, the direction of Clark Field. He also kept the 37th Division and 129th RCT in reserve to help in the push forward if needed. The problem Griswold faced in confronting Japanese defenses was that the Americans had little information about Japanese troops strength in this area. War planners estimated that there were between 4,000 and 8,000 Japanese soldiers around Clark Field, and American intelligence believed most of these troops were members of the Air Force, meaning only a few soldiers would be experienced in ground combat. American military officials therefore believed that there would only be weak resistance to the American advance at Clark Field.

In actuality, the Japanese stationed the Kembu Group at Clark Field, which was composed of 15,000 men from the Army and Navy. Of these 15,000 men, roughly 8,500 were experienced ground combat soldiers split into four units defending the area surrounding Clark Field, and the Japanese defenses protected not only Clark Field but also the route south toward Manila. The American 40th Division, which probed Japanese defenses to the west and southwest, made contact with enemy positions on January 23rd and then began an attack against them, but American soldiers encountered problems with the landscape as they had to climb hills devoid of any kind of protection while facing machine gun and mortar fire. The unit attacking what was called Hill 1800 was able to overcome Japanese defenses, but on the next hill, Hill 500, American soldiers were unable make any progress up the slope against intense Japanese fire.

Even with a detachment of the 40th Division being stopped at Hill 500, American commanders still believed that they were encountering a small defensive force rather than the Kembu Group's defensive perimeter, so they believed American forces could quickly overcome the defenses and take Clark Field. On January 25th, the 160th Infantry attacked Hill 636, overcoming one defensive position before meeting heavy resistance halfway up the hill. To the north, other members of the

160th attacked other hills in the area, first taking Hill E before attacking Japanese defenses on Hill G. Even though Japanese defenses were much heavier than the Americans had planned for, their attacks took a heavy toll on the Japanese center and the 160th Infantry was threatening to outflank Japanese positions on their right. While the Japanese expected their defenses to hold for at least a week, they were already in danger of being overrun in the first few days of fighting.

Griswold next ordered the 160th and 108th Infantry Regiments to move toward the south and attack Hill 636, which blocked the path to Clark Field. Once they overcame defenses at Hill 636, they could secure Clark Field and then move toward nearby Fort Stotsenburg. As was the case in nearly all American attacks on Japanese hilltop defensive positions, Japanese troops fired machine gun, artillery, and mortar rounds at American soldiers, pinning them down and forcing them to call for mortar and artillery support. American fire then allowed the ground troops to move forward a bit at a time until they could take a Japanese machine gun or artillery position before having to repeat the process. This meant that the process of overcoming Japanese defenses was painstaking and slow, with each American battalion involved in the fighting losing an average of 20 casualties per day. At the same time, while Japanese soldiers slowly wore down American units, they were unable to halt the slow and steady gains that American troops made day after day.

On January 26th, the 160th Infantry made a big push on the Japanese right, taking Hill 636 and Hill 600 against soldiers who were unable to hold their positions and had to retreat in the face of the American attack. Meanwhile, the 108th Infantry attacked closer to the center, where Japanese defenses held and stalled their progress. By this time, American commanders had realized they were up against strong Japanese defenses and scrapped their plans for a quick victory at Clark Field. Even though their progress was slowed by the stronger Japanese defenses, as of January 27th, they had dealt damage to Japanese positions and had also captured major transportation points at the Manila Railroad and Route 3 near the town of Bamban. Japanese forces were also suffering heavy losses, with the Takayama Detachment of the Kembu Group alone losing nearly 1,000 men killed in the fighting up to this point.

On January 28th, the 40th Division began a new attack against the Kembu Group's positions, with the 129th Infantry coming in from the west with support from the 754th Tank Battalion. To the north, the 160th Infantry gained quite a bit of territory near Hill 620 before getting pinned down by gunfire and artillery. They were later hit by a counterattack that pushed them backward. On the 29th, the 160th Infantry regrouped and broke through the center of the Takaya Detachment's position.

The 129th Infantry also saw major action when they were ordered to take a Japanese hill-position called Top of the World. This location was a strongly defended, 1,000 foot high hill that was the major objective in the area. The 1st Battalion, 129th Infantry began the attack on the morning of January 31st, where they were quickly pinned down by enemy fire, but the 1st

Battalion was ultimately able to make some headway during the afternoon, and by nightfall, they had gained a precarious foothold halfway up the hill. On February 1st, more units of the 129th climbed the hill, and after fierce fighting, they were able to take the crest by midday.

The result of these engagements on the right led to huge losses for the Kembu Group. American troops had penetrated areas along the flanks and center of their position and had also effectively destroyed the armored units that were attached to the group. Over 2,500 Japanese soldiers had been killed or injured, and a further 750 casualties had occurred among reinforcements that had been sent to aid the Kembu Group. By early February, the XIV Corps had taken Clark Field and had secured critical areas of Route 3 and the Manila Railroad. This meant that while the Kembu Group was still a threat, they had been sufficiently weakened that the Americans could begin to turn their attention toward Manila.

Pictures of abandoned Japanese planes at Clark Field

At San Jose, roughly 100 miles north of Manila, along with the towns of Lupao and Munoz, Japanese commanders placed the 10th and 105th Divisions, along with the 2nd Tank Division. These units were reinforced by the 7th and 10th Tank regiments and the 2nd Mobile Infantry. These would be the troops tasked with opposing the I Corps as it moved south. For the I Corps, their plan of attack against San Jose involved a pincer maneuver, with an attack from the northeast through Munoz being carried out by the 6th Division while the 25th Division would attack from the southeast through Lupao.

The drive toward San Jose began on February 1st, and the I Corps would have to cross flat land with little cover against a defense that consisted of dug-in Japanese medium tanks, with support from infantry units and machine gun positions. The 3rd Battalion, 20th Infantry led the line, and they were confronted by Japanese tanks and artillery south of Route 99, the road leading into Munoz. On the 2nd, the 1st Battalion, 20th Infantry again was halted by the Japanese defense, while the 2nd Battalion also failed to make much headway against Japanese defenses near Route 5. The 1st Battalion, 35th Infantry advanced close to Lupao before taking artillery, mortar and machine gun fire from Japanese defenses in the town. This forced the 1st Battalion to retreat, and on the next day they resumed the attack but were unable to make gains, and like the 20th Infantry, were unable to take their town.

Because of the slow progress, American commanders decided to bypass both towns, thus sending reinforcements to keep Japanese forces confined within Lupao and Munoz while the main body of troops moved forward toward their objectives. The 35th Infantry, along with the 6th Division, advanced near San Jose, and on February 4th, they were able to take the town almost unopposed. With that, American commanders realized that the Japanese had committed the bulk of their forces to defending the paths leading into San Jose at Munoz and Lupao, and had virtually no remaining troops to defend San Jose proper. The Japanese troops remaining in these towns were increasingly isolated and surrounded by American units, and the Japanese defenders at Munoz attempted to break out on February 7th. They failed to realize that Route 5, their escape path away from town, was in the hands of the Americans, and they were quickly engaged by strong American positions along the road that virtually wiped them out.

At Lupao, the 35th Infantry advanced, pushing Japanese troops further and further back until they too decided to attempt a break out. A group of 11 tanks attempted to break through the 35th Infantry's line, and five of them were able to get away. Their crews left the tanks in the foothills near town and retreated on foot. Japanese infantrymen also retreated away from the town, and by February 8th, American troops held Lupao.

Across the Central Plains, the 40th Division continued fighting the Kembu Group in mid-February, and American units continued to deal with the difficult task of assaulting dug-in Japanese troops. The XIV Corps had taken Clark Field and controlled an important point in the Japanese defenses at Top of the World, but the Kembu Group still had roughly 25,000 soldiers holding strong positions in the foothills near the Bamban River. For General Krueger and the XIV Corps, the task of defeating the Kembu Group would involve coordinated attacks involving air support and artillery fire that would force the Japanese troops into their trenches and caves for protection, which would be followed by American infantry operations.

On February 6th, General Kruger ordered the XIV Corps to re-engage the Kembu Group. The plan of attack involved the 185th and 160th Infantry Regiments attacking the center of the Kembu Group's position, while the 108th moved on the right and the 129th on the left. On February 6th, the 160th Infantry began operations against McSevney Point, a major defensive position for Japanese troops. The 160th was aided by support from tanks, planes, and artillery, which pinned down Japanese troops in their foxholes and caves as American infantry advanced behind them to attack the enemy troops as they emerged from their shelters. It took three days for the 160th to take the summit of McSevney Point, followed by a series of ferocious Japanese night counterattacks. On the morning of February 10th, the 160th realized that the Japanese had withdrawn from the position following their last unsuccessful counterattack.

The loss of McSevney Point convinced the commander of the Kembu Group to withdraw from that portion of the defense perimeter to their last-stand positions, which created a gap in the defensive line that isolated the two wings. The gaps created by this maneuver allowed American units on both flanks to drive the Japanese troops back. On the Japanese right, the Eguchi-Yanagimoto Detachment held out for nearly a week, but by February 12th, they had lost everything except Hill 7. With that detachment defeated at Hill 7 on the afternoon of the 12th, the 108th Infantry had overcome the Japanese right.

On the left, the 185th Infantry was making important gains against the Japanese defenses, while in the center the 160th Infantry had pushed forward into the Japanese's last-stand line. American units continued moving forward in the painstaking task of taking hill after hill, and between February 10 and 12, American troops took three of the last major Japanese hill positions. On February 15th, with continued American advances on the left, right and center, and with heavy casualties among its soldiers, the Kembu Group was effectively destroyed. Isolated units of the Kembu Group still remained, but the XIV Corps now only needed to engage in mop-up operations, and American commanders could fully turn their attention to the drive to Manila. Overall, the XIV Corps lost 285 men killed and 1,180 wounded, while the Kembu Group suffered 12,000 deaths (Smith, p.206)

The rest of XIV Corps had been moving toward Manila since late January. While they were harassed by Japanese units during this time, they were not appreciably slowed in their drive toward the capital, and by early February, American commanders had planned for a pincer maneuver involving the XIV Corps from the north and the 11th Airborne Division moving in from the south. The 11th Airborne landed in southern Luzon on January 31st at Nasugbu, a site that allowed them to isolate Japanese forces in southern Luzon (so they would not be able to reinforce defenses at Manila) and position themselves for the drive north to that city.

After landing, the 11th Airborne's 511st Infantry led the line in moving north to Manila, but they were delayed when they had to fight a series of actions against small Japanese units defending the bridges leading to the capital city. In fact, the major obstacle for the 11th Airborne involved the logistics of their movement, as Japanese destruction (and attempted destruction) of bridges challenged their ability to move men and supplies to their staging points for the attack on Manila. Army engineers had to work quickly, using pontoons and reinforcing roads and undamaged bridges to keep the 11th Airborne moving.

There were roughly 10,000 Japanese troops stationed at Manila, and they were broken up into three combat groups that defended the north, south, and center of the city. However, aside from breaking their troops up into these groups, the plan for defending the city was not well-conceived, with Japanese officers looking to inflict heavy casualties on American troops and to stop them from controlling Manila for as long as possible. They also planned to demolish infrastructure that could be useful to the Americans, such as the port area, bridges, water supply system and power grid. Japanese troops cannibalized guns from wrecked aircraft and ships, and many of their heavier weapons were 20-mm and 25-mm airplane guns that were modified for use on the ground.

The XIV Corps reached the outskirts of Manila on February 3rd and promptly began operations against the suburb of Santo Tomas, where the 8th Cavalry experienced the first instance of close-quarter city fighting in Manila when they were attacked by Japanese troops hiding in buildings at the intersection of Quezon Boulevard. The Japanese hid among numerous buildings, including Bilibid Prison and Far Eastern University. The 8th Cavalry was able to retreat away from the intersection, and while there was potential for heavy fighting at Santo Tomas, this did not materialize because Japanese troops stationed there were surprised by the American advance and had not expected their arrival for another two weeks. Thus, the Japanese units stationed there retreated following the engagement at Quezon Boulevard and the Americans were able to take control of the suburb.

Along with the 8th Cavalry, the 37th Division made its way into the city from the north, and its 145th Infantry began clearing the Tonto District, which they accomplished on the morning of February 9th. To the left of the Tonto District, the 148th Infantry cleared the Binondo District before moving on to the Santa Cruz District. As this was occurring, Japanese troops in the area blew up the Pasig-Jones and Santa Cruz Bridges, the two western bridges into the city. The Japanese Northern Force also began destroying military stores and installations along the northern entrance to the city, setting off large-scale fires that were intensified by strong winds. These fires lasted until February 6th before they were finally brought under control by American troops and Filipino citizens.

Aside from the fires, the 37th Division and 1st Cavalry Division had little problem clearing the northern suburbs of Japanese forces. In fact, the Northern Force had executed its orders to destroy certain key points and had withdrawn south over the Pasig River, where they destroyed the bridges after they had crossed. American troops killed roughly 1,500 Japanese soldiers in various engagements throughout the northern sector prior to the withdrawal, and this had given the Americans experience in what to expect in the fighting to follow.

On the morning of February 7th, the 37th Division was ordered across the Pasig River, where they would engage the Central Force's 1st Naval Battalion in the western portion of Paco District, and especially Provisor Island. The 37th Division had no problems making their way to Paco District, but upon reaching the Paco Railroad Station, they faced heavy fighting from Japanese troops stationed there, as well as those in the nearby buildings of Concordia College and Paco School. On the night of February 9th, most of the Japanese troops withdrew from these positions, and when the 148th Infantry stormed the Japanese positions the next day, they faced a much smaller force than expected.

Meanwhile, the 129th Infantry crossed the Pasig on February 8th and then moved west toward

Provisor Island. A small force in two boats tried to sneak across the river to the island to take one of the outbuildings and create a landing spot for the invasion of the island, but they were quickly attacked by Japanese troops and were only saved from being wiped out because of mortar support that kept Japanese troops from surrounding them. That night, they were evacuated off the island, but the force had sustained 17 casualties in the aborted mission. The next day, the 129th fired artillery and mortar rounds at the island to soften up defenses for another attempted amphibious landing, this time involving 90 men. Three boats were sunk by machine gun and mortar fire, but the rest were able to make it to the island, where they took the boiler building while mortar and artillery fire pounded the rest of the island. The mortar and artillery fire dealt heavy damage to Japanese positions, and American troops were able to secure the island on February 11th. Their goal in taking the island was to control the power plant located there to provide power for the city, but the Japanese troops had destroyed some of the equipment prior to the American landings, so they were unable to use the power plant.

The 1st Cavalry was ordered across the Pasig River around the same time as the 37th Division, and as it moved to into the Santa Ana District, it encountered little resistance and quickly set up patrols to secure the area. Thus, by February 10th, the XIV Corps had secured two sectors across the Pasig River, and along with the 11th Airborne to the south, they now had the ability to deploy their forces to encircle the city and cut off withdrawal routes for the Japanese soldiers stationed there. The 5th Cavalry moved from the west, taking the strategic area of Nielson Field, while the 8th Cavalry, and later the 12th Cavalry (which relieved the 8th Cavalry), made its way to Manila Bay. Furthermore, the 37th Division made contact with the 11th Airborne coming up from the south, completing the encirclement of Japanese forces in Manila.

The Japanese commander tasked with defending Manila, Admiral Sanji Iwabuchi, had originally planned to defend the city until the end, but as American forces began moving toward the city, Iwabuchi decided that the situation was so dire that he began planning for a withdrawal. First, he moved his headquarters to Fort McKinley, a few miles outside of the city, and then began planning a more general retreat.

As this was occurring, General Yokoyama of the Shimbu Group was planning for a counterattack against American forces near Manila. Yokoyama believed there was only one regiment of American troops near Manila and believed he had an opportunity to cut them off from the main attack force on Luzon. With Iwabuchi away from the city, Yokoyama halted the Manila Naval Defense Force from retreating out of Manila and had them hold their position in Manila pending the outcome of the Shimbu Group's counterattack.

The counterattack would consist of two columns. The northern column would attack across the Markina River, aiming for Novaliches Dam and Route 3 north of the city, while the southern column would also move across the Markina, then through the Balara Water Filters, before establishing contact with the northern wing at Grace Park. The 112th Cavalry, which had replaced the 12th Cavalry, faced the brunt of the northern column's counterattack between February 15th and 18th. After a series of skirmishes in which 300 Japanese soldiers were killed, the counterattack fell apart and the northern column retreated, and the southern column was caught as it was crossing the Marikina River when American artillery units attacked it on February 16th. For the next three days, the 7th and 8th Cavalry fought off their attempts to break through American lines, and when the southern column finally withdrew on the 19th, American troops had killed roughly 650 enemy soldiers. With the failure of the counterattacks, there was no hope of Japanese forces opening a gap in the American circle, and from that point on, the Shimbu Group had no further contact with the Manila Naval Defense Force, which was left on its own to attempt to repel American forces at Manila.

After stopping the Shimbu Group's counterattack, American forces turned their attention back to taking Manila. As the XIV Corps pushed in from the north and west, the 11th Airborne held their lines around Manila and also cut off the Abe Battalion of the Southern Luzon Force at Mabato Point. Between February 18th and 23rd, three infantry battalions, with support from artillery and tanks, attacked the Abe Battalion, killing 750 men while suffering only 60 casualties.

Within Manila, engagements between American and Japanese troops took the form of street fighting, with American troops being forced to slowly push forward and clear buildings and streets one at a time. As this was occurring, American artillery units and bombers took out most of the remaining Japanese mortars and artillery, reducing them to using light weapons, grenades and machine guns against the oncoming Americans.

Filipino citizens running from the fighting in Manila in February 1945

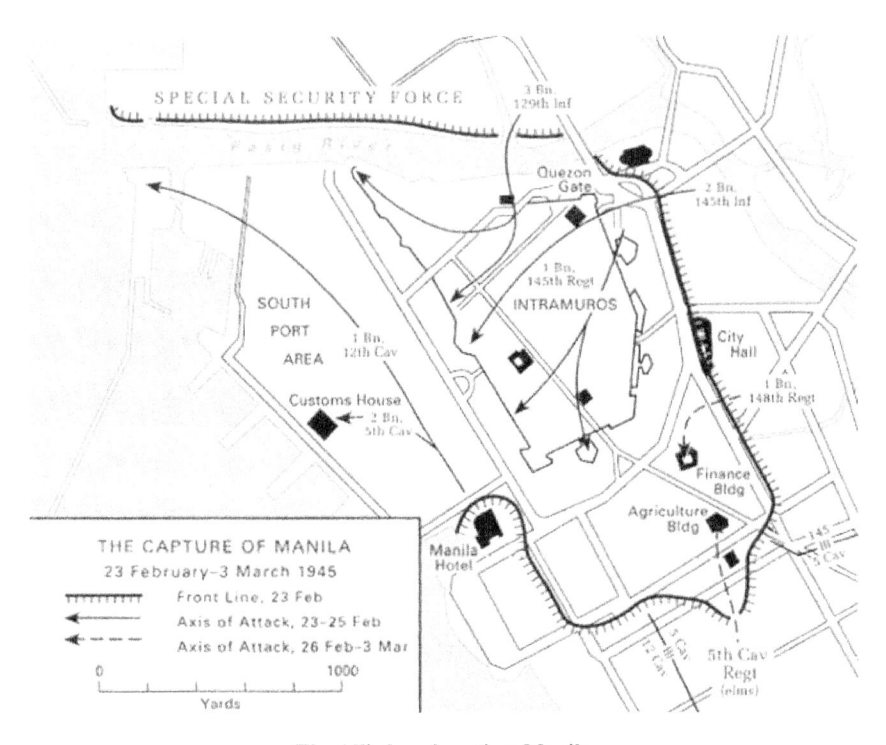

The Allied push against Manila

American troops pushed Japanese forces back block by block, finally leading up to the last stand by Japanese forces at the cluster of governmental buildings known as the Walled City. The Americans resorted to artillery bombardments for several days because American commanders believed Japanese troops had constructed a series of tunnels and bunkers in the Walled City that would be difficult for American infantry to assault without heavy bombardments before the final attack. On February 23rd, the ground assault began with the infantry advancing into the Walled City while being supported by tanks, artillery and mortars. Much of the subsequent fighting occurred between American infantry units and isolated pockets of Japanese troops who had sought cover from the artillery fire.

It took a little more than a day to finish clearing Japanese troops from the Walled City, and by late on the 24th, they had finished operations at the Walled City and nearby Fort Santiago. In total, the battle of Manila cost the XIV Corps 1,000 men killed and 5,500 wounded. The Japanese lost 16,000 men killed in the area around Manila, and the Manila Defense Force itself lost 12,500 men killed, with the rest being members of the Shimbu Group who had engaged

American troops either during the failed counterattack or in skirmishes around periphery of Manila.

In addition to the military casualties, large portions of the city were destroyed by the fighting, and the damage done to Filipino civilians was extensive. The Japanese had fought to the death across Manila, and Admiral Iwabuchi and his men had also presided over the systematic murder and rape of Filipino civilians. MacArthur had refused outright to countenance tactical airstrikes in support of his own troops for fear of killing civilians, which slowed the advance and increased American casualties. While this presented a classic moral-military conundrum, nobody can deny the moral integrity of MacArthur's command, but when the city fell at the end of February, an estimated 100,000 civilians were dead.

American troops in the Walled City on February 27, 1945

An aerial view of the devastated ruins of Manila in May 1945

As Manila was falling, Japanese commanders on Luzon had a decision to make regarding how to proceed with their defense of that island. Their main remaining goal was to deny the Americans the use of Manila Bay, a port that could be used as a staging area for an assault on the Japanese home islands. They could either deny the use of the bay by holding out at the Bataan peninsula, as the Americans had done in 1941-1942, or they could position themselves in northern Luzon and attempt to hold out there.

After securing Manila, the Sixth Army began moving to engage and destroy the Shobu and Shimbu Groups, the two largest Japanese troop concentrations remaining on Luzon. While the XIV Corps was fighting in Manila, the I Corps had positioned itself along the northern portion of the Central Plains, and after its victory against the Manila Defense Force, both portions of the Sixth Army were now ready for the next part of the operation. However, after the victory at Manila, MacArthur shifted tactics in a way that hampered the Sixth Army's ability to quickly engage and defeat the remaining Japanese soldiers on Luzon. With Japanese defeat at Luzon seemingly assured, MacArthur ordered a garrison force to be established in Manila and also siphoned off troops from Luzon to help retake central and southern Philippine islands that had been bypassed in the initial invasion of the nation.

Given the reduction in troop strength, the attacks against the Shimbu and Shobu Groups would be more difficult than had been originally anticipated. The Shimbu Group consisted of roughly 30,000 soldiers, and they were deployed along a defensive line that was aided by rugged, mountainous terrain. American operations against the Shimbu Group commenced on February

20th, when the 7th Cavalry marched through the Marikina Valley that led up to the Shimbu Group's positions. Behind the 7th Cavalry was the 8th Cavalry, which secured the town of Tagig and then also made its way through the Marikina Valley.

On February 23rd, the 7th Cavalry made contact with the forward elements of the Shimbu Group's defensive line and came under attack near Antipolo. The 7th and 8th Cavalry faced heavy fighting for the next week, during which they were barely able to gain any ground. The fighting was made more difficult by the fact that Japanese soldiers based their defense around a series of caves that were difficult for artillery to hit, forcing American troops to engage each cave and bunker and either kill or drive out the Japanese soldiers stationed within them.

The 6th Division also began marching toward the Shimbu Group's positions on February 22nd. They headed toward the northern section of the Japanese defenses, where they attacked positions located at Mount Pacawagan and Mount Mataba. Under fierce fighting, they were unable to dislodge Japanese soldiers from these locations, and by March 4th, American commanders decided to revise their plans. In their new plans, American forces would concentrate their efforts against the Shimbu Group's left, where they hoped to outflank Japanese positions. If this was successful, American troops could then get around Japanese defenses and attack their most fortified positions from behind.

On March 8th, the 1st Cavalry and 6th Infantry began their attack, while to the south, the 20th Infantry and 1st Infantry cleared what were believed to be the Shimbu Group's main supply route. The 1st Infantry was able to force its way a mile and a half forward, and by March 11, they had created a gap in the Japanese defenses. The 20th Infantry then moved in behind the 1st Infantry before heading to the east to attack a second section of the defense.

The Shimbu Group's commanding officer, General Yokoyama, became concerned about the penetration into his defenses and ordered that section of the perimeter to fall back to its secondary defense lines. He then ordered a counterattack on March 12th that involved a three-pronged assault by seven infantry battalions. Even in the beginning, this counterattack seemed destined to fail as American artillery quickly knocked out communication and command post positions that were crucial to coordinating the elements of the attack. The counterattack then devolved into isolated endeavors by Japanese units, and Yokoyama called it off on March 15th after having suffered losses amounting to two battalions of soldiers.

In the aftermath of the counterattack, American troops put renewed pressure on Japanese defenses. While their progress continued to be slow, American units advanced at four points along the defense perimeter, and they also drove a deep wedge along the Japanese left. American forces were unable to make further gains in the next few days, but General Yokoyama, believing that his situation was precarious, decided to pull his units on the left back across the Bosoboso River. However, due to communication problems along the line, these units did not begin their retreat until March 22nd, and on that day, an attack by American 6th and 43rd Division units coincided with the retreat. The Americans therefore encountered little resistance as they pushed forward and gained important positions at Mounts Baytangan, Yabang, and Caymayuman.

With the withdrawal and loss on their left, Japanese forces in that area were able, in the short-term, to remain in the field, but they now faced the possibility of being flanked and encircled, thus destabilizing the entire Japanese defense perimeter. As this was occurring, a renewed push against the center of the Japanese line in late March further weakened their position. Although fighting would be slow as American troops advanced, the defense had been compromised, and after taking Ipo Dam, the center of the Japanese line had collapsed. Thanks to the strength of the Japanese defense along hill and mountain positions, coupled with their use of caves, trenches and tunnels, continued fighting would occur through late May, but the Shimbu Group had lost cohesiveness, and their ability to mount a serious threat to American troops had been negated. From this point forward, American units engaged in mopping up operations that involved slowly moving forward and killing or driving out isolated groups of Japanese soldiers who remained in the field.

The Shobu Group was the second major Japanese force remaining in the field in Luzon, and unlike the Shimbu Group, they had planned to withdraw into northern Luzon, where they would attempt to hold out for as long as possible against American forces. The Shobu Group deployed its units to create a triangle, with its points at Baguio, Bontoc, and Bambang, and with a fourth sector in the Cagayan Valley which supplied Japanese forces. The 32nd Division was ordered to attack the Shobu Group, and they began moving out in early February where they reached the town of Santa Maria and then continued further on toward the entrances of the Arboredo and Agno River Valleys. For the next week, the 32nd Division engaged Japanese a series of outpost defenses before finally coming across the main Japanese defensive line in the area on the Villa Verde Trail.

Like the 32nd Division, the 25th Division also began operations in northern Luzon in early February. During reconnaissance operations, the 25th Division found that Japanese troops had concentrated in their area, meaning that they had positioned troops to defend the approaches to their defensive triangle from this direction as well. Aerial reconnaissance during this period also discovered the Baguio-Aritao supply road, which connected Japanese troops at Bagui and Bambang. American commanders realized that if they could take the supply road, they would be able to isolate Japanese troops at the two locations, so they decided to target the supply road in their attacks against the Shobu Group.

Aside from the two American divisions, Filipino guerrilla units (known as the USAFIP) also operated in tandem with the Americans in northern Luzon. Guerrilla units were tasked with reconnaissance operations and attacking Japanese patrols. Over time, their operations expanded to the point that Filipino guerrillas comprised roughly one division of combat troops against the Shobu Group.

American commanders chose to begin their efforts in northern Luzon against Bambang. The 25th and 32nd Divisions would be involved in these efforts, while the 44th Division would occupy Japanese forces at Baguio to keep them from reinforcing Bambang.

During late February and early March, the 33rd Division probed Japanese defenses. On the east side, 33rd Division troops were able to take Japanese positions in a ridged area that was referred to as the Hill 600-1500 line. Elsewhere, American troops had problems gaining traction against entrenched defenses, such as along Route 11, where the 71st Infantry was only able to get within a mile and a half of its stated objective of an area called Camp 2.

Meanwhile, the 33rd Division commander, Major General Percy Clarkson, was upset that his forces were only being used to hold Japanese forces in place at Baguio during this initial phase of the mission. When he realized that Japanese forces were engaging in a withdrawal all along its line, he argued that he should be allowed to push his troops forward to take a more forward position. 33rd Division reconnaissance units moved forward beginning on March 7th, and they were surprised to find almost no resistance along the western portion of the Japanese defenses, which allowed them to take Aringay and Caba. Other units pushed Japanese troops back from the hills at the entrance to the Tuba Trail. The seeming lack of defenses in this area convinced Clarkson to focus on this area, and by mid-March, he had made plans to utilize both regular troops and guerrilla units to make a push on Baguio. American forces first took the port town of San Fernando against a 3,000 man defense force, and this cleared the way along Route 9 for the drive on Baguio.

Aside from losing territory leading up to Baguio, Japanese forces had the added problems of supply difficulties, with American air strikes on supply roads restricting the supplies that made it to Japanese troops. Before the end of March, front-line troops were receiving less than a quarter of their daily rations, and starvation and diet-related diseases were taking its toll on Japanese troop-strength. Yamashita, realizing the precarious position that his forces at Baguio were in, ordered Japanese civilians and governmental officials to evacuate the city. For his soldiers, however, he ordered them to remain to defend the city for as long as possible.

In early April, American forces made their push for Baguio. The 129th Infantry broke through at Sablan in a battle involving artillery and medium tanks. The 148th Infantry then secured Route 9 through the town of Calot, and other American units secured supply depots along the area that Japanese troops were retreating from. Finally, between April 11th and 15th, American artillery, airplanes, and tank units targeted and destroyed nearly all artillery pieces that Japanese forces in the area had at their disposal. In order to try to shore up his position, General Sato, commander of Japanese troops at Baguio, sent two infantry companies to a barrio two miles southeast of Calot, but before they arrived, American troops had passed that point and had taken the town of Yagyagan. This episode highlighted the dysfunction that Japanese commanders were experiencing by this point.

Beyond Yagyagan, Japanese forces had created a defensive position at the Irisan gorge, an area with defensible high ground positions that were well positioned to fire down into Route 9, which passed through the gorge. Elements of the 148th Infantry began the assault by engaging in a frontal attack on the Japanese positions, while other units made an enveloping maneuver from the sides. After heavy fighting, the 148th was able to secure the area. American units continued to push forward, where they overcame a series of hill positions leading into Baguio, and by April 22nd, they were ready to make their final push into the town.

On April 22nd, two battalions from the 130th Infantry moved in from the west, while a battalion from the 75th Infantry came in from the south. These units met heavy resistance from Japanese troops, but elsewhere the 123rd Infantry was able to make important gains that triggered a withdrawal by some sections of the defense. The speed of the American advance forced a general Japanese withdrawal at this location as well, and by April 24th, the 33rd Division held most of Baguio. While losing this important location was a blow to the Japanese, they were able to get 10,000 troops out ahead of the American advance, which they could subsequently use to reinforce other sections of the their defensive perimeter.

The 25th and 32nd Divisions on the Bambang front they quickly made contact with Japanese troops and then began assessing plans for an assault on Bambang. In late February, the 126th Infantry of the 32nd Division attacked two Japanese delaying positions, while American patrols in the nearby Agno Valley found no sign of Japanese troops. To the west, in the Arboredo Valley, American units found the opposite: Japanese forces had set up strong outposts here to stop an advance. Units attacking from three directions compressed the defense line, and after heavy fighting accompanied by artillery support, elements of the 127th Infantry were able to break through the outpost line on February 24th. As Japanese troops from the 10th Reconnaissance division (which had been manning the outpost) retreated, they were pursued by the 127th, which continued forcing contact with the retreating troops and harassing them. Finally, as the 10th Reconnaissance withdrew to the Salacsac Pass area, they were reinforced by two companies of infantry and one under-strength artillery battalion. As the Japanese units were being reinforced, the 127th Infantry was joined by the 2nd Tank Battalion to increase their troop-strength in that vicinity.

Since Salacsac Pass was a strong defensive position, it seemed as though the opposing forces were headed toward a stalemate, and much of the month of March involved American attempts to dislodge Japanese troops from their high-ground positions, while Japanese troops made use of their terrain advantage to repulse American attacks. The 10th Reconnaissance and their reinforcements also were able to fall back to secondary and tertiary defense positions at Salacsac Pass, giving them an increased ability to delay and harass the American advance. In fact, the 128th Infantry and 2nd Tank Battalion had not yet broken through by April 5th, and between the 5th and 17th, American soldiers at Salacsac Pass were suffering large numbers of casualties.

After more reinforcements, American troops spent the month of April attacking a series of Japanese hill positions. Japanese soldiers delayed the push as long as possible, and in late April they sent a counterattack that failed to allow them to gain territory against the Americans. American forces finally began to make headway in early May as they engaged in an enveloping movement involving battalions from the 127th and 128th Infantry as the 126th Infantry engaged troops in adjacent areas. The attack was successful and occurred so quickly that American forces reached the Villa Verde Trail.

It was at this point that the 32nd Division was close to linking up with the 25th Division near Santa Fe. With that, the last obstacle for American forces before Bambang was Balete Pass, which the 27th Infantry began attacking on April 27th. Aiding the 27th Infantry was the 35th Infantry, and these two units fought their way up Kapintalan Ridge while the 161st Infantry came in from the west to begin an enveloping movement against Japanese positions. This movement surprised the Japanese troops, and by May 4th, the Americans had captured Balete Pass and had moved beyond it. Helping the troops engaged on the Bambang Front was that at this point, Baguio had been secured, and reinforcements could now help bolster the American troop-strength.

The last major action along the Bambang Front occurred at Santa Fe. From May 14-22, the 27th Infantry cleared enemy troops around Kanami Ridge while the 161th Infantry took a strong enemy position at Mount Haruna. Continued fighting occurred along the Bambang Front, but this mainly took the form of invading pockets of Japanese forces. By May 29th, American units were in the process of surrounding Japanese troops at Bambang when Yamashita sent orders for a withdrawal from that location. The fighting had been extremely costly for both sides, as the 2nd Tank Division and 10th Division suffered casualties amounting to 13,500 men, while roughly two-thirds of the 20,750 soldiers at the Bambang Front were killed. (Smith, p.538)

The withdrawal at Bambang, coupled with the losses at Baguio, forced General Yamashita to order a general withdrawal of the Shobu Group to their last-stand positions, known to American commanders as the Kiangan Pocket, on June 15th. At the Kiangan Pocket, the American 6th Division moved up Route 4 before quickly breaking through a portion of the perimeter that was being manned by the Japanese 105th Division. As this was occurring, UFAIP guerrillas attacked from the direction of the Cagayan Valley. The situation for Japanese troops was one of extreme disorganization. Some troops were still trying to make their way to the last-stand position, while others were trapped by American forces.

General Krueger took advantage of the confusion among Japanese units by pressing his advantage, looking to move his forces quickly forward with the 37th Division moving up Route 5 through Santa Fe and Bagabag while the 6th Division would move in a more northerly direction through Route 4. This movement would surround and restrict the retreating Japanese troops. Between June 1st and 4th, Japanese antitank units tried to slow the American pursuit, but although they engaged the 775th Tank Battalion which was reinforcing the 129th Infantry, they were unable to do enough damage to delay their progress. Within the next few days American troops secured the towns of Aritao, Bayombong, and Bagabag.

The American advance continued through mid-June, where they reached the Cagayan Valley. Fighting within the valley occurred when the American 37th Division engaged with Japanese soldiers from the Yuguchi Detachment, who were retreating up Route 5. The 37th Division killed 600 Japanese soldiers and captured another 285 (Smith, p.569). By this time, Krueger believed that Japanese forces were on the verge of defeat, so he sent additional troops in the form of the 11th Infantry of the USAFIP.

By the end of June, Japanese troops, who had been harried and harassed for the majority of their retreat, had reached their final positions. American units had penetrated into northern Luzon to the point that there were two separate elements of the Shobu Group. One, comprised of 13,000 soldiers, was located at Sierra Madre. Meanwhile, the main body of 52,000 troops was positioned at the Japanese last-stand area. Although in raw numbers it seemed that Japanese troops still had the ability to threaten American forces, most of these soldiers were ill-equipped and were suffering from starvation and disease. As it turned out, a final confrontation in northern Luzon never occurred. Instead, American troops focused on containing Japanese forces, and the remaining Shobu Group units actually stayed in the field until the end of the war, at which point they finally surrendered. Mopping up operations also occurred on islands in the central and southern Philippines, but with the capture of Luzon, American forces were now prepared to begin building the military infrastructure for bombing missions and a possible invasion of the Japanese home islands.

Iwo Jima

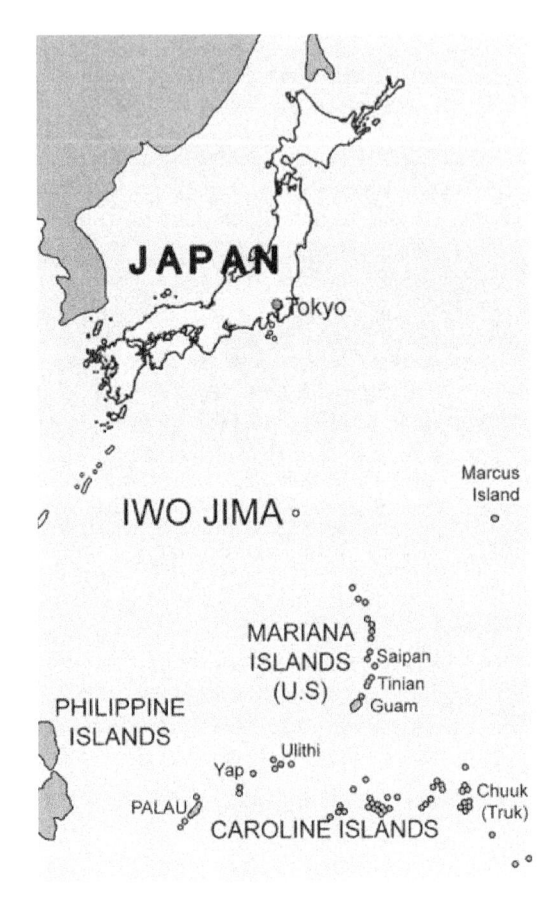

Map of the region

Iwo Jima is more officially known as "Sulfur Island," and it lies in a chain of volcanic islands south of the Ogasawara Islands. In total, the area is known as the Ogasawara Archipelago or the Bonin Islands, and it was critically important because Iwo Jima is situated approximately 650 nautical miles south of Tokyo. For U.S. naval and air forces, the island had tremendous strategic importance as an air base for fighter escorts in support of long-range bombers hitting the mainland, and as an emergency landing strip for B-29s returning from raids. The B-29 was essential to movement toward and eventual victory over the Empire. The B-29 "Superfortress," built by Boeing, possessed superior technology such as remote control machine gun turrets and pressurized cabins for high altitude work, and two of them would eventually carry the atomic bombs to the Japanese mainland. Of equal importance were the fighter escorts, such as the P-51 Mustangs, though these single seat fighters saw less action in the Pacific than they had in Europe. In the entire war, they shot down almost 5,000 enemy aircraft.

The B-29 "Superfortress"

P-51 Mustangs

These raids fell under the operative name of "Operation Scavenger," and Iwo Jima would not only hasten "Operation Downfall" (the ultimate destruction of the Japanese homeland), but would figure into logistics for delivery of the two atomic bombs ultimately dropped on the Japanese cities of Hiroshima and Nagasaki in the following months. Iwo Jima allowed blockades from both the sea and air, and from its location, aerial attacks could be conducted on enemy air and naval forces. In addition, Japanese kamikaze pilots, who had proven themselves an incredibly deadly threat to the American navy, would have to operate out of Okinawa or Kyushu if Iwo Jima was lost to them.

Japanese military commanders were fully aware that if Iwo Jima was lost, invasions of the mainland would soon follow, and even though this small patch of land in the sea covered an area of only 8 square miles, the Japanese had other reasons for defending it so passionately. It is commonly thought that the Japanese leadership did not want the Empire to be seen as an "easy" enemy, and furthermore, the island sat on the flight path of American B-29 bombing raids. If the Americans were able to use Iwo Jima, the distance and fuel requirements would be shortened, not to mention that emergency landings would require a much shorter distance. Japan needed the island airfields for its own planes, which were still conducting almost daily attacks on B-29s in the Marianas to the southeast, and Japanese planes had succeeded in destroying a healthy number of B-29s on the ground. Finally, the Japanese had an important radar station on the island that could signal ahead with news of American raids two hours in advance.

Initial raids against Iwo Jima were carried out from aircraft carriers that would distinguish themselves in the overall move toward Japan itself, commencing in June 1944 and comprised chiefly of B-24 bombers from the 7th Air Force in the Marianas. The island would be bombarded for over 70 days ahead of the actual amphibious invasion of Iwo Jima, which would not occur until over half a year after the first bombardment. The number of days spent bombarding the island was the most in the Pacific during the war.

When the actual invasion did commence, the offensive was on an epic scale. Over 800 warships, including six battleships, were involved, and after a lengthy bombardment during which 6,000 tons of shells and bombs were launched against the island by noon of the first day, an extra 10 days of naval bombardment was requested by Marines involved in the projected landing. As the U.S. Navy's website put it, "Prior to the invasion, the 8-square mile island would suffer the longest, most intensive shelling of any Pacific island during the war."[1]

The USS *New York* bombarding Iwo Jima on February 16, 1945

However, due to unfavorable weather conditions and the heavy aerial bombardment already accomplished, the Marines were granted only three extra days of bombardment, forcing them to

---

[1] Battle for Iwo Jima, 1945, The Navy Department Library – http://www.history.navy.mil/library/online/battleofiwojima.htm

prepare for the set date of February 19 as landing day. Unfortunately, the prolonged bombardment, although certainly softening the Japanese positions to some degree, did not have the far-reaching effects that the Americans expected or hoped for, given the use of such heavy ordnance. In fact, many Marines mistakenly believed that the bulk of Japanese soldiers on the island had been killed by the bombardment. In reality, once the landings were complete, there would be about 100,000 men fighting within an area 1/3 the size of Manhattan. While American planners optimistically thought Iwo Jima could be taken in a week, the island would be one of the most densely populated spots on the planet for 36 days.

A strategy briefing before the invasion of Iwo Jima

In 1945, the Allies would quickly understand and fear just how ferociously the Japanese were willing to fight, and much of that was a result of the Battle of Iwo Jima. In fact, the Japanese defending the island had no illusions about victory and did not even consider it a realistic option. They merely hoped to bloody the enemy so badly that the Allies would reconsider invading Japan. As Japanese military officers reported after the war:

> "In the light of the above situation, seeing that it was impossible to conduct our air, sea, and ground operations on Iwo Island [Jima] toward ultimate victory, it was decided that to gain time necessary for the preparation of the Homeland defense, our forces should rely solely upon the established defensive equipment in that area,

checking the enemy by delaying tactics. Even the suicidal attacks by small groups of our Army and Navy airplanes, the surprise attacks by our submarines, and the actions of parachute units, although effective, could be regarded only as a strategical ruse on our part. It was a most depressing thought that we had no available means left for the exploitation of the strategical opportunities which might from time to time occur in the course of these operations."

In command of Japanese forces on the island was General Tadamichi Kuribayashi, and he arranged a defensive scheme for Iwo Jima that flew in the face of all previous Japanese viewpoints on defense, particularly island defense. While the previous commander, General Hideyoshi Obata, had arranged artillery close to the beach and had positioned infantry to defend an island from the very water's edge, Kuribayashi decided instead to turn the inner island, from the back of the beach line inward, into an impenetrable and invisible fortress. The first Japanese troop reinforcements for Iwo Jima began to arrive well before the American bombardment from sites such as the naval base at Yokosuka and Chichi Jima.

Kuribayashi

Kuribayashi had the benefit of having traveled in the United States, and he had even attended Harvard for a short time. In his travels, he learned that American industry could be militarized at the touch of a button, and that American popular opinion was sensitive to high casualties in conflicts. If anything, his openly stated view that the U.S. should not be engaged as a military enemy may have contributed to his being given the task of defending Iwo Jima by leadership who may have viewed the defense of the island as a suicide mission. Once assigned his post, however, he took on the matter of American sensitivity to casualties as a tangible strategy – "If American casualties are high enough, Washington will think twice before launching another invasion against Japanese territory."[2] As for the Japanese view of casualties, a different mindset altogether was predominant: the strategy of sacrifice with no survivors.

---

[2] IwoJima.com – Japanese Iwo Jima Strategy

When the new General arrived on Iwo Jima on June 8, 1944 to relieve Obata, 80 fighters were positioned there. By the next month, all but a few were gone, and those remaining were destroyed in the American naval bombardment. Kuribayashi's first step was to evacuate all civilians from the island, and in direct opposition of General Obata's positioning, his beach strategy was based on an intention not to have one aside from minimal light-arms fire from infantry. The amphibious invaders would not face significant fire for the first 500 yards after landing. Meanwhile, Japanese artillery was positioned on high ground, particularly that over the Chidori Airfield and on the slopes of Mount Suribachi, the highest point of land on the island at 560 feet high. This included all artillery pieces, rockets and mortars.

In the next phase of arranging the defense, an extensive network of caves and tunnels were created, in full knowledge that no structure built above ground could stand up against the naval bombardment. Kuribayashi and his Japanese defenders were eventually in possession of 361 artillery pieces of 75mm or larger, 5 anti-tank battalions, a dozen 320mm mortars, 65 mortars of 150mm and 81mm, 33 naval guns and 94 anti-aircraft guns. Standard weapons included a small detachment of the Type 95 light tanks (employing three crewmen and 37mm guns), field guns in and around caves, Arisaka 7.7mm bolt action rifles with attachable bayonets, Nambu 8mm automatic, magazine-fed pistols, machine guns, knee mortars and standard issue grenades, not of the pin type but those that required striking to activate. Tank defenses were originally intended to be mobile, easily switching from firefight to firefight, but given the difficult terrain, Kuribayashi decided to install them in static positions and bury them, with turrets that were camouflaged to the point of virtual invisibility from the air.

The black ash that inundated the island was suitable for a superior quality of concrete, and the resulting caves, bunkers, pillboxes and large rooms were elaborate. Up to one quarter of the entire garrison was enlisted in the tunneling, and while some of the caves were suitable for two to three men with gear, others could hold up to 400, with multiple entrances and exits to prevent forces from becoming trapped. Ventilation systems were engineered to contend with the danger of sulfur fumes common to the island. On Mount Suribachi itself, the 60 foot-deep crater with a 20 foot ledge on which one could walk the entire circumference of the rim was particularly well-developed as a fortress. The Japanese had constructed elaborate caves all the way around the crater, and according to one of the 28th Marines who took the summit, "It was down in the crater that the Japanese were honey-combed."[3] Approximately 800 of the so-called "pillbox" structures were erected in a short amount of time, an impressive and rare feat of engineering given the distance from supplies and the time available. Men of the 28th found the crater to be naturally warm, but not nearly so much as the north end of the island, as one noted, "some of our boys received burns just from sleeping on the ground."[4] It was said that Marines who preferred hot food could have it simply by burying it for a short time throughout much of the island.

---

[3] Oral History: Iwo Jima, the Flag Raising: John Bradley Interview – www.history.navy.mil/flags/faq87-31.htm
[4] Oral History: Iwo Jima, the Flag Raising: John Bradley Interview

Mount Suribachi on the southern end of Iwo Jima

On the other hand, the black ash, according to accounts of veterans who were there, made advances particularly difficult. This "black sand" is described as large-grained, like coffee or BB shot, and climbing any slope was far more difficult than climbing in sand. Where one might sink to the top of the shoes in sand, advancing Marines sank from the ankles to the knees depending on the particular terrain. Vehicles also sank to hubcap height.

Kuribayashi's command post was installed on the north side of the island, northeast of Kita village and south of Kitano Point, and it was built 20 yards underground and connected to over 150 yards of tunnels. The enormous chamber featured a complete war room. On the second highest point of the island, Hill 382, a radio and weather station was established, and Colonel Chosaku Kaido, the artillery commander, occupied an enormous blockhouse nearby. The main communications center was over 50 yards in length, 20 yards in width, and far underground. An underground passage was to connect all major installations and comprise approximately 17 miles in length, but by the time the American bombardment began, only 11 miles had been completed.

In order to protect the two operating airfields, Kuribayashi ordered the construction of anti-tank ditches along all airstrips, and Japanese forces mined every conceivable ground approach. On January 2, 1945, B-24 Liberator bombers inflicted heavy damage on one of the fields, but Kuribayashi took 600 men from their units to repair the damage quickly. Using 11 trucks and a handful of bulldozers, the field was operational again within 12 hours, with 2,000 men filling the bomb craters.

In terms of strategy, Kuribayashi's plan included not only allowing enemy forces to cross the beach with minimal to no opposition but also not to return fire against American naval vessels. This was mostly to avoid divulging the locations of Japanese positions. The only light-arms resistance by the Japanese defenders would be over occupied areas above the Motoyama Airfield, the north beaches and Mount Suribachi. Once artillery was first deployed, pieces would be moved to the ground above the Chidori Airfield. This kind of operation required enormous stockpiles of ammunition, food and supplies, and even though many transport ships had been sunk before reaching Iwo Jima, the island's occupiers were well-entrenched in time for the attack. As late as February 1945, personnel continued to arrive before the island was encircled.

On August 10, 1944, almost six months prior to the amphibious invasion, Rear Admiral Toshinosuke Ichimaru arrived with over 2,000 additional personnel, many of them aviators and ground crews (Ichimaru himself was a famed aviator). While Iwo Jima's airfields had been used for conventional purposes, they would also be used for the notorious kamikaze attacks, which truly began to increase as a Japanese strategy in October 1944. Translated as "God Wind," "Divine Wind" and "God Spirit," kamikazes would sink 47 Allied vessels and damage over 300 by the end of the war, but the rise in the use of kamikaze attacks correlated the loss of the Empire's air superiority and its waning industrial might. This method of fighting would become more common by the time Iwo Jima was fought over, and it was especially prevalent during the invasion of Okinawa. The "privilege" of being selected as a kamikaze pilot played directly into the deep-seated Japanese mindset of "death before defeat." The pilot training manual assured each kamikaze candidate that when they eliminated all thoughts of life and death, fear of losing the earthly life can be easily overcome.

Still, not all cases of those chosen to be kamikazes were equally noble. Recruits were trained with torturous regimens or corporal punishment, and stories of mental impairment caused by drugs or saki abound. Some were described as "tottering" and dazed, being carried to their planes by maintenance officers, and forcibly pushed in if they backed down. Pilots who could not find their targets were told to turn around and spare their own lives for another day, but if a pilot returned nine times, he was to be shot. At the moment of collision, he was instructed to keep his eyes open at all times, and to shout "Hissatsu" ("clear kill").

In January 1945, Ichimaru informed troops on Iwo Jima that the Philippines had been lost and the Japanese fleet largely destroyed, leading to a high likelihood that Iwo Jima would be attacked soon. 127 American ships were reportedly heading northeast from Saipan toward Iwo Jima in an apparently unexpected change of American tactics, and anticipating that the assault would come sooner than it did, defenders on Iwo Jima were prepared, with the exception of the central tunnel's completion.

These defenses would have to contend with U.S. soldiers who were likely to carry an M1 Garmand, Thompson M1 or M1Carbine. Flamethrowers were well-designed for dealing with this kind of defense and would be used throughout the battle. American aircraft over Iwo Jima were predominantly Vought F4U Corsairs, and the landing craft included LCTs (Landing Craft Tanks that carried four), LSTs (Landing Ship Tanks that carried 20 in the U.S. version) and LVTs (Landing Vehicle Tracked, an amphibious, sometimes armored personnel carrier commanded by Army personnel, not Navy. American soldiers were commonly equipped with satchel charges and backpack explosives as well.

A Marine equipped with a flame-thrower at Iwo Jima

In sum, the strategic intent of the overall defensive scheme, no matter what was to occur, called for "strong, mutually supporting positions…defended to the death. Neither large-scale counterattacks, withdrawals nor bonsai charges were contemplated."[5]

---

[5] *Battle of Iwo Jima: Japanese Defense* – http://www.battle-fleet.com/pw/his/Battle-Iwo-Jima-Defense.htm

Photo # NH 104135 Relief map of Iwo Jima, 1945

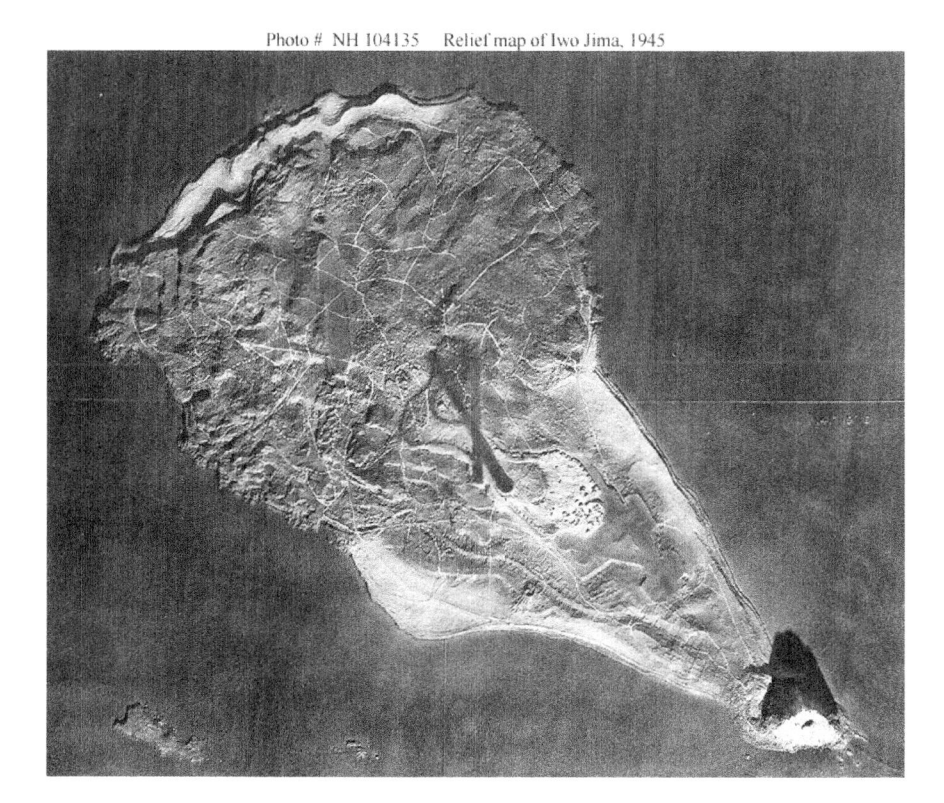

Aerial photo of Iwo Jima in 1945. The airstrips are visible

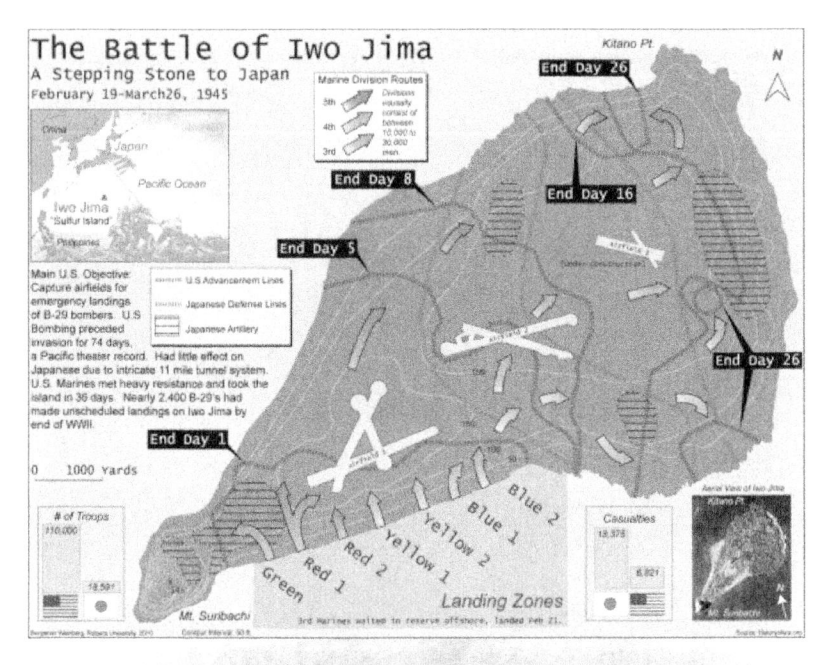

LVTs approaching Iwo Jima

At 2:00 a.m. on the 19th of February, battleship guns announced the beginning of the Iwo Jima offensive, also called D-Day like its more famous European counterpart. Soon after, over 100 bombers assaulted the island, followed by more bombs dropped by carrier aircraft. At 8:59 a.m., a minute ahead of schedule, the first of 30,000 men from the 3rd, 4th and 5th Marines began to land, and they would be followed by 40,000 more later in the day. The first aim was to neutralize and capture Mount Suribachi, and though these landing forces weren't fought on the beach by Japanese infantry, they had to deal with heavy artillery being fired at them by well-hidden units. The Japanese would open the steel doors to let their artillery pieces fire, close the door while reloading, and fire again. Kuribayashi also wisely waited for as many Marines as possible to land on the beach, thus offering more targets for the Japanese artillery.

Thanks to Kuribayashi's strategy of offering light resistance (at least from Japanese infantry), the Marines quickly found their landing zones congested, so much so that the 21st Marine regiment was boated and prepared to land but couldn't due to lack of space. With space so limited, some troops re-embarked onto their respective ships and landed later in the afternoon. When the Marines who landed encountered no Japanese forces, they mistakenly thought most of them had been killed in the bombardment. In fact, the Japanese were merely waiting for their approach, and the first lines of Marines that did approach on the 19th were quickly mowed down by machine gun fire once they got within range of the hidden Japanese positions.

Marines burrowing in on the beach

While the Marines had to contend with artillery on Mount Suribachi, important naval actions took place around the area and mitigated the potential damage. On February 18, the U.S. carrier *Enterprise* task groups 58.5, 58.4 and 58.1 separated from the main group, and headed for a refueling rendezvous to the southwest of Iwo Jima. The next morning (D-Day for the Marines), *Enterprise* refueled and set course 60 miles northwest of Iwo Jima. *Enterprise's* primary responsibility on the 19th was to protect amphibious forces from air attacks, and at 1630, she launched six Night Air Group 90 Hellcats to cover the forces at dusk. Two hours later, four VF (N)-90 fighters encountered eight interceptions, but most of the Japanese planes turned away and declined to engage. Before 1930, an enemy "Helen" (twin-engine heavy bomber) was knocked out of the sky (or as the Navy and Air Force was fond of saying, "they splashed it.").

On the 20th, the Marines advanced from the south of Mount Suribachi, north of the airfield, and satchel charges and flame throwers were used to reach entrenched Japanese forces on the mountain, all while cruisers and destroyers bombarded Japanese positions. Furthermore, ravines were set with gasoline fires to force the enemy out of entrenched positions. However, the elaborate tunnels dug by the Japanese allowed their men to flee further inward from the use of fire instead of being smoked out, and when the attacks would stop, the Japanese defenders could simply move right back into position. Another problem hampering the Marines was that the use of tanks in this theater of operations had a major disadvantage: a Sherman tank was difficult to disable, often requiring that Japanese attackers come out in the open, but the terrain throughout most of the island was not suited for armored movement.

A Sherman tank equipped with a flame-thrower attacks Japanese positions on Iwo Jima

At 0830 on the morning of the 20th, the 23rd advanced after a 15 minute period of shelling, naval bombardment and air preparation, and at the appointed "King" hour, the artillery was lifted approximately 400 yards and fired continuously for five minutes, supported by the 4th Tank. This advance was met with machine gun, mortar and artillery fire, but by noon, the northern limits of the airfield had been taken after "a series of well-concealed pillboxes and infantry strong points [were] reduced."[6] For the rest of the day, little progress was made by the 23rd, as they formed a seaward wall of defense against the airfield.

The 24th Marines took moderate to heavy losses on the second day, from after midnight to dawn. The 3rd and 4th Platoons of Regimental Weapons Company were ordered not to land until the beach's condition had been improved, a large enemy mine field was cleared, and a road for the tanks was "taped" through the field. For the 5th Marines, the day was marked by a series of counterattacks and Japanese attempts at infiltrating American lines. They were shelled by artillery and mortar fire throughout the night, and when "K-Hour" came, advances were slow, with "extreme difficulty in completing proper re-supply and reorganization of front line units on time."[7] Supply and evacuation problems persisted on the beaches, and LTVs were used primarily for bringing in supplies. In the late afternoon, an enemy air strike brought 50 caliber strafing, rockets and bombs to the top of the quarry, and the distance was so near that the markings were clear. Five were killed, with six wounded. Only 200-300 yards had been gained in two hours, and the Americans' left flank was mostly unable to move throughout the day. Orders were received to consolidate, dig in and establish firm contact.

For the 26th Marines, few supplies or equipment could be received from the beach, but they managed to defend against a morning Japanese counterattack with help from artillery fire. Advance was all but impossible given the abundance of mines; the Japanese had planted yardstick mines tied to 63kg bombs. Two or three of the enemy artillery pieces had been destroyed by naval guns, and an enemy dog-tag identified the Japanese unit opposing them as the 145th Infantry Regiment. A captured enemy document identified a second Japanese unit as well: the 312th Independent Infantry Battalion. Where the advanced stopped, 300-400 enemy dead were counted.

The 28th Marines, as they did every night, received a heavy barrage of shelling from Mount Suribachi, which by now had already been appropriately dubbed "Meatgrinder Hill." In the early morning, an enemy barge landed on the west beach, and 39 enemy soldiers were killed trying to reach shore. The Marines were fearful of "banzai" attacks at night, a tactic frequently used by the Japanese that simply attempted to overwhelm Allied positions with massive numbers of men, so they were alert at all hours. To help prevent such attacks, the American navy would shell the island throughout the night in an effort to actually brighten the night sky and prevent Japanese soldiers from sneaking up on the American lines. At 0800, the 28th was ordered to attack, seize Suribachi, and mop up the west beach. Tanks arrived, and the advance went through 200 yards of reinforced concrete pillboxes, but Major Allen and Captain Young of D and I Company were severely wounded and evacuated.

---

[6] *Iwojimahistory.com* – http://www.iwojimahistory.com/content/view/13/35/1/0/
[7] *Iwojimahistory.com*

Meanwhile, the 21st Marines were in the boats by 0800, and landed at Beaches Yellow 1 and 2 at 1345. A warning was issued that friendly Marines of the 4th Division were moving through on that day. Recon was limited by darkness, and there was heavy artillery and mortar fire on the assembly area, although no casualties were reported. Three enemy tanks were spotted on the airstrip by the 23rd Marines. Naval artillery destroyed one, and the other two retreated. At 0045, orders were received for continuation of the attack, after pre-arranged strikes at selected targets. With the advance came increased resistance, and removal of mines slowed progress. Due to the number of casualties, units began to merge with others, and contact with adjacent units was lost during daylight hours only to be reestablished at night.

Tanks, once thought to be essential in all advances, were maintained at the rear with terrain and mines continuing to pose significant problems: "the mere appearance of a tank forward with the infantry during the attack resulted in heavy artillery and mortar fire."[8] Employment of half-track, 75mms became impractical, and they were returned to the rear, where their absence was keenly felt. The 24th endured heavy fire from throughout the night, and a half-track platoon of Regimental Weapons Company landed on "Yellow" Beach 1 on the morning of the 21st. The entire day was spent scanning advanced routes and removing mines.

---

[8] Iwojimahistory.com

Supplies landing at Iwo Jima

While the Marines inched their way toward Mount Suribachi and the airfield on the southern end of Iwo Jima, the navy was attempting to prevent attacks by Japanese planes taking off from nearby islands. After 0900 on the 21st of February, the *Enterprise* and the *Saratoga* CV-3 split up. *Saratoga* and her three escort destroyers went to join Task Group 52.2, Rear Admiral Calvin Durgin's forces of escort carriers to the northeast of Iwo Jima. *Saratoga* operated in tandem with *Lexington* CV-16 and *Hancock* CV-19. "Saratoga was now 'Queen of the Jeeps" (escort carriers), but her reign was short-lived."[9] Before 1600, she picked up a large "bogey" on radar that turned out to be a mass of 20-25 planes at a distance of approximately 75 miles. They were first identified as friendly due to the belief that American air patrols were returning, but when planes were sent aloft to confirm it, they shot down two Zeroes. The body of enemy planes emerged from the low fog and descended on *Saratoga*, which took three direct hits from the planes' bombs, while two enemy planes fell off the starboard side and one crashed directly into the flight deck. The crew fought the fires for 90 minutes as the carrier sped up to 25 knots, but a second attack began four hours later and *Saratoga* was targeted by five suicide planes. In the attack, the *Saratoga* was badly damaged, and the USS *Bismarck Sea* was sunk, making it the last carrier to sink during World War II.

Enterprise turned to the north rather than follow the route of *Saratoga*, to strike at the airfields that supported the suicide missions over Iwo Jima. She was now the only fleet carrier operating at Iwo Jima, and her added mission was now to inflict as much damage as possible on the enemy airfields of the region. Instead of a full-out launching of fighters, she launched pockets of 4-8 Hellcats on the hour around the clock. Outright kills were few, but many potential threats were turned away, and the carrier inflicted significant damage on the airfields and the harbor of Chichi Jima. Many Japanese cargo ships were sunk, along with other important structural and resource damage. The USS *Gregory* joined *Enterprise* at Chichi Jima to assist in the rescue of ditched pilots, and before leaving, *Enterprise* targeted the airfield at Susaki and the seaplane base at Futami. By the beginning of March, enough of Iwo Jima was controlled that landings and take-offs could be maintained without fear of suicide attacks, and *Enterprise* remained off the island until March 9. "If the [USS Carrier] Enterprise and Task Group 58.5 had played a secondary role during the Tokyo raids, they made up for it at Iwo Jima."[10]

Two hours before dawn on the 21st, an attack by approximately 100 Japanese soldiers was repelled, but explosions occurred in the rear area and two fires erupted on the beach "Blue" 1 in ammunition dumps. Lieutenant Colonel Mustain was killed in action, and Major Fenton Mee took command, and in the course of the confusion, an unintended gap formed between elements of 1/25 and 2/25. All units were ordered to consolidate for the night. Thousands of Marines had to shift position that night, all while small enemy groups remained active on the beach after dark.

---

[9] USS Enterprise: 1945 Iwo Jima
[10] USS Enterprise: 1945 Iwo Jima – http://www.cv6.org/1945/iwo-2.htm

Making matters worse, the American supply lines from the beach were poor, at a time when flame-thrower servicing was needed and supply materials such as radio battery replacements would have been helpful. Several Marines of the 27th were stabbed in the night, and general rules of combat as a tactical code did not exist for either side. Japanese who spoke English continued to call for help, then shoot whichever American responded.

   The Americans' right flank also dealt with heavy resistance early on the 21st. The right flank met heavy resistance and had to deal with increasing artillery, even as naval gunfire destroyed two pieces. Tanks and infantry reported cases of booby-trapped saki bottles and terra cotta mines, also found in shell holes and foxholes. One of the most harrowing incidents of the day involved 24 Japanese soldiers committing mass suicide by jumping together off of a cliff around airfield I.

The flag atop Mount Suribachi

During the 21st, pyrotechnics were set off atop Suribachi over the heads of the 28th Marines, the unit charged with the taking of Suribachi, and if that wasn't enough for the Marines to sit through, a 40 plane strike was called in before the K-hour advance only 100 yards from the Marines' position. For the advance itself, both tank and air support would soon become impossible, and the tanks were ultimately unable to make it by K-hour, so there would be no advance until they arrived. When they did, multiple pillboxes and blockhouses were knocked out, and the armor was able to "bore through the main defenses in front of the mountain."[11] There were multiple incidents of cave attacks before the 28th reached the base of the mountain, but the various units consolidated at late afternoon.

All told, the enemy dead for the day totaled 508, and despite all the difficulties, the Marines achieved a major milestone in successfully encircling Mount Suribachi by the 22nd of February. The 21st Marines were ordered to relieve the 23rd by 0730, and this was accomplished under cover of darkness, although the First Battalion received heavy enemy fire that resulted in severe casualties as they made their way across a stretch of Airfield I. They were not able to be in position at the appointed time, so a request was offered to have the 2nd Battalion of the 24th Marines attached to initiate the next attack on schedule. However, that request was inevitably canceled. The right flank gained only about 50 yards of ground, with 250 on the left for the entire day, but many enemy fortifications were compromised.

---

[11] Iwojimahistory.com

Members of the 24th Marines

February 23rd would go down as perhaps the most auspicious day in the overall invasion of Iwo Jima, as it was on this day that Marines reached the top of Suribachi after non-stop heavy fighting. At 1020, a patrol under command of Lieutenant Harold Schreir of the 28th Marines reached the top and raised a small flag on the summit. That flag was raised by five Marines atop the same mountain as part of a 40 man patrol and was hoisted by Platoon Sergeant Ernest I. "Boots" Thomas of Tallahassee, Florida. A Marine Corps photographer captured the first raising on film, just as an enemy grenade caused him to fall over the crater edge and tumble 50 feet. The lens of his camera was shattered, but the film and soldier were safe. Historian James Bradley described in *Flags of Our Fathers* why this would not end up being the iconic moment of the battle:

> "The Secretary of the Navy, James Forrestal, had decided the previous night that he wanted to go ashore and witness the final stage of the fight for the mountain. Now, under a stern commitment to take orders from Howlin' Mad Smith, the secretary was churning ashore in the company of the blunt, earthy general. Their boat touched the beach just after the flag went up, and the mood among the high

command turned jubilant. Gazing upward, at the red, white, and blue speck, Forrestal remarked to Smith: 'Holland, the raising of that flag on Suribachi means a Marine Corps for the next five hundred years.'

Forrestal was so taken with fervor of the moment that he decided he wanted the Suribachi flag as a souvenir. The news of this wish did not sit well with 2nd Battalion Commander Chandler Johnson, whose temperament was every bit as fiery as Howlin Mad's. "To hell with that!" the colonel spat when the message reached him. The flag belonged to the battalion, as far as Johnson was concerned. He decided to secure it as soon as possible, and dispatched his assistant operations officer, Lieutenant Ted Tuttle, to the beach to obtain a replacement flag. As an afterthought, Johnson called after Tuttle: 'And make it a bigger one.'"

Picture of the first flag-raising atop Mount Suribachi

A larger flag would be brought by an LST, and when that flag was raised, the iconic photograph of Joe Rosenthal taken. Rosenthal noted, "Out of the corner of my eye, I had seen the men start the flag up. I swung my camera and shot the scene. That is how the picture was taken, and when you take a picture like that, you don't come away saying you got a great shot. You don't know."

As it turned out, Rosenthal had taken a picture that would win a Pulitzer, but initially, a lot of people assumed it was a staged shot. As one writer asserted, "Rosenthal climbed Suribachi after the flag had already been planted. ... Like most photographers [he] could not resist reposing his characters in historic fashion." Rosenthal would be forced to argue for decades that he had spontaneously captured the flag-raising, insisting, "I don't think it is in me to do much more of this sort of thing ... I don't know how to get across to anybody what 50 years of constant repetition means." Thankfully, a film of the very same moment, shot by Bill Genaust, proved that Rosenthal hadn't staged the iconic picture.

A 1945 stamp commemorated the flag-raising atop Iwo Jima

The second flag raised by Marines atop Mount Suribachi. Photo by Mark Pellegrini

The first platoon to reach the top stayed for three days before being relieved, and the flag always flew throughout the Iwo Jima offensive. Unlike certain mythologies that were constructed around famous historical events elsewhere, the flag-raisings of Iwo Jima occurred during a month of stark reality and were not documented for cinematic glorification. The raising of the flag on Suribachi created a national "ecstatic moment…a quintessential moment of American heroic triumph, and a celebration of the virtues of the common soldier."[12]

After the colors were raised, elements of the different Marine units met at the southernmost point as ordered. Congratulations were sent from Lt. General Smith, Vice Admiral Turner and Maj. General Rockey of the 5th Marines. The rest of the day was spent demolishing caves and mopping up the remaining pockets of resistance, and a night defense of just 40 men from E Company was left on the summit.

Although every American now remembers Rosenthal's picture and associates it with Iwo Jima, there was still plenty of work to do. While that moment unfolded atop Mount Suribachi, Marines were advancing toward the second airfield at the island's opposite end. At the same time, the Marines had to strengthen their own defensive positions during February 24th and 25th because enemy units attempted night infiltrations in groups of two and three.

---

[12] Edward T. Linenthal: Review of "Iwo Jima in American Memory," Karal Ann Marling, John Wetenhall, p. 9

Accurate and intense enemy fire fell on the 25th Marines throughout the night, and such a bombardment became more the rule than the exception. All the while, enemy patrols that harassed front lines were repelled, but these attacks still inflicted American casualties, and just as importantly, they slowed the American advance. The 25th Marines made only moderate advances over these few days, but when they fired two rocket barrages against the hill, it drove a bunch of Japanese out of the structures and out into the open, where most were immediately killed. The total enemy dead in that action was 200. When the 25th Marines were counterattacked at mid-day by 100 Japanese soldiers following a heavy mortar barrage, they pushed back that attack but suffered even more casualties. As if the fighting wasn't miserable enough, a cold rain began to fall on the island during February 26 as well.

Thus, the 5th Tank of the 26th Marines moved out at daybreak through February 27th in a steady rain and under heavy fire, but the unit managed to extend 200 yards into the 4th Marines' zone, and the attack managed to advance 400 yards. This was considered an enormous gain in perspective, but the right flank was unable to advance at all. A bluff to the right stymied their progress, and fire from the top pinned down the advance. This bluff would end up harassing and delaying the entire invasion of Iwo Jima for a number of days, since the effectiveness of the tanks was largely negated by the Japanese positions on this higher ground.

As the progress was halted, uncoordinated counterattacks came from the left and somewhat in the center, but both were repelled by the Japanese on the afternoon of the 27th. A couple of units reached ground in advance of the main lines but were forced to withdraw, and due to conditions on the beach, with the rain and volcanic ash mixing, it was even harder for supply items to reach the front. On top of that, the 27th Marines' beach defenses reported a counter-landing of 50 Japanese during the day, with another 400 landing during the night. These were repelled by a combination of beach defenses and naval fire. No offensive enemy action was reported during the morning hours, but the Marines were shelled consistently. The total enemy dead for February 27 came to 515.

During the early morning hours of February 28, flares from Suribachi were again sent up by night over the 28th Marines, the closest unit to the mountain's base. This helped the Marines defend against any nighttime attacks, and enemy swimmers were killed coming ashore on the west beach. During daylight hours, the forward advance continued, with three teams landing abreast, but since the rain had mixed with volcanic dust, almost all automatic weaponry was reduced to single-shot weaponry.

The attack on Iwo Jima was only supposed to take a week, but Marines had been on the ground for 10 days and still had plenty of work to do.

Marine machine-gunners attacking Japanese positions

As symbolic and encouraging as the taking of Suribachi might have been, the mountain made up only one point of the island and one mission. The northern end, with its airfield and Japanese fortifications, was equally defended and arguably possessed a heavier arsenal of resources, including eight infantry battalions, a tank regiment, two artillery and three heavy mortar battalions. The fight for Iwo Jima was far from complete after Suribachi.

Likewise, the center of the island offered a strong resistance and was dubbed the "meat grinder" by attacking forces. The highest point of this area was Hill 382, also known as "Turkey Knob," which housed a large Japanese communication center. The southern extension of Hill 382 was known as the "the Amphitheater." Toward the northern tip, Marines did experience one minimal "banzai" charge, which contradicted direct orders of General Kubayashi, and the desperate act was a deadly mistake. The 700 Japanese dead spelled the end of organized resistance in the center of the island.

On the northern end, the 22nd Marines continued attacks on known targets with artillery and tank support. The First Battalion "jumped off" on time, but the 2nd found itself in an intense firefight, with no advances made until mid-morning. By early afternoon, after Suribachi had been taken on the 23rd, American units had reached the southwest edge of Airfield II. Some of the men crossed the runways before being driven back, and ultimately, by the end of February 23, no change of position had been gained due to heavy incoming fire. Meanwhile, the beach and rear sections were shelled, and by early evening, a Condition Red alert was issued to all units. Soon after, enemy planes appeared, but their subsequent bombing was ineffective.

As different Marine units prepared to advance on the morning 24th, The 27th Marines were held in Division Reserve, and even before the advance they reported that tactical maps distributed among the officers had been compromised due to copies lost in battle. Sure enough, at 0300, enemy infiltrations began along the west coast. Pull-type booby traps were found tied to saki bottles, helmets, and even dead Japanese soldiers. The heaviest concentration of enemy fire was directed at roads to the west of Airfield I, but the Americans held out, and enemy dead for the day was listed at 645. Failed enemy infiltrations against the 28th were attempted throughout the night, but to no avail.

February 24th's daily advance began at 0730 with a friendly air strike along the front lines, and about two hours later, the entire line moved forward under heavy fire and bad terrain. A gap developed between the Marines during the day, and heavy fire was received from Airfield II, but at 1700, all units consolidated for the night. The furthest units had advanced about 400 yards with the support of two airstrikes and artillery, and they maintained contact with the enemy throughout. By now, the Marines had grown accustomed to the Japanese's constant attempts at infiltration in the darkness, which were supported by heavy artillery and mortar fire, but the forward units managed to repulse those attacks during the early morning hours of February 25. The forward units were relieved at 0900, and the day was spent reviewing the Division front.

Beginning the next northern advance on the 24th of February, following 75 minutes of naval bombardment, the 4th and 5th Marine Divisions attacked again in the north, supported by tanks. The Japanese were successful at stopping the tanks with anti-tank guns and mines, and throughout the entire day, the 5th Division gained only 500 yards. However, the 21st Marines fared better. The 2nd Battalion of the 21st Marines sighted enemies behind their lines at 0630, and the infiltrators were killed immediately. Excellent progress was made in the day's advance, with the 3rd Battalion gaining 600 yards against well-organized pillboxes and other entrenchments. Attacks continued at 1330, and at 1445, twelve "Blue" Tanks were at last operational on the second airfield. Enemy fire and mines produced heavy tank casualties, but the 2nd Battalion circled west of the airfield, and by 1545, two companies had crossed it. The high ground above changed hands several times, with much hand-to-hand fighting, and at 2145, units were consolidated for the night. The 21st Marines could be proud of their accomplishments on February 24.

Not all of the Marines were so fortunate. The 23rd Marines drew heavy shelling during the night of the 24th, and although attempts were made to pinpoint the origin of fire, success was minimal. The 24th had to content itself marking mines during the day. Meanwhile, the 3rd Marines advanced along the troublesome bluff to the right of the central invasion, which helped to suppress Japanese fire being rained down on Americans from that position. The 3rd advanced

500 yards throughout the afternoon, far enough that contact was lost for a time between the 3rd and the other Marines.

At the end of February 24, the 27th continued as a reserve unit. 30 enemy dead were found in a sulfur hole, and several had committed suicide, including three officers. This was a sight encountered with increasing frequency as the month wore on. New mine fields were discovered, overrun mortar positions were found to be booby-trapped, and roads around the airfield received concentrated enemy fire. Enemy dead totaled 645, and well over 100 enemy infiltrators had been killed, with many of the Japanese soldiers tied to crude demolition as booby-traps. The early daylight hours were spent mopping up on and around Suribachi.

At 0930 on the morning of the 25th, the 3rd Marines began their attack to the north, and as with the day before, movement was slow and casualties high. The 9th Marines saw their first action in the Iwo Jima offensive on the 25th. They were passed through the 21st and commenced their attack at mid-morning, but the source of enemy fire was difficult to locate even at 25 yards. Progress was slow against enemy fire, and tanks received heavy resistance around the Airfield II area. The 1st Battalion of the 9th Marines managed to cross the runways toward Hill 200-P and gain a foothold on the hill, but they suffered heavy casualties. The 2nd Battalion tank support was a good deal more effective; since the area was small in dimensions, two or three tanks wielded enormous influence. The 2nd Battalion advanced 400 yards before being stopped abruptly under heavy fire.

After a 95 minute artillery barrage, the 23rd advanced and flanked Airfield II, an objective that would be denied them until late afternoon, but ultimately, the Japanese defense of the field was weakened by aggressive infantry and tank attacks. All Marine units consolidated on favorable ground in late afternoon, and orders were issued for attacks the following day. Small groups of enemy infiltrators were spotted by night, and elements of the 24th were ordered to the assembly area. They were pinned down for the day and requested two airstrikes, neither of which ever came. With the continued enemy strength on the bluff line right continuing to stymie progress, all advances were halted until it could be neutralized.

The 23rd Marines, also in the vicinity of Airfield II, continued the attack during the early morning of the 25th against pillboxes, bunkers, emplacements and caves. Mine fields were discovered on the airfield runway and in the area of the Radio Weather station on TA 200W and heavy enemy tank fire was received from Hill 382, but by the afternoon, the southwest slopes were taken, with American units consolidating by dusk. Tanks were brought up, but their presence drew much heavier fire, exacerbating the situation. The center of the line gained 75-150 yards but sustained heavy casualties, and the Marines were forced to withdraw from its positions below the cliff line under cover of smoke screens.

By February 26, the Marines had still failed to take the bluff line that was causing them so many problems as they advanced, but enemy fire from that position had decreased. They had also managed to destroy a large number of pillboxes by now, and a group of 20 Japanese were killed in a cave on the northwest slope of Suribachi.

The second airfield was finally taken by the 3rd Marines on the 27th of February, and the 9th Marines were still in the vicinity of Airfield II. Tanks increased in importance as the Marines' advance was almost immediately blocked by caves and pillboxes to the front and at the flanks. Heavy fire came from the right, and only small gains were made in the morning. The Japanese continued trying to infiltrate the American lines that night, in tandem with artillery bombardment, but the 28th Marines again fought them off. 103 enemy dead were confirmed.

During the 27th, the 25th Marines advanced after dawn with the cliff line to the right. The advance went 150 yards before immediately halting as the Marines found themselves in an open area with no cover. They took heavy casualties, and two of the three tanks in support were destroyed. By evening, it was decided that the objective ground could not be reached, so the 25th withdrew through the lines back to the positions of the preceding night. The center and right gained 200-300 yards, and all units halted the advance on favorable ground to consolidate as night fell. The 26th Marines withdrew into the assembly area for "reorganization, salvage and evacuation of the dead."[13] Almost all enemy dead were recovered under cover of darkness, with the 27th Marines using phosphorous to camouflage the troop movements. The total Japanese dead for February 27 was listed at 840.

By the last day of February, the third airfield was occupied by Marines, but the surrounding hills were still held by the Japanese. Soon after, Marines assaulted the hills, 362A and 382, successfully taking and holding them by the 1st of March. The following night, an after-dusk attack was staged by Marines on Hill 362A, but the hill would not be secured until the 8th of March. On March 4th, a damaged B-29 landed on the island during the fighting, an important sign that Marines were sufficiently in control of the airfield to make landings possible. The first P-51s would arrive at the island as air support for Marines by March 6th, and Task Force 58 was relieved in preparation for a subsequent assault against Okinawa.

By the end of the first week of March, the southern airfield was fully operational for the Americans, and evacuation of the wounded proceeded without interruption. Since Iwo Jima was interconnected with so many simultaneous actions proceeding in the South Pacific, the bombing of the airfields in Chichi Jima was of great parallel importance, and attacks on Paulus and Yap in the western Carolines ensured that the strategic air importance of Iwo Jima would not simply be transferred to another site by the Japanese. Somewhat symbolically, of all the flag-raisings on Suribachi, the final one was hoisted by the U.S. Combat Team 28 on March 14, 1945, near the end of the conflict.

Over the course of March, the Japanese continued desperately attacking, including mounting a

---

[13] www.Iwojimahistory.com

counterattack on the 23rd and 24th Marine Regiments, but that assault was stopped by artillery, and 650 of the enemy were killed. Resistance continued throughout the following days as Japanese units repeatedly penetrated American lines in attempts to sever communication, but the defense had just about reached its last gasp. The final Japanese resistance was overcome at Kitano Point on March 25th, and the last Japanese unit to attempt a penetration of the American lines was allegedly led by Kuribayashi himself. The result of that action left 250 more Japanese dead, including Kuribayashi. At 8:00 a.m. on March 26, the island was declared secure, although a lengthy time would go by before final resistance was rooted out of the caves. Either way, the 147th U.S. Army Infantry arrived for garrison duty on Iwo Jima by March 20 and would have full control of the island by the 4th of April. By April 7, 100 P-51s were able to land on the island and subsequently escort a B-29 bombing raid against the Japanese mainland. It would be incorrect to assume that once the island came under American control, the fighting stopped or the environment became safe. It was clearly operational, but not necessarily safe, and casualties were suffered through the last day of American occupation.

The island of Iwo Jima remained under American control for several years even after the war, until it was eventually returned to the Japanese in 1968. In the last months of the war, the aircraft carrier USS *Iwo Jima* was under construction at Newport News, Virginia, but she was canceled on August 12, 1945 and her partial hull was scrapped. Her namesake, however, was launched from Bremerton, Washington in 1960 and commissioned in 1961. Today, no civilians are allowed on the island, and the Japanese operate a naval base there. American carriers still use it for landing training, and nuclear weapons are said to have been located at one time or another on Iwo Jima, Ton Chichi, Okinawa and other Japanese sites.

Final casualties for the entire Iwo Jima offensive have been estimated at 6,821 American dead and 19,189 wounded, compared to 20,000 Japanese dead and 1,083 wounded and/or captured. Clearly, fighting to the death and committing suicide were prevalent among the Japanese ranks. In this strategy of sacrifice, the Japanese remained true to their word, and of the few prisoners taken, many were conscripted Korean laborers. It has even been estimated that up to 6,000 Japanese fighters are still entombed within the network of caves.

Cyril O'Brien recalls that of the 3,400 soldiers of the 28th who came ashore with him, the unit that would scale the summit of Suribachi first, only 600 were standing when the battle was ended. In his words, Iwo Jima was a battlefield "with no front lines, no rear, every inch a battleground...the enemy was nowhere and everywhere...the Japanese were not on Iwo Jima. They were in it!"[14] This small island, only a few miles in length, inflicted about 33% of all Marine casualties during World War II, and it was the first major Pacific battle in which American casualties exceeded those of the Japanese. According to O'Brien and others who have fought in multiple theaters, the Iwo Jima experience could only be measured by itself.

---

[14] Cyril O'Brien, Iwo Jima Retrospective – www.military.com

That assertion is also supported by the fact that Iwo Jima stands as one of the most highly decorated engagements in modern American history. The Medal of Honor, created during the Civil War and often awarded posthumously, was bestowed on 27 heroic men who participated in the battle, 22 of whom were Marines and 5 of whom were Navy men. The Medals of Honor received for service at Iwo Jima comprised a quarter of the total awards given for the entire war. Half of the Iwo Jima Medals of Honor were granted posthumously, and the last living recipient, Herschel "Woody" Williams, was invited aboard the USS *Iwo Jima* in 2011 to participate in a remembrance ceremony. The youngest of the recipients, to whom the award was given posthumously, was Jacklyn Lucas, who had turned 17 on Valentine's Day, days before the offensive. Upon his recruitment, he was actually 14 but effectively hid the fact.

Iwo Jima was so important to the men who fought there that the 133rd Naval Construction Battalion is still seeking a unit citation for their work alongside the invading Marines, and the 31st Naval Construction Battalion and their comrades stormed the beaches, "fought alongside their Marine counterparts, and provided essential resupply efforts during the invasion. They provided staging areas for supplies, transported wounded back to our ships and helped bury the dead. They established a base camp to provide food and shelter to those on the island, built a road up Suribachi, and a runway that would be used for forward refueling and repair of B-29s headed for Japan."[15]

---

[15] 31st Navy Seabee's Association – www.31st-Seabees.com/iwo%20jima.htm

The memorial atop Mount Suribachi. The inscription reads, "'Among the Americans who served on Iwo Jima, uncommon valor was a common virtue.' - Nimitz"

Iwo Jima was also notable for the participation of Native American code-talkers, particularly the Navajo, who served in every major Marine action from 1942-1945. Some Native American languages had been used effectively in the First World War, and Navajo was perfectly suited to work against the Japanese because the language was oral, not written, and consisted of multiple dialects, all of tremendous complexity. It was thought that only 30 or so non-Navajos understood the language, and that none of them were Japanese. "Navajos could encode, transmit, and decode a three-line English message in 20 seconds. Machines of the time required 30 minutes."[16]

Six Navajos worked around the clock during the first two days of the assault on Iwo Jima, and in that time, they sent and received approximately 800 messages. The Japanese, adept code-breakers, nonetheless remained baffled by the Navajo language and never came close to cracking it. As one soldier at Iwo Jima put it, "Were it not for the Navajo, we would never have taken Iwo Jima."[17] Several members of the code-talkers unit were decorated for their actions in September

---

[16] www.history.navy.mil/faq61-2.htm

1992.

Naturally, the Battle of Iwo Jima instantly became a source of pride among Americans, and it was almost immediately glorified in the 1949 movie *Sands of Iwo Jima*, starring John Wayne and including cameos of a few of the Marines who had famously raised the flag on Iwo Jima. However, a lot of historians have second-guessed the need for fighting the battle of Iwo Jima at all, and the question of whether it was truly necessary is still debated by modern scholars. Considering the horrific casualties suffered as a result of "the bloodiest fight in Marine history,"[18] it is a sensitive question for Americans, particularly the families of Marines, but it is known that leading officers debated each other on the subject at the time. By April 1945, just a few weeks after the battle had ended, retired Chief of Naval Operations William V. Pratt openly questioned in *Newsweek* magazine the "expenditure of manpower to acquire a small, God-forsaken island, useless to the Army as a staging base and useless to the Navy as a fleet base…" Pratt went on to openly wonder "if the same sort of airbase could not have been reached by acquiring other strategic localities at lower cost."

Some historians have asserted that the battle took place in part due to rivalry between the service branches. Historian Robert S. Burrell argued that the Battle of Iwo Jima was only justified in hindsight and that it could have been avoided entirely, writing, "This justification became prominent only after the Marines seized the island and incurred high casualties. The tragic cost of Operation Detachment pressured veterans, journalists, and commanders to fixate on the most visible rationalization for the battle. The sight of the enormous, costly, and technologically sophisticated B-29 landing on the island's small airfield most clearly linked Iwo Jima to the strategic bombing campaign. As the myths about the flag raisings on Mount Suribachi reached legendary proportions, so did the emergency landing theory in order to justify the need to raise that flag."

Occasionally, Burrell and others have argued that in making the decision to go ahead, larger mission objectives, local plans and dates were altered, the same sort of questions that plagued the aftermath of the Battle of the Bulge. As Burrell noted, "The Marine Corps, which paid the heaviest price, remained completely excluded from the decision-making process."[19] These theories purport that the Navy moved strategically on its own behalf, as it did by not waiting for the Army to complete the Philippines mission and free up troops for an invasion of Formosa, by conspiring with the Air Force to create stronger post-war departments for themselves at the expense of the Army in going ahead with Iwo Jima.

Conversely, those who argue Iwo Jima was essential point to several facts. For example, when Admiral Spruance asked Curtis LeMay directly, "What do you think about the value of Iwo

---

[17] www.history.navy.mil/faq61-2.htm
[18] Robert S. Burrell, "Breaking the Cycle of Iwo Jima Mythology: A Strategic Study of Operation Detachment", in Journal of Military History, Vol. 68 No. 4 (Oct. 2004) p. 1143
[19] Robert S. Burrell, p. 1144

Jima?"[20]. Le May is said to have responded that it would "...be a tremendous value to me. Without Iwo Jima, I couldn't bomb Japan effectively."[21] Taken at face value, this would appear to be an authentic response. Furthermore, Burrell's argument, according to Officer Brian Hanley, is "disabled by an impaired understanding of historical analysis and weakened further by a tendency to disparage beyond reason the motives and judgment of Navy and United States Air Force leaders."[22] While Hanley admits that inter-service rivalry is omnipresent in joint actions, the Battle of Iwo Jima (as in most cases) was based on less than perfect intelligence, and the results were not profound in relation to hopes and expectations, leading Hanley to conclude that "one conspicuous defect of Burrell's argument is the absence of sound strategic analysis."[23]

Today, of course, the Battle of Iwo Jima is almost synonymous with the famous photograph of servicemen raising the flag atop Mount Suribachi. Rosenthal's iconic photo of the flag raising was able to identify the soldiers who participated, which included Marines Ira Hayes, Mike Strank, Rene Gagnon, Harlon Block, Franklin Sousley, and U.S. Navy Corpsman John Bradley. The flag was raised during the fourth day of the Battle of Iwo Jima, and it would win the Pulitzer Prize for Photography. The tragic postscript that's often forgotten is that the picture did not capture the end of the campaign; in fact, three of the soldiers pictured in the photo died over the course of the next month on Iwo Jima.

So inspired was sculptor Felix de Weldon by Rosenthal's photo that he recreated it in a life-sized model, casting it in bronze and having it erected across the Potomac River by the Arlington Cemetery in September 1954. During the 179th anniversary of the United States Marine Corps (which was founded in 1775), the memorial was dedicated to then President Eisenhower. The 32 foot figures hoisting a 60 foot flag stand upon a 10x3 base, upon which all major engagements in Marine history are inscribed.

Okinawa

Okinawa was home to 450,000 people, and along with Formosa, "formed a kind of eastern protective barrier for preserving Japan's lifelines through the East China Sea as well as the last barrier to an invasion of the homeland up through southern Japan" (Gow, p. 21). As American forces moved closer and closer, and especially after their victory at Saipan, Japanese military planners began to see Okinawa as the site of a potential attack, so they sent 100,000 soldiers to the Ryukyu islands and began constructing fortifications, all while moving thousands of civilians off the islands.

---

[20] Robert S. Burrell, p. 1145
[21] Robert S. Burrell, p. 1145
[22] Brian Hanley, "The Myth of Iwo Jima: A Rebuttal", in The Journal of Military History, Vol. 69 No. 3 (July 2005), p. 802
[23] Brian Hanley, p. 802

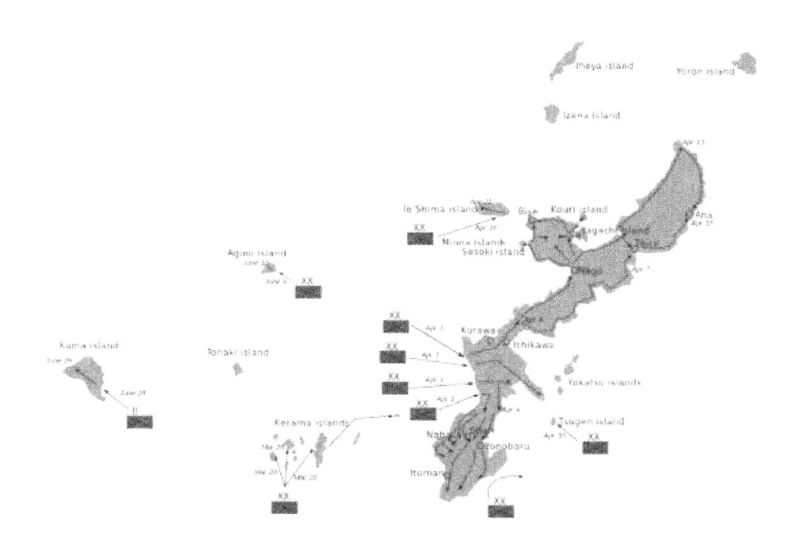

The Ryuku islands and Allied (blue) plans for operations.

Aerial view of Okinawa

In terms of Japanese airpower, a directive initiated on March 1, 1945, called Operation Ten-Go, featured kamikaze units as important avenues of attack, a strategy the Japanese increasingly relied on starting around the end of 1944. Translated as "God Wind," "Divine Wind" and "God Spirit," kamikazes would sink 47 Allied vessels and damage over 300 by the end of the war, but the rise in the use of kamikaze attacks was correlated to the loss of the Empire's air superiority and its waning industrial might; due to the growing lack of experienced pilots, the Japanese military turned to kamikaze pilots who were able to deal large amounts of damage even with their lack of training. Not surprisingly, Allied leaders and soldiers who fought against kamikazes were amazed by the pilots' determination and bravery, as Vice Admiral C.R. Brown noted, "There was a hypnotic fascination to the sight so alien to our Western philosophy. We watched each plunging kamikaze with the detached horror of one witnessing a terrible spectacle rather than as the intended victim. We forgot self for the moment as we groped hopelessly for the thought of that other man up there."

Earlier in the war, kamikaze units were voluntary, but by 1945 they were compulsory, and

Kikisui, or massed attacks by kamikaze pilots, would be the method used by the Japanese to attack Allied vessels off the coast of Okinawa. The "privilege" of being selected as a kamikaze pilot played directly into the deep-seated Japanese mindset of "death before defeat." The pilot training manual assured each kamikaze candidate that when they eliminated all thoughts of life and death, fear of losing the earthly life can be easily overcome. Still, not all cases of those chosen to be kamikazes were equally noble. Recruits were trained with torturous regimens or corporal punishment, and stories of mental impairment caused by drugs or saki abound. Some were described as "tottering" and dazed, being carried to their planes by maintenance officers, and forcibly pushed in if they backed down. Pilots who could not find their targets were told to turn around and spare their own lives for another day, but if a pilot returned nine times, he was to be shot. At the moment of collision, he was instructed to keep his eyes open at all times, and to shout "Hissatsu" ("clear kill").

The American plan for seizing Okinawa was very ambitious, in part because the military did not anticipate the maniacal resistance put up by Japanese defenders, but an ambitious campaign was also a necessity for logistical reasons. They not only planned to invade and defeat Japanese forces concentrated there but then also quickly develop the infrastructure with which to create the military bases that would be so important in attacking the Japanese home islands. Since Japan was not engaged in any other military operations in the Pacific at the time, and because they were cut off from their forces in the south, the bulk of Japan's military manpower and machinery would be focused on the Ryukyus during the campaign. Adding to the difficulty of the operation was the fact that Okinawa was far from Allied bases in the Pacific. American strategists believed the Japanese would respond to the attack by launching all available aircraft in both Formosa and the Chinese mainland, and if the Japanese managed to overwhelm American airpower, the ground forces fighting on Okinawa would then be isolated and in danger of being overwhelmed by Japanese forces. In order to combat the airpower at Japan's disposal, American military leaders believed Allied aircraft carriers would have to stay in the combat zone for a long period of time, where they would be attacked by an estimated 3,000-4,000 land-based Japanese aircraft (Gow, p. 24)

Crucial to American efforts was the need to gather intelligence about the island, a difficult prospect considering Okinawa was still roughly 1,200 miles away from the nearest American air base in late 1944. During the early part of 1945, the Americans focused on gaining intelligence on Okinawa, and that January, they estimated that there were 55,000 Japanese soldiers on the island. Military planners also assumed the Japanese would send further troops to the island, and that the defense force would probably be in the region of 66,000 by the time of an attack.

The plan that came together for Okinawa, called Operation Iceberg, set the invasion date for April 1, 1945, and the plan called for taking other Ryukyu islands such as Okina Daito, Kume, Miyako and Kika by April 8. From there, American forces would quickly move to attack Kyushu, the southernmost of Japan's home islands. The responsibility for the attack on Okinawa would be given to the Central Pacific Task Force, a joint army-navy force that was headed by Vice Admiral Spruance. Spruance would also have command over Task Force 50, which was made up of naval covering forces and special groups, along with Task Group 58 and Task Force 57, which consisted of an American fast carrier force and a British air carrier force. In terms of naval operations around Okinawa, the fast carriers would strike Okinawa, Kyushu, and other nearby islands in order to neutralize Japanese air power. The carriers of this group would then station themselves to the east of Okinawa and engage in support duties after American troops landed and began their attack. Meanwhile, the British carrier group would continue with strikes and patrols and would also be ready for any further operations against Kyushu (Frank, p. 29).

In terms of ground troops, Operation Iceberg relied on the element of surprise. One week before the planned invasion, the 77th Division would attack Kerama Retto, an island to the west of the home islands, which would then subsequently be used as a base for supplying ammunition and fuel for the forces engaging in the attack. They would then begin a diversionary attack on southeast Okinawa and then attack the beaches of western Okinawa near the island's two main airfields. Then, the XXIV Corps would take the southern portion of the island as well as any islands that would be needed for navy installations.

As Allied troops began the campaign, they quickly took the Kerama islands, which Japan had failed to fortify because they did not believe the islands possessed sufficient importance to be targeted by an American attack. American forces occupied all of the islands by March 29th, while the British Task Force 57 reached its position for the attack on Okinawa on March 26th. As American naval vessels moved on Okinawa, the last task before the attack was to clear the waters off the coast of mines. In the last week of March, 5,182 tons of shells were fired at the Ryukyus to soften their defenses. The next part of the plan would involve landing ground troops on Okinawa.

Allied soldiers landing on the Kerama islands.

The ground invasion was set to begin on April 1, 1945, and on that day, over 1,300 ships were involved in landing soldiers on the island. American forces had gained plenty of experience in amphibious landings over the past two years, but unlike at Guadalcanal or the Marianas, the Japanese did not contest the beach areas, allowing 60,000 troops to come ashore by the end of the first day. As they moved toward Okinawa's two main airfields, they experienced little resistance and quickly captured them.

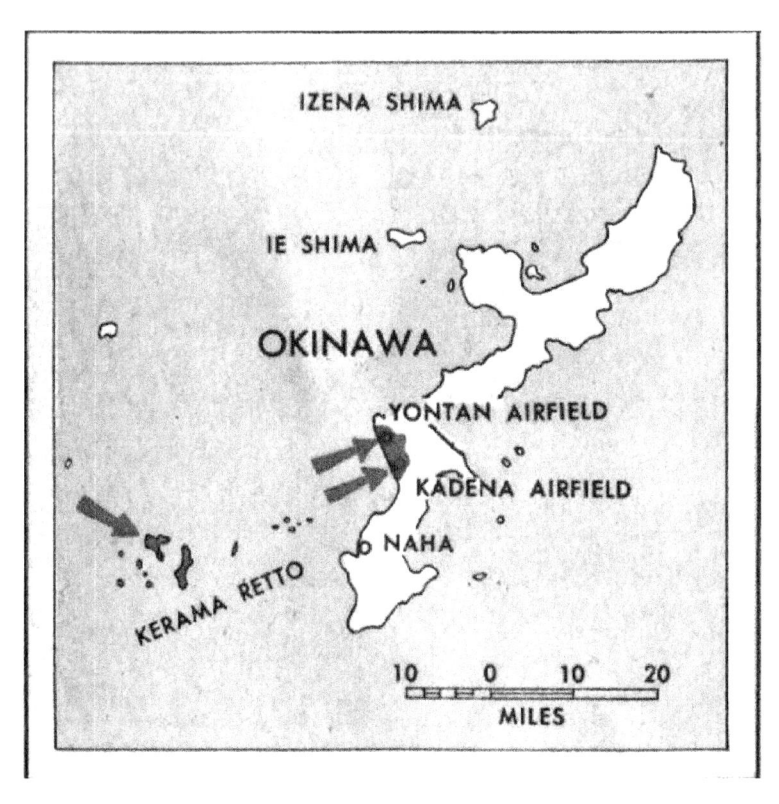

The invasion plan on April 1.

The USS *Idaho* shelling Okinawa on April 1.

Marines coming ashore on April 1.

American forces moving on the beaches of Okinawa, April 1.

Unlike American ground troops on day 1 of the assault, naval forces positioned off the coast were attacked. Admiral Spruance's flagship, the *Indianapolis*, as well as the battleship *West Virginia*, two transports, and one landing ship were all hit by suicide attacks. The British carrier *Indefatigable* was also hit by a kamikaze plane, but it remained able to continue launching and recovering planes. As the first day came to an end, casualties were much lighter than military estimates had assumed, and it was a surprise that American forces had captured the airfields so quickly. However, Allied officials understood that the Japanese would not simply capitulate, especially not on an island so close to the home islands.

Ahead of the invasion of Okinawa, the Japanese commander at Okinawa, Lieutenant General Ushijima of the 32nd Army, positioned his troops to execute the commands that had been given to him: to hold Okinawa until the end and exact as heavy a price as possible on the Allied forces invading the island. The 32nd Army had been weakened when its 9th Division was sent to Formosa, but they still possessed an important artillery arsenal greater than any the Americans had faced in the Pacific so far. In fact, Ushijima's decision not to contest Okinawa's beaches probably stemmed from his desire to keep his artillery from being attacked by American warplanes and naval guns. Instead, he positioned them inland where they would be safer, a similar tactic to the one the Japanese used at Iwo Jima. Ushijima also conceded the airfields as indefensible and opted to position his troops in fortifications around the island.

Ushijima

A picture of Japanese commanders on Okinawa in February 1945. (1) Admiral Minoru Ota, (2) Lt. Gen. Mitsuru Ushijima, (3) Lt. Gen. Isamu Cho, (4) Col. Hitoshi Kanayama, (5) Col. Kikuji Hongo, and (6) Col. Hiromichi Yahara.

On the second day of their attack, the invading forces altered the plan due to the ease with which they had captured the airfields. Instead of first attacking the southern portion of the island before moving to the north, American troops would now simultaneously take both areas of the island. From the beginning of their advances, however, both thrusts, made up of Lieutenant General Simon Bolivar Buckner, Jr.'s Tenth Army (moving north) and Major General John R. Hodge's XXIV Corps (moving south), began to encounter resistance in the form of camouflaged Japanese positions surrounded by minefields.

Hodge

Bolivar, Jr.

Spruance, Nimitz, and Buckner

On Hodge's drive south, the 7th Division, which was positioned along the left flank, fell behind the 96th Division when they were engaged by Japanese forces positioned along a ridge parallel to the coastline near the town of Kuba. After an aerial bombardment of the Japanese position, the 7th Division engaged in a frontal assault that was turned back by the Japanese units. A second aerial bombardment was followed by a second frontal assault, but that attack also failed. On their third attempt, the men of the 7th Division again proceeded with a frontal assault, but this time the division's Company C broke off and flanked the Japanese position. The Japanese were completely surprised by this maneuver, and Japanese soldiers defending the ridge were wiped out when Company C brought the brunt of their grenades and flamethrowers on them. This would establish a pattern in American engagement with Japanese troops on Okinawa, because while the Japanese were very skilled at defending against a frontal assault, they were constantly unable to cope with flanking maneuvers. After gaining the sightline of the ridge, American reconnaissance could start to determine the positions of Japanese forces in the defensive zone around the town of Shuri (Frank, p. 70).

Meanwhile, the 96th Division was also facing stronger resistance from Japanese forces as it moved south. When the Americans came up to a ridge near Mashiki, they faced Japanese defenses that included a tank moat, barbed wire, and minefields. After aerial bombardment of the Japanese position, the American 2nd Battalion, 383rd Infantry charged, forcing the Japanese to retreat, and in subsequent charges, the Americans were able to gain control of the entire ridge. The 96th Division then made its way forward to the defensive zone surrounding the Kakazu area, where the fighting would be bloody and fierce. In this defensive zone, American troops would face three Japanese battalions, which were each composed of 1,200 troops.

In the north, Japanese defenses were not as strong as those in the south. As progress to the south was made, the American forces pushing north destroyed two pockets of Japanese resistance on their way to the town of Nagahama during the first week. The northern expedition then increased their advance in the hopes of coming upon Japanese units before they had time to adequately prepare a defense. Japanese troops in the area withdrew toward the Motobu Peninsula, and by April 7th, Americans forces had sealed off the peninsula from the rest of Okinawa and moved to destroy the Japanese forces there. By April 8th, the Japanese had retreated to prepared positions on the Motobu Peninsula, where American forces in that sector (the Marines of the III Amphibious Corps) were ordered to eliminate them. While the Americans encircled the Japanese positions on the Motobu Peninsula, the Japanese forces decided to engage in a guerrilla-style defensive strategy.

While the northern and southern campaigns in Okinawa pushed on, Allied naval vessels unloaded goods and equipment for the ground troops. Naval strategists were aware of the threat still posed by Japanese aircraft and naval vessels, so they placed vessels to screen the Allied transports at Okinawa. They also created an anti-submarine screen stretching from the northern coast of Okinawa to the Keramas. Finally, a radar picket lay beyond this, and then the Fast Carrier Force and British Carrier Force lay beyond this.

Along with early air attacks against naval ships, the Japanese Navy decided to utilize the remaining ships from its Combined Fleet: the battleship *Yamato*, as well as the cruiser *Yahagi* and seven destroyers. Because the *Yamato* only had enough fuel to make it to Okinawa, Japan's plan was to beach the battleship at Okinawa and then use its guns against the Allied forces off the coast.

As the *Yamato* task force moved toward Okinawa, Japanese aircraft began attacking American vessels, and during attacks on April 6th, roughly 355 of the 900 planes used were manned by kamikaze pilots. The fact that over 1/3 of the aircraft used were kamikazes reveal the great lengths Japanese military leaders were willing to take to defend the island, and during the fighting, the Americans lost three destroyers, two ammunition ships and one landing ship. The next day, kamikaze planes damaged the battleship *Maryland*, the destroyer *Bennet*, and the destroyer escort *Wesson*. The carrier *Hancock* was also hit by a kamikaze plane, and though 72 men were killed in the incident, *Hancock* was still able to recover its planes and continue operations.

As the ships dealt with Japanese planes on April 6, American reconnaissance identified the *Yamato* heading for Okinawa, and the Allied navy sought to destroy the ship before it was able to reach Okinawa and attack Allied vessels with its incredible firepower. American Rear Admiral M.L. Deyo made preparations to deal with the *Yamato* group by sending a force of six battleships, seven cruisers and 21 destroyers to form a wall between the *Yamato* group and the Allied transports.

A map showing the route of the Allied forces (red) intercepting the *Yamato* group (black).

The first attacks took place when planes from the Task Group 58 (280 in all) attacked the *Yamato* Group, and after multiple waves of aerial bombardment, the cruiser *Yahagi* was disabled, the destroyer *Hamakaze* had been sunk, and the *Yamato* had been hit by two bombs and a torpedo. Although the *Yamato* continued to move forward, its speed had been affected and its slower movement now made it an easier target for Allied bombers. Eventually, both the *Yamato* and and *Yahagi* were destroyed, killing 3,665 men in all, and with the loss of the *Yamato* group, the Japanese navy lost almost all ability to contest the Allied forces at sea. From that point forward, their only capabilities to challenge the Allied naval forces were through air attacks (Gow, p. 92).

Aerial view of the attacks on the *Yahagi*.

Aerial view of American planes attacking the *Yamato*.

Aerial view of the *Yamato* under attack.

The *Yamato* shortly after exploding on April 7.

Back on Okinawa, intelligence reports were still hazy as to Japanese positions, but the Americans understood that they would soon be facing the main body of Japanese forces. On April 7th, the 7th Division was still heading south when its western wing, made up of the 184th infantry, encountered a major Japanese position near Minami-Uebaru that was called Red Hill. Red Hill consisted of a hill with trenches and caves that were covered with mines and barbed wire. The 184th attempted a frontal assault to take the position, but they were forced to abandon it when they encountered heavy machine gun and mortar fire. A second attempt at a frontal assault included tanks, but one hit a landmine and another was blown up by a satchel-charge. Japanese heavy artillery fire drove the infantry units once again, and some more tanks were disabled in the engagement. Finally, when the 3rd battalion of the 184th moved in a flanking maneuver on the enemy's right, it caught the Japanese by surprise and allowed the Americans to take the hill.

The 184th Infantry would come across two more fortified positions over the next few days. The first, called Tomb Hill, was located northwest of Ouchi, while the second was called Triangulation Hill. While the 184th managed to take both positions, they again faced problems when trying to attack Japanese positions with tank-infantry teams. Tanks were susceptible to the heavy artillery fire from these Japanese positions, and once they were disabled and their infantry escorts driven off, the tank crews were bayoneted and the tanks were incorporated into the Japanese defensive works.

After capturing Tomb Hill and Triangulation Hill by April 8th, the 184th came upon the Shuri Fortified Zone. Meanwhile, the other half of the American forces moving southward, the 96th Division, also came across a heavily fortified area near Kakazu. Unaware that they had come upon the outer rim of a heavily fortified defensive position and believed they were only engaging in another Japanese defensive pocket. In actuality, the Japanese 32nd Army had set up their headquarters here, and their position was heavily defended with tank moats, trenches, mortars, heavy artillery support, and reinforcements that could be sent to shore up any potential breaches in their defense.

As Companies A and C of the 1st Battalion moved forward to engage with Japanese forces on the western portion of Kakazu Hill, they were able to reach the crest of the ridge without being detected, but when Japanese soldiers finally spotted them, Company A was pinned down by heavy fire. Company C attempted to reach them, but they were forced back by Japanese fire. Finally, all three companies were forced to retreat away from the hill. The surviving troops from the three companies of the 1st Battalion were so badly injured that army medical personnel deemed them all unfit for further combat duty.

The western edge of the Kakazu ridge

At the same time that the 1st Battalion began their attack from the west, Company L charged up the ridge from the other side without being spotted by the Japanese and also reached the crest. However, Company I, which was supposed to support Company L, had been delayed in initiating its attack and was pinned down by enemy fire. This isolated Company L at the top of the ridge, where they were forced to repel a Japanese attack. Company L was later able to retreat under smoke cover, but by the time this engagement ended, the 1st Battalion had been reduced to about half strength and was no longer operational. These assaults, which took place on April 9th, had failed to gain the Americans any ground, but they had managed to kill roughly 400 soldiers, thus weakening the manpower of the Japanese defense.

The Japanese 32nd Army was carrying out its plan of inflicting as much damage as possible, but at this point, military leaders in Tokyo gave the 32nd a new directive for a counteroffensive against American positions. While the leadership of the 32nd Army had conceded the two main airfields in Okinawa and had instead focused their attention on creating a strong defensive zone in the southern portion of the island, military commanders in Tokyo considered the airfields to be of strategic importance, and their orders for a counteroffensive were aimed at reclaiming the airfields. The plan that the 32nd Army created involved sending Japanese troops into close proximity with American units, thereby neutralizing American artillery, naval guns and air support because they would be reluctant to hit their own soldiers. The Japanese offensive began on April 12th, but was quickly defeated. From that point on, the 32nd Army focused its attention on defending their base in the south, with the only offensive operations being nighttime infiltrations of American camps.

By the end of fighting on the 12th, American casualties had grown to 2,900 with 451 dead, while Japanese casualties were at 5,750.

American soldiers pass a dead Japanese soldier on Okinawa, April 1945.

An American plane firebombing northern Okinawa.

During the second half of April, American troops faced heavy fighting in the south, while the units in the north surrounded Japanese positions in the Motobu Peninsula. One critical region in the north, called Ie Shima, was deemed to be important as a place where the Allies could install an early warning air defense system for units on Okinawa, as well as being a launch point for the invasion of Japan. The Japanese were aware of the strategic importance of Ie Shima, and in the early part of 1945, they ordered 2,000 soldiers and civilians to destroy the airfields and military installations there. They had also constructed defensive positions from which they hoped to repel invading soldiers.

The Japanese strategy for Ie Shima was based on trying to entice American troops to land on the lightly guarded beaches and trick American military commanders into believing the area was only lightly defended when in fact there were 2,000 Japanese soldiers stationed there. The Americans encountered not just a strong military force on Ie Shima but also resistance from civilians (including women), who attacked American soldiers with anything from modern weapons to wooden spears. As a result, American soldiers at Ie Shima were among the first to experience the "fanatical resistance" of civilians, something that would represent considerable danger for any American invasion of the Japanese mainland as well.

American soldiers in a foxhole with a Japanese orphan, April 1945.

As the Americans began their attack, Japanese forces were centered around the town of Ie, which was protected by ridges surrounding the area. The largest ridge, called the Bloody Ridge by the 77th Division, was the main natural defensive barrier. For U.S. ground forces, it was important for them to capture defensive positions on the high ground, because from those positions, Japanese troops could fire artillery at the transport ships unloading troops and equipment on the beaches. To soften up enemy positions, American planes flew bombing missions during the two days preceding the attack, and on April 16th, American ground troops commenced their attack. American troops quickly took the airfields and made progress moving inland before Japanese forces counterattacked. The 3rd Battalion, 305th Regimental Combat Team (RCT) took the brunt of this assault, as Japanese soldiers armed not only with guns but also grenades and satchel charges sought to either shoot Americans or blow themselves up in the vicinity of American troops. During the attack, one American soldier broke his arm when the leg of a Japanese trooper who had blown himself up hit him (Gow, p. 112).

Aerial view shows the town of Ie and the high ground along the eastern end of the island.

American tanks on Bloody Ridge knocked out by Japanese artillery, April 20.

The Americans faced a difficult situation when they came upon the ridges of Ie Shima. The 1st Battalion, 305th RCT attempted to secure the Bloody Ridge on April 17th but were driven back. What amounted to a stalemate at the Bloody Ridge turned when the Americans decided to approach the ridge from the south and west rather than the north. The 305th and 307th moved slowly up the ridge and were able to take the fortifications at the top of the ridge, but then they had to face a major Japanese counterattack to hold it. The Japanese sent 300 troops, along with civilians, and after marching through their own mortar fire, they got within 15 feet of the Americans before they were driven back. While the Americans suffered heavy casualties, the Japanese lost 280 soldiers.

As this battle was raging at the Bloody Ridge, the 3rd Battalion, 305th Infantry destroyed Japanese positions around the town of Ie, which opened up a path to the ridge network from the south. As the rest of the 305th approached from the south, a simultaneous attack allowed American forces to make their way up the ridges and destroy the remaining Japanese defenders. Even after being driven from the ridges, Japanese troops and civilians mounted a counterattack on April 22nd, but these attackers were defeated with no further casualties suffered by the Americans. In all, the Japanese lost 4,706 casualties, including at least 1,500 civilians who had been forcibly armed and placed in uniform. For the Americans, the 77th Division suffered 1,100 casualties. (Gow, p. 115) Although the cost had been very high, capturing Ie Shima allowed the Americans a base from which to launch support operations for ground troops still fighting on Okinawa, as well as providing them airfields from which to launch a potential attack against the Japanese home islands.

Meanwhile, Marine commanders began planning an assault on the last remaining Japanese forces in northern Okinawa (the soldiers who had retreated to Motobu Peninsula). The plan, devised on April 13th, involved having the 1st and 2nd Battalions of the 4th Marines, the 3rd Battalion of the 29th Marines, and the 1st and 2nd Battalions of the 29th Marines attack simultaneously from all directions. The various battalions maneuvered into position, and on the 16th, the Americans commenced their attack. The 3rd Battalion (29th Marines) and 2nd Battalion (4th Marines) attacked Japanese forces to the west, while the 3rd Battalion (4th Marines) pushed north. At the same time, the 29th Marines moved into position to attack the stronghold of Yae Take. All of these units were supported by artillery and aerial bombardment of Japanese positions, and by the late afternoon, the crest of Yae Take had been captured and many Japanese units had fled the area. Many were killed later when they attempted to reengage American troops.

By April 18th, Japanese troops at the Motobu Peninsula were in flight, and the 4th and 29th Marines were tasked with chasing them. The 4th Marines killed over 700 soldiers as they tried to retreat away from the peninsula, and from this point forward, the biggest danger of Japanese attacks in northern Okinawa would be from small groups engaging in guerrilla warfare.

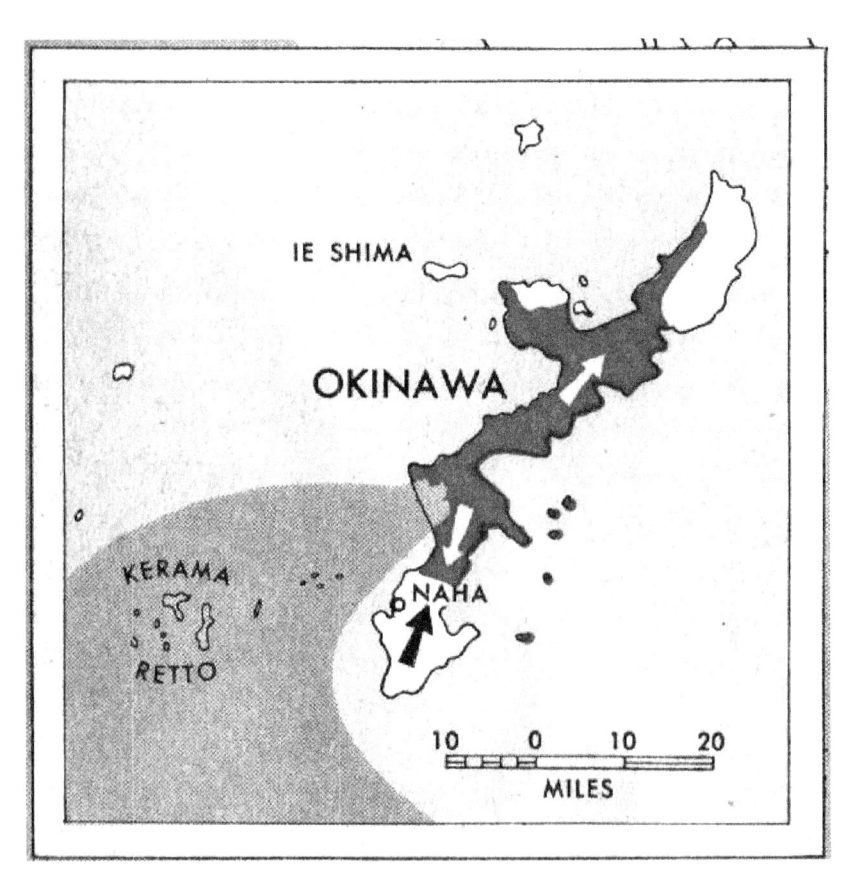

American advances (in red) across Okinawa by April 15.

With Japanese forces effectively neutralized in the north, American troops began preparing the area for support operations. But while the north had mostly been cleared of enemy soldiers, the south would continue to be a major area of operations because American units still had to breach the 32rd Army's fortifications around Shuri. In fact, the fighting around Shuri would represent the last major ground battle by American forces against the Japanese in the Pacific War.

The Japanese defenses at Shuri represented a "tightly-held, fortified coast-to-coast defense line relying on a series of intricate and skillfully constructed underground positions. American veterans now expected accurate and heavy light mortar and machine gun fire backed by artillery, ferocious counterattacks and infiltration attempts plus excellent reverse slope defense." (Gow, p. 119) As General Hodge relayed to his troops on the eve of American attacks on the Japanese position, "It is going to be really tough, there are 65,000-70,000 fighting Japanese holed up in the south end of the island. I see no way to get them out except to blast them out yard by yard." (Gow, p. 119)

As American forces in the south prepared for their attack on Shuri on April 19th, they captured a Japanese document suggesting that the Americans never advanced at night and therefore Japanese troops did not have to be as vigilant during that time. As a result, the Americans moved some units during the night of April 18th without being seen by Japanese soldiers. However, the Americans faced a problem in that they needed to build bridges over an inlet leading up to the outer portions of the Shuri defensive positions. The 27th Engineering Division was ordered to build two 90-foot bridges, and they did so by building the bridges during the night and placing them into position at 3:00 a.m. on April 18th.

As three U.S. army divisions moved toward the Japanese 62nd Division's forward defensive line, naval vessels stationed off the coast engaged in a massive bombardment of Japanese positions. Beginning at 6:00 a.m., six battleships, six cruisers, and six destroyers shelled the 62nd's position for 20 minutes, and then they targeted the rear for 10 minutes in hopes of drawing Japanese troops back toward the forward areas of their defensive perimeter. After that, the ships started shelling the forward areas once more. Meanwhile, the 10th Army, with 27 corps and division artillery units, also began shelling the Japanese positions. Together, this was the greatest concentration of artillery used in the Pacific Theater, and it was estimated that 19,000 shells hit Japanese positions over 40 minutes of bombing (Gow, p. 121), but the grand bombardment of Japanese positions had little effect because Japanese soldiers were able to hide in underground shelters and caves.

In their initial engagement against Shuri, which occurred on April 19th, the XXIV Corps was unable to break through the Japanese forward line. Further fighting occurred between April 20th and 24th, but American troops once again found it extremely difficult to break the Japanese defense. An important problem that developed during the four days of fighting was the creation of a mile long gap between the 27th and 96th Divisions that the Americans needed to close, since American commanders feared that the Japanese could counterattack through this gap to flank both the 27th and 96th Divisions. The 165th Infantry was ordered to close the gap, but they encountered problems almost immediately when the 1st Battalion lost contact with the 2nd Battalion. Both battalions then found themselves in a heavy firefight when they made contact with a heavily fortified Japanese position that they called the "Item Pocket", which was manned by 600 soldiers as well as several hundred civilians.

The 165th faced the Japanese defenses in this area without mortar or tank support, and even though they suffered heavy casualties, they had established an unbroken line by April 26th and began an advance to the south. After securing the area west of the Item Pocket, they were joined by tank-infantry units that assaulted the Item Pocket and were able to conquer the position by the evening of the 27th.

Another position that the Japanese had heavily fortified was the area surrounding the village of Iso. At Iso, the Japanese 21st Independent Infantry Battalion was joined by the 1st Heavy Mortar Division. Two peaks jutting out of the ridge network surrounding Iso were the keys to the defense of the area; East Pinnacle rose 50 feet above the ridge and Japanese soldiers had constructed fortifications and tunnels there, while West Pinnacle was also fortified and included machine gun positions. As the 2nd and 3rd Battalions of the 27th Division's 105th Infantry began their attack, they suffered heavy casualties but were able to take East Pinnacle when two assault battalions of the 105th Infantry scaled the peak and surprised the Japanese soldiers stationed there. The West Pinnacle was also captured after the Japanese soldiers positioned there decided to wildly charge the American soldiers who had surrounded it.

The Japanese 32nd Army's leadership determined early on that its outer defense perimeter would eventually be breached, so they decided to withdraw the bulk of their troops to the second Shuri defense line. This meant that American advances after April 24th only came up against small pockets of Japanese troops instead of facing the full brunt of the Japanese defense, but the withdrawal also gave the Americans time to regroup and reshape their plans for taking southern Okinawa. With the successes in northern Okinawa, General Buckner now decided to shift III Amphibious Corps to the south, where the increase in manpower would help him in the frontal assault that he planned against the Shuri defense rings. In addition, the Americans began rotating units. The 96th Division, which had engaged in much of the fighting in southern Okinawa up to this point, was replaced on the front line by the 77th Infantry Division. After a week of rest, the 96th was then sent back to the front lines to replace the 7th Division. The 27th Division had also suffered heavy casualties and was replaced by the 1st Marine Division, which moved south from northern Okinawa.

Japanese strategists originally believed the most likely American attack would be a flanking maneuver attempting to catch the Japanese by surprise, but on April 26th, General Ushijima abandoned his defense of possible flanking maneuvers and instead met the threat of a frontal assault by redeploying these troops to help hold the second Shuri defense ring. He deployed the 44th Independent Mixed Brigade behind the 62nd Division to prevent American penetration of the western area. He then sent the 22nd Regiment of the 24th Division to relieve the 62nd Division in the east, while sending the rest of the 24th Division to the northeast, where they would act as reserves.

As each side maneuvered units into strategic locations in southern Okinawa and braced for the next attack, Allied naval forces were still stationed off the coast to provide support for the ground troops. At the same time, the navy had to protect itself from constant Japanese aerial attacks. Naval units off the coast of Okinawa became more vulnerable every day, and throughout April, as many as 20 planes attacked the fleet each day. These planes included kamikazes, divebombers, and torpedo bombers (Gow, p. 135). During the month of April, 20 Allied ships were sunk and 157 were damaged, but even with these successes, overall Japanese naval forces were losing the ability to contest the seas. The *Yamato* Task Force had been the last of the Japanese Navy's vessels capable of launching offensive maneuvers, and the Japanese had lost 1,000 planes during the month. As a result, even though the Japanese had inflicted large amounts of damage to the Allied fleet off the coast of Okinawa, they had also sustained heavy losses, which were made all the more important by the fact that Japan was having trouble replacing the pilots and warplanes that they were losing. Furthermore, by the end of April, the Allies had moved planes onto airstrips they controlled on Okinawa, and the increased number of planes meant the ships in the vicinity of Okinawa now had air cover protecting them around the clock.

American anti-aircraft fire at night from one of the Okinawan airstrips.

The Japanese High Command was aware of the staggering losses suffered by the Japanese army and navy as the battle for Okinawa continued, and they understood the enemy had superior manpower and technology. Facing those realities, the Japanese believed that losing Okinawa was only a matter of time, and they now hoped the 32nd Army could simply hold out long enough and inflict enough damage on American ground troops to discourage any attempt to invade the home islands. But even as the Japanese commanders lost faith in Okinawa's defenses, Ushijima and the 32nd were still a dangerous force, and they were even considering a counterattack on American positions.

By the end of April, American commanders had brought the III Amphibious Corps to southern Okinawa and began planning for a three-division offensive against Shuri. On the right, the 27th Division made some progress before being stopped near the town of Nakama, roughly three miles north of Shuri, but in the center, the 106th Infantry engaged in heavy fighting and was unable to advance far before their troop strength was depleted to the point that they were unable to continue the offensive. The 106th subsequently had to be relieved by the 6th Marine Division. Also in the center, the 96th Division failed to gain much ground, but they did manage to kill hundreds of Japanese soldiers in the Urasoe-Mura escarpment.

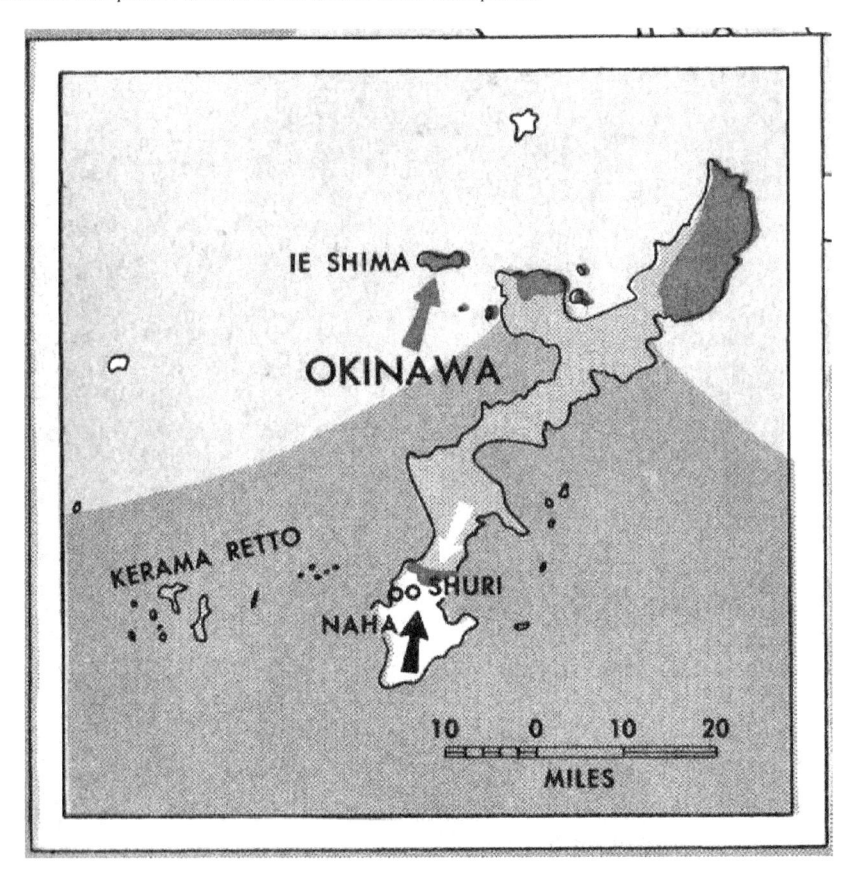

The battle lines (in red) on May 1.

An American reconnaissance plane flying over Okinawa in May.

On May 2nd, American scouts reported that the Japanese were moving their artillery further south, and with that, commanders believed that the rigid structure of the defensive positions meant the Japanese only had two choices: hold their position until the end or withdraw to the south. The Americans did not believe the Japanese had the capability to counterattack, so they were completely unprepared when the Japanese actually did mount a counterattack. At the time, the Japanese commanders had become increasingly worried about the troop losses they were sustaining. The 62nd Division, for example, was down to less than 50% of its fighting strength, and additionally, it seemed that many Japanese soldiers were suffering from a loss of morale. These two factors convinced the 32nd Army's leadership to consider mounting an attack against the Americans. Lieutenant General Isamu Cho, Ushijima's chief of staff, believed Japanese forces were being slowly eroded, and that the best course of action was to attack while they still had the manpower to do so.

As a result, on May 2nd, the Japanese officers announced the plan for their attack. They would engage in a large-scale counterattack on May 4th in coordination with an assault on Allied naval forces off the coast. The goal of the attack was to destroy the XXIV Corps on Okinawa and also to cripple the Allied fleet, an action which they believed would turn the tide of the battle. The main attacking force would be the 24th Division, which was comprised of 15,000 men. The 24th Division was supposed to lead breakthroughs of the American lines at the center and eastern sectors, and once through, other units would pour into the gaps and destroy the isolated American forces. In conjunction with the advance on the ground, suicide boats and planes would hit the Allied fleet, disrupting the supply lines to the ground forces on Okinawa and giving Japanese troops an opportunity to strangle American ground forces on the island.

On May 4th, the attack commenced, and Japanese troops were ordered to "kill one American devil for every Japanese," which was asking a lot considering that the kill ratio on Okinawa to that point had been 10 Japanese dead for every American killed. (Gow, p. 143). At the same time, the complexity of the Japanese plan helped bring about its undoing. For instance, the 26th Shipping Engineers were supposed to make an amphibious landing but missed their landing point and instead came to an area between the Yontan and Kadena airfields that was heavily defended by the Americans. All the boats were destroyed, and the men who managed to reach shore were cut down by American machine-gun fire. A small group did manage to elude the Americans, but they were killed the next day when they were engaged by American forces near Chatan. On the east coast, Japanese forces encountered similar problems; when native Okinawan boatmen tried to row several hundred troops behind the American 7th Division for an attack, they were spotted by naval ships and destroyed. In total, the Japanese lost between 500-800 men in the two botched attacks, and they also lost all their boats.

The main attack began with an artillery barrage that was perhaps the heaviest the Americans faced in the Pacific Theater. The 24th Division then surprised American forces by marching through their own mortar fire. However, after overcoming the initial element of surprise, the American 7th Division was able to hold its ground, and as Japanese troops were caught in open ground and not able to continue pushing forward, they were exposed to American artillery and gunfire that had a devastating effect on the Japanese soldiers.

At a second point, the Japanese attempted to open a breach in the American lines by pushing infantry, tanks and engineers forward, but here too the Americans stopped their forward momentum by disabling the Japanese tanks with artillery fire. This left Japanese forces unable to concentrate their forces in the spearhead maneuver that had been planned, and again, they were unable to open a gap in the American lines.

Even though reports coming back to the Japanese commanders indicated that they had been unsuccessful in breaching the American lines, Lieutenant General Tatsumi Amemiya, commander of the 24th Division, continued the attack by launching another wave of attackers at the American lines on the evening of May 4th. In this second attack, Japanese troops succeeded in opening a gap about 1,000 yards behind American lines, but they withdrew later in the evening for unknown reasons. In the early morning of May 5th, the Japanese attacked this area again with a combined force of infantry and tanks, but this time, the Americans held their lines. By the end of the engagement, the Japanese had lost 248 soldiers as well as much of their equipment.

The only real success occurred in the 77th Division's sector, where the Japanese managed to occupy Tanabaru and Tanabaru Ridge, which cut off supply lines to some of the American front line troops in that area. American commanders were very worried by this turn of events and pushed for American troops to retake Tanabaru Ridge. It took three days of fierce fighting, but eventually, the Americans regained control of the ridge, and in the process they killed another 460 Japanese soldiers.

By the evening of May 5th, it had become obvious to Japanese commanders that the offensive had failed, and in order to save face, they announced to the Japanese military leaders that they had inflicted a large amount of damage on the Americans and were now going to temporarily suspend the offensive to go revise their plans for a future engagement. In all, 5,000 troops had been lost, and the 24th Division, which spearheaded the attack, had suffered the largest number of casualties. The loss of equipment was equally important, because the Japanese lost much of their tank capabilities and had also exposed their artillery placements to American fire. On May 4th, 19 pieces of field artillery had been destroyed.

Meanwhile, the Americans had also endured heavy casualties. The 1st Marine Division had lost 352 men, while the 7th and 77th Divisions had lost 379 men. Had the Japanese offensive occurred before the Americans had rotated their forces on the front lines, they might have been able to force open the gaps they had planned, but since they were facing relatively fresh American troops, they were unable to achieve their objectives.

Once the Japanese offensive had been halted, the 10th Army began a renewed push south. In the southeast, on May 6th and 7th, the 7th Division sent patrols to sweep the area in front of them for enemy soldiers, and, after finding none, they began an attack. They took an area called Gaja Ridge with little resistance before finally being pushed back at Conical Hill, where Japanese troops mounted a strong defense and used mines that had been placed in the area to prevent tanks from supporting the American soldiers there. Over the next two days, the 7th Division made incremental progress against the Japanese 22nd Regiment of the 24th Division, which had been ordered to hold their ground for as long as possible. At the same time, the 7th Division was under pressure from American commanders to make better progress, and by May 9th, the 7th Division had pushed forward into an area called Kochi Ridge, where exhausted soldiers were finally replaced with troops from the 96th Division.

Although the Americans were making progress in their southern drive, it was taking a lot of time, and total American casualties were mounting, reaching 20,000 by early May. General Buckner, who was becoming frustrated by the Japanese defense, decided to launch an all-out attack on Japanese positions that would begin on May 11th. This general offensive involved two corps that would align themselves across the island; the American units involved included the 6th Marine Division and 1st Marine Division of the III Amphibious Corps and the 77th Division and 96th Division of the XXIV Army Corps. The 27th Division was given the responsibility to control northern Okinawa, while the battle-weary 7th Division was allowed to rest.

General Buckner's ultimate goal was to use the two corps to envelop the Shuri defenses along the west and east while attacking heavily through the middle of the Japanese position. Buckner's staff believed the Japanese were weaker along their right flank, so they placed their freshest troops there in the belief that they could break through the Japanese lines. However, because Ushijima had previously removed units guarding the coastal areas and redeployed them facing the American ground troops, the Japanese defenses were now strengthened beyond what American planners had assumed.

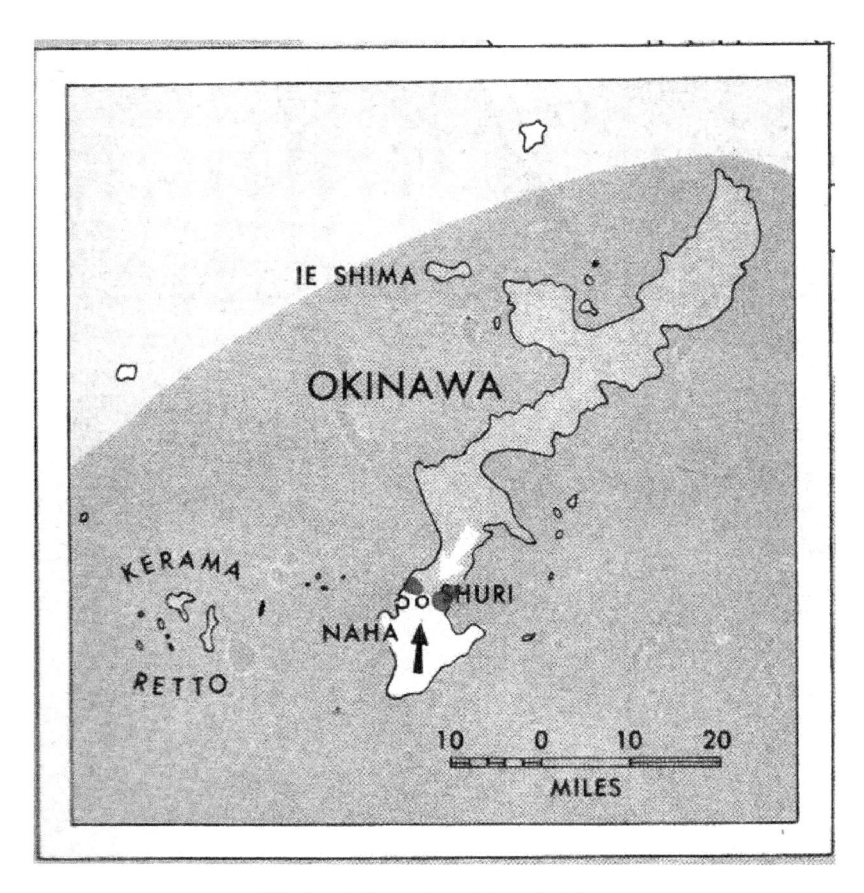

The battle lines (in red) in mid-May

Even though the Americans had planned on a coordinated attack involving their western, eastern, and central units, things devolved quickly into uncoordinated battles in all three sectors. In the west, American forces were making slow progress as they had to construct and cross bridges while also getting their heavy equipment across, all while facing heavy fire from Japanese troops. The most difficult area that the troops in the west had to face was at Sugar Loaf Hill, a three-hill complex that was covered by artillery positions at Shuri. The fighting at Sugar Loaf Hill was extremely intense, and the 2nd Battalion suffered 400 casualties over a three day period. The 6th Marine Division also suffered heavy casualties, but American troops were finally able to take the hill on May 18th after four days of heavy fighting. After that, American troops were quickly confronted with another strong defensive position at Horseshoe and Crescent Hill.

At Horseshoe and Crescent Hill, American troops not only had to take another well-defended Japanese position, but Japanese troops counterattacked, forcing the Americans to call on battle-weary reserve troops to help stem the tide.

A demolition crew from the 6th Marine Division blowing up a Japanese cave in May.

On the left, the 77th Division faced a tough defensive position at Chocolate Drop Hill. Not only was the hill heavily fortified, the ground leading up to the hill was completely open and had no cover that could shield American infantry units from artillery and small-arms fire as they moved toward this position. Even worse, portions of the ground were marshy, and when it began to rain, tanks were unable to provide support for infantry units storming the hill. It took the 77th Division a number of days before they were able to take the hill, and as on the right, once they captured Chocolate Drop Hill on May 20th, they were immediately faced with more fortified positions in Flattop Hill and Dick Hills. These two positions were right on the inner edge of the Shuri Defense Zone, and Japanese soldiers stationed at these two areas held out for 10 days before they were overcome by a combined force of the 77th an 96th Divisions.

The breakthrough of the Shuri Defense Zone finally occurred on this left side of the American attack, and it involved the Tenth Army, which attacked Conical Hill, a 476 foot high hill that was a key defensive position. In addition to its mortar and artillery placements, Conical Hill was manned by the Japanese 89th Regiment of the 24th Division, with support from the 27th Independent Battalion. American commanders launched a frontal assault against Conical Hill with the 96th Division, which the Japanese expected, but the Japanese did not expect two American platoons to concentrate their efforts against an area that had strong natural defenses but was weak in terms of manpower. Focusing on this weak spot ultimately allowed the 96th to take the hill.

Once the 96th Division had taken Conical Hill, the American forces in that area had created a narrow path through the Japanese defenses between Conical Hill and the coast, where American naval vessels were positioned. The 7th Division, back in action after receiving a rest period, was ordered to move through the path created by the 96th Division. Japanese forces were not ready for the suddenness of the American attack, which began on the night of May 19th and commenced without tank support. The 184th Infantry made the initial push into the Japanese lines, and as they moved to protect the western flank, the 32nd Infantry continued the push forward to cut Shuri off from the south.

The 32nd Infantry's progress was slowed as the weather turned, and without tank support, they faced a succession of Japanese counterattacks alone. From May 23-26, the 32nd Infantry made little progress, and for American commanders, it seemed as though the Japanese were planning on holding out and fighting until the last man. What they did not realize was that Japanese leaders had planned a coordinated retreat from their positions. The Japanese 32nd Army had been in contact with their superiors in Tokyo and told them that they had engaged their last reserves. From this point forward, the 32nd Army would have to either engage the enemy in guerrilla warfare or hold out until the end at Shuri, after which the Americans would be able to plan their assault of the Japanese mainland unimpeded.

With no reinforcements from Japan forthcoming, the 32nd Army's commanding officer, Ushijima, decided that fighting until the end at Shuri was not the optimal decision. Given that a number of his 50,000 men were unarmed, packing his men into the small area of Shuri could cause chaos, and standing until the last man at Shuri would shorten the amount of time military planners in Tokyo would have to prepare for an American assault of the home islands. Instead, Ushijima decided on a retreat to prepared positions on the Kan Peninsula. As the retreat began, Ushijima left a few units behind at Shuri to engage the Americans and delay them beginning a pursuit of Japanese forces.

American units saw Japanese movements as early as May 22nd, but at this time they assumed these were civilians and disregarded their importance. It was not until a few days later, on May 26th, that the Americans finally understood a withdrawal was in progress. On that day, they saw

3,000 troops and 100 trucks moving south. This meant that only a skeleton force was left at Shuri, and American units commenced to storm Shuri positions, taking Shuri Castle by the end of the month. With Shuri under American control, they now moved to the last Japanese position at the southern tip of Okinawa.

U.S. Marine Lieutenant Colonel R.P. Ross, Jr. placing the American flag on a parapet of Shuri castle at the end of May.

At the end of May, American forces had been on Okinawa for two months, and they had killed over 62,000 Japanese soldiers, with another 9,500 estimated as killed. About 8,000 of these deaths had occurred in northern Okinawa, with the rest occurring in southern Okinawa. The Americans had also suffered heavy casualties, with the III Amphibious Corps and XXIV Corps suffering 26,044 casualties. The Marines had suffered 6,315 casualties, while the army had 7,762 casualties, but even with these casualties, the ratio of Americans killed to Japanese killed was still roughly 1:10 (Gow, p.166-167). Added to the casualty numbers were issues of exhaustion; over 61 days of fighting, the 96th Division had fought for 50 days, the 7th Division had fought for 49 days, and the 77th Division fought for 32 days.

Even though the Americans saw the Japanese retreat, they believed it was not an organized withdrawal but actually the end of organized resistance. General Buckner believed there was nothing left to do but mop up the last pockets of Japanese resistance. However, the Japanese forces that had withdrawn from Shuri were still organized, even though they now split into two groups. The 32nd Army comprised the bulk of the forces, and they had cooperated during the defense of Shuri with the remnants of the Okinawa Naval Base Force, which was under the command of Rear Admiral Minoru Ota.

During the retreat, the Naval Base Force's 2,000 men moved to the southwestern area of Oroku, but as the 4th Marines moved to seal off and then destroy the Naval Base Force, they faced off against a mixed Japanese unit that included conscripted Okinawans, administrative troops, and construction and submarine crews. Few of these men had experience in ground combat, and as the 900 American troops and 24 tanks moved against the Naval Base Force on June 4th, they were able to quickly move in against little resistance. However, after that first day, the American soldiers moved within range of the Naval Base Force's machine guns and 40 mm cannons, and the 4th Marines were without tank support because they had to cross marshy ground. By June 7th, the Japanese forces here had blocked the American advance, but the 4th Marines were eventually joined by the 29th Marines from the west, the 4th Marines from the south, and the 22nd Marines from the southeast. With these reinforcements and the possibility of multiple points of attack, the Japanese Naval Base Force was surrounded and slowly pushed together into an area near the town of Tomigusuki. On June 11th, the Americans began their attack on this final position, and by the next day, nearly all of the Japanese soldiers had either been killed in the fighting or had committed suicide, with the exception of a group of 159 who surrendered. This turned out to be the largest surrender of Japanese forces on Okinawa.

A group of Japanese prisoners who surrendered rather than commit suicide.

While the Naval Base Force moved to its position on Oroku, the 32nd Army retreated to prepared positions at Yuza-Dake and Yaeju-Dake. These positions were located on ridges, with the ground leading up to them pocked with hills from which small bands of Japanese soldiers could harass and delay American troops. At this point, Ushijima's 32nd Army consisted of roughly 11,000 men, and they were ordered to fight to the death. The bulk of this force consisted of the 24th Division, which was deployed along the west from Yaeju-Dake to the town of Itoman. Ushijima held the 62nd Division back as reserves, and in the east, he deployed the 44th Independent Mixed Brigade. While Ushijima still had a core of veteran soldiers, many of his remaining men had been poorly trained and were not likely to put up much of a fight against the Americans. Moreover, the 32nd Army had little artillery and mortar support this time, which would obviously hamper their efforts at holding off American attacks.

On June 1st, American forces moving toward Ushijima's positions attempted to close the gap quickly, but the marshy, muddy terrain was difficult for the soldiers to move on, and they also experienced delays while moving supplies to the frontline troops. As they came upon pockets of Japanese resistance, the defenders also slowed their progress. When the first American units finally reached the Japanese positions, on June 6th, the 381st Infantry was driven back at Yaeju-Dake, but they were eventually able to take the lower section of the ridges. The Americans next planned to attack from the west against a strongly defended hill area that they called the "Big Apple."

As the 381st Infantry moved up toward the Big Apple, they were caught in machine gun and 20mm fire and were forced off the lower ridges they had previously taken, so the Americans took a different approach the next day. This time, they called in airstrikes against the Japanese positions and also fired artillery barrages against it. The 381st were able to move higher up the ridges by utilizing smoke shells to screen an advance, aided in this effort by the fact the Japanese soldiers thought the smoke was a cover for a retreat. When they began showing themselves along their position, many were killed by artillery fire.

Although the 381st continued to make progress, by June 12th, American commanders realized that the terrain on Big Apple made it nearly impossible for these troops to continue to push forward in a timely manner. Instead, they shifted their attention to the advance by the 7th Division, which was moving along the right flank. The 7th Division's task since the beginning of June had been to move southward and eliminate any threats along the Chinen Peninsula. They spent the first week of June gathering roughly 10,000 civilian prisoners at Chinen, and then on June 8th, they moved into position for an attack on Yaeju-Dake. Since the paths leading up Yaeju-Dake were in open view of Japanese soldiers, the 7th Division decided to attack at night, and a heavy fog that rolled into the area further shielded their movements from the Japanese.

Once again, the Japanese did not believe the Americans would attack at night, so they actually withdrew from the high ground that night to avoid artillery fire and planned to return early the next morning before American troops began their movements for the day. Instead, when the Japanese troops returned to their positions the next morning, they found American soldiers manning their posts. Many of the Japanese soldiers were killed in the morning's engagement, and by the time it had finished, the Americans had taken a key defensive position. Further American advances occurred in the southeast, where the 96th Division engaged the Japanese 44th Independent Mixed Brigade, and by June 12th, the Mixed Brigade had suffered enough casualties that their lines were beginning to give way. As the 44th Mixed Brigade lost its cohesiveness in the face of the American assault, Ushijima committed his reserves to shore up the southeastern defenses, but even with the reserves, the Japanese had insufficient manpower to hold the line. On June 12th, the 96th Division entered the town of Yuza, and by June 16th, Yuza Peak also fell into American hands, representing another major blow to the Japanese defense.

Men from the 96th Division look for hidden Japanese soldiers on Yaeju-Dake.

While the 7th Division was holding its position and the 96th Division continued its push forward, the third part of the plan involved the 1st and 7th Marines near Kunishi Ridge. Like the 96th Division, the 1st and 7th Marines decided on a nighttime attack that began shortly after midnight on June 12th, but this attack, which utilized both tanks and infantry, was quickly met by Japanese machine gun and artillery fire that pushed both the soldiers and tanks back. The Japanese positions at Kunishi Ridge proved so strong that the Marines were unable to overcome the defenses even after attacking over the next several days. The Marines suffered heavy casualties from Japanese machine gun and mortar fire, and it was only after the Americans called in a series of airstrikes that the Japanese defenses were weakened to the point that they could be taken. On the 16th, the 1st and 7th Marines were reinforced with the 22nd Marines, and it was only at this point that they were able to take the ridge and deal another blow to the Japanese 32nd Army.

By June 17th, the Americans had breached the final Japanese positions, and the 32nd Army had finally lost its ability to hold out. As the 32nd Army lost its cohesiveness, the ensuing chaos allowed the Americans to chase random groups of Japanese soldiers and kill them. The one portion of the 32nd Army that remained intact, the 24th Division, withdrew to its former command post at Medeera and held out for four days before being overrun by American troops.

Even after Medeera was taken, Ushijima ordered the last of his troops to engage in guerrilla tactics against the Americans. Many did continue fighting until the end, but roughly 3,000 of them eventually surrendered over the rest of the month, as did 1,000 Okinawan labor troops. For General Ushijima and his second in command, Lieutenant General Cho, surrender was not an option even though General Buckner offered them the chance to surrender. Instead, Ushijima and Cho decided to commit seppuku, a ritual disembowelment that was a part of the Japanese samurai and Imperial Japanese Army traditions. Ironically, Ushijima committed suicide just 4 days after Buckner himself had been mortally wounded during the mop up by a Japanese artillery shell. Buckner had often drawn enemy fire by wearing a helmet with his three stars visible, but he was wearing an unmarked helmet when he was hit on June 18.

A picture of Buckner (far right) taken on June 18, shortly before he was killed.

On June 22, the Battle of Okinawa officially concluded as American troops finally controlled the entire island, but Okinawa has remained an endless source of both fascination and controversy. One of the most notable aspects of the battle was the Japanese's determination to fight to the death, but they also forced civilians into fighting and even forced civilians to commit mass suicide when the end was near. A recent documentary has asserted "there were two types of orders for 'honorable deaths' - one for residents to kill each other and the other for the military to kill all residents." As a result, it's believed that over 100,000 civilians may have been killed, a number made all the more difficult to estimate due to the fact that an untold number evacuated into caves and were entombed in them when American soldiers sealed them as they advanced in order to protect themselves. American troops also used flamethrowers to smoke the Japanese out of caves, and in the process, it was impossible to distinguish civilians from soldiers.

An American Marine using a flamethrower on a Japanese cave.

Most importantly, the Battle of Okinawa was so ruthless that it convinced Allied leaders that the invasion of Japan would be an absolute bloodbath for all sides. American military officials estimated that there would be upwards of a million Allied casualties if they had to invade the Japanese mainland, and if they were successful, Japan would suffer tens of millions of casualties in the process. As the Battle of Okinawa was about to finish, America's secret Manhattan Project was on the brink of its final goal: a successful detonation of a nuclear device. On July 16, 1945, the first detonation of a nuclear device took place in Alamogordo, New Mexico.

Dropping the Atomic Bombs

Before World War I, research in atomic theory was concentrated solely in Europe. The United States clung to old fashioned physics while the Europeans moved on to more sophisticated topics. Only after the war did the United States embark into the realm of atomic research, first in California, at Berkeley.

Ernest Lawrence, a Berkeley physics professor, began toying with generating high energy through particle acceleration. Because a linear accelerator would have to be miles long to generate enough energy, Lawrence opted for a spiral model, which he dubbed a cyclotron. Throughout the 1920s and into the 1930s, Lawrence accelerated atoms faster and faster, increasing the amount of energy (measured in electron volts) he was able to produce.

Ernest Lawrence

Lawrence's experiments received a boost in the early 1930s from events taking place in Europe. With Adolf Hitler's rise to power in Nazi Germany, Jews were facing violent persecution at a time when many of them held positions of high prestige in German universities. Nations around the world offered to give the fleeing Jews a new home, including the United States, which recruited many Jews to its universities. Among them was Albert Einstein, who arrived in Princeton, New Jersey, in 1932, and Leó Szilárd, who came to Columbia University in 1938. Others escaped Europe because of the rise of fascist dictatorships; Enrico Fermi fled to the United States during the rise of Benito Mussolini. This flood of scientists into the United States helped propel the country's interest in atomic physics.

Albert Einstein

On the eve of the outbreak of World War II in Europe, Albert Einstein and Leó Szilárd, both European Jews who had immigrated to the United States, sent an urgent letter to President Franklin Roosevelt. Szilárd had been working alongside Enrico Fermi to develop a nuclear chain reaction using uranium to generate vast amounts of power, and he hoped to convince the President to provide more funding and resources to his research.

The now-famous Einstein-Szilárd Letter, written by Szilárd but signed only by Einstein, asserted that "it appears almost certain that [the creation of nuclear power] could be achieved in the immediate future." It then goes on to discuss the potential of converting this energy source into a bomb, though they cautioned that such a weapon might "be too heavy for transportation by air."

Ominously, the letter discussed an important ingredient in building nuclear technology, access to uranium ore. The United States had only moderate quantities of the ore, though Canada and the Belgian Congo were deemed to have bounties of uranium. Another location, Czechoslovakia, was particularly rich in uranium deposits. However, the two informed President Roosevelt that the German annexation of Czechoslovakia had led the Nazis to stop all sale of uranium from Czechoslovakian mines. They correctly suggested that Germany was probably using the uranium to develop nuclear technology of its own, and that it was important for the United States to outpace Germany in the race to develop nuclear energy.

Though the letter was written in August 1939, about a month before Germany's invasion of Poland and the outbreak of World War II, Roosevelt did not receive the letter until October 11th, 1939. Perhaps this was for the best. With war now raging in Europe, Szilárd's suggestions about a German arms race were all the more potent.

One of Roosevelt's close confidants, Alexander Sachs, presented the letter to the President. He did so by also recalling a story about an American inventor who offered to build steam ship technology for the French Emperor Napoleon. Napoleon was short sighted and rejected the American's offer. The American later took his offer to England, where it was accepted. England, of course, went on to win to win the Napoleonic Wars, and Napoleon met his Waterloo. Would Roosevelt also suffer from such shortsightedness?

With that, Roosevelt was convinced, though hesitant. He called on Lyman Briggs, the Director of the Bureau of Standards, to set up a committee to investigate the uranium issue. The Advisory Committee on Uranium began meeting on October 21st, with Szilárd in attendance. By the end of the meeting, a paltry $6,000 was given to the scientists to further their studies. While the President had committed funds to nuclear research, his generosity was clearly quite limited.

Meanwhile, across the pond, Great Britain was considering nuclear weaponry amid the urgency of a continental war. British scientists Otto Frisch and Rudolf Peierls, both Jewish immigrants from Austria and Germany, authored a letter very similar to that delivered by Einstein and Szilárd.

Both were working at the University of Birmingham when they made a critical discovery. The two had found that, contrary to existing beliefs, a nuclear bomb would require only a tiny bit of uranium – about one kilogram, or 2.2 pounds. Einstein and Szilárd had cautioned that the construction of a bomb rested on the idea that the weapon's weight would be too much to transport by air. On the contrary, Frisch and Peierls' discovery made clear that a bomb could be delivered by air.

The two penned a memorandum and sent it to Henry Tizard, head of the Scientific Survey of Air Defense. Still undecided, he formed a committee to investigate the idea, much as Roosevelt had done in the United States. The MAUD (Military Application of Uranium Detonation) Committee was formed in April 1940, just months after the American Advisory Committee on Uranium had been formed. The United Kingdom had now joined the United States, and possibly Nazi Germany, in the quest to create a nuclear bomb.

Unlike the Americans, however, the British experiments with nuclear weaponry initially advanced much more quickly, no doubt because of the urgency of war. By mid-1940, the Nazis were on the verge of overrunning France, and with the Nazis and Soviets having a nonaggression pact, the Axis were about to be unopposed on the European continent. Britain had to worry about the Nazis turning the full force of their military against them. Naturally, the discovery that a bomb could be produced with potentially decisive effects on the war increased political support for research, reaching all the way up to the highest levels. Even Prime Minister Winston Churchill was offering his seal of approval.

Although weaponry innovations were slow back in the United States, researchers nonetheless made advances in nuclear technology. Most important among these was Glenn Seaborg's discovery of plutonium in March 1941. He had isolated a gram of element 94 and named it plutonium after the recently-discovered planet, Pluto. This discovery yielded another fissionable material in addition to uranium, but political interest in the United States was still tepid at best. The British, however, had hopes of working with the Americans to speed up bomb production. With the Battle of Britain on the verge of reaching its climax, British resources were limited, and safe spaces for research were equally sparse. Hoping to spur American interest, MAUD sent a report detailing its discovery of the feasibility of a nuclear bomb to the American committee headed by Lyman Briggs.

To MAUD's surprise and consternation, the memorandum seemed to have gone unnoticed within the American nuclear community. In August 1941, Australian physicist Mark Oliphant flew to Berkeley, where he met with the American atomic researchers. Oliphant had been working on the British nuclear research with the MAUD Committee, and he came to the U.S.

hoping to ignite increased research efforts in the country. Most importantly, Oliphant met with Ernest Lawrence and managed to convince him of the potential for an atomic bomb. Until then, Berkeley researchers, including Lawrence, had been focused primarily on harnessing nuclear physics as a source of energy, not weaponry.

Convincing Lawrence was a critical moment in the developed of British-American cooperation on the nuclear project. Once Lawrence was convinced, the Berkeley professor spread the word to his fellow American scientists. In particular, Lawrence spoke with Arthur Compton, a leading scientist in the government agency, the Office of Scientific Research and Development (OSRD). The agency was charged with developing scientifically-advanced weapons, though nuclear weaponry was not yet on its agenda. Compton spoke with the Office's leader, MIT professor Vannevar Bush, and convinced him to approve a unit devoted to nuclear research.

By October 9, 1941, this scientific chain, stretching from Australia to Berkeley, had now reached the President of the United States. From the MAUD Committee to Oliphant, then on to Lawrence and Compton, the news of nuclear weaponry had finally reached Bush, a high-level U.S. government official. Before funding and cooperation could be secured, Bush needed to speak directly with President Roosevelt.

That day, Roosevelt shifted his position on nuclear weapons from reluctant to assertive, and he gave the official go-ahead for secret nuclear weapons research, agreeing to collaborate with the British government at the highest levels. Two days later, the President sent a message to Prime Minister Winston Churchill suggesting the two nations work together on the matter. Full cooperation was not yet at its highest levels, however; the British remained uncertain that the Americans were up to the job.

In October, the President had authorized the Army to take over the management of the project, which was still in its baby stages. With this authorization, research into nuclear weaponry catapulted from a snail's pace to greater urgency, with physicists from around the nation now working toward one coordinated effort. Einstein, Fermi, Szilárd, and Lawrence, along with the help of British scientists, were now working under the administrative leaders Briggs and Bush. It was a literal "dream team" of physicists.

Still, events in October hadn't quite brought nuclear bomb manufacturing to fruition. Roosevelt only authorized funds and organization for *research*, stressing that the production stage could not proceed without further presidential authorization. The President wanted a first report from the scientists about the projected costs and timeline of the program.

On a casual Saturday, December 6, 1941, President Roosevelt signed an Executive Order authorizing the creation of the Manhattan Engineering District to coordinate the manufacture of an atomic bomb and giving the program $2 billion. At the time, the act was of questionable legality; Congress had legislated neutrality in the European war, and the Manhattan District opened the doors to British-American weaponry cooperation. When Roosevelt implemented the Lend-Lease program that facilitated arms sales to the British earlier in the war, isolationists were furious, and the America First Committee lobbied strongly against intervention of any sort into the war. Thus, this Executive Order was given in secret, and the President went on to spend the rest of his Saturday relaxing.

The very next day, Roosevelt's relaxation was over for good, and the legality of the Executive Order became a moot point following the attack on Pearl Harbor. The nation was now engaged in an unprecedented battle, and the importance of the Manhattan Engineering District elevated overnight. American nuclear research was about to speed ahead frenetically.

With the creation of the Manhattan District, the central problem associated with nuclear research switched from too little interest to too little time. The Allies and the U.S. had faced setbacks of all sorts entering 1942, and the outcome of the war in Europe and in the Pacific was very much in doubt. The situation remained precarious and uncertain.

Vannevar Bush

On December 18, less than two weeks after President Roosevelt's Executive Order, Vannevar Bush and his co-leader Arthur Compton created the S-1 Uranium Committee to divvy up research projects on nuclear energy. Ernest Lawrence was to research electromagnetic enrichment techniques while Harold Urey was to direct research into gaseous diffusion for uranium enrichment. Together, these top leaders coordinated with research scientists from across the country to create a unified and efficient nationwide effort. The entire relevant intellectual resources of the United States were now being put to use in creating a nuclear bomb.

Meanwhile, President Roosevelt was trying to coordinate research efforts with the British at a higher level. Despite early desires for intervention from British scientists, the lag in American research had put a damper on British hopes for transatlantic cooperation. Despite discussions between Roosevelt and Churchill, the British government was now convinced that the United States was not up to the job of creating a nuclear bomb, given the country's slowness in the early years of British development. The British and Americans thus continued to operate independent programs that were mostly uncoordinated, even though the country's scientists shared information and discoveries with each other as research progressed.

By the summer of 1942, American research into a nuclear weapon had advanced considerably. Lawrence had found enormous success with electromagnetic enrichment of uranium-235, leading American scientists to conclude that the amount of enrichment needed would be even less than previously thought. However, researchers were running into problems elsewhere. Isotope separation processes at Columbia and gaseous diffusion efforts were encountering enormous stumbling blocks.

With the urgency of war providing pressure, Vannevar Bush, as the administrative head of the project, felt that the production stages could wait no longer. Research was important, but having the infrastructure in place to build the bomb when the time was ripe was equally critical. He authorized the S-1 Committee to begin offering projections for the infrastructure that would be needed to actually build the bomb, irrespective of costs.

To initiate production, the Army Corps of Engineers became directly involved. That summer, the transition from S-1 control to Army control was complete, with Colonel James C. Marshall in control of the Manhattan Engineering District. But Marshall was an army man, not an engineer, and knew nothing about theoretical physics. Bush thought he was inadequate for the job of coordinating the creation of a nuclear bomb, so a reshuffling of administrative leadership took place in September, with Brigadier General Leslie Groves replacing Marshall as head of the Manhattan District. Unlike Marshall, Groves was an engineer with the perfect credentials for handling the project. With Groves as the military head, he appointed a man named J. Robert Oppenheimer as the project's scientific leader.

Oppenheimer

Oppenheimer's appointment surprised many. While he had made significant insights into fast neutron calculations, Oppenheimer did not have a Nobel Prize, as many other lead scientists (including Lawrence) did. Furthermore, Oppenheimer lacked administrative experience, and his associations with the military were loose at best. Some suggested he was a communist. Regardless, Groves saw great intellect in Oppenheimer and considered him the perfect fit for the position.

Together, Oppenheimer and Groves began selecting sites to build infrastructure for producing the nuclear bomb. At this point, the Manhattan Project was headquartered in New York, near Columbia University, but the construction of the bomb was anticipated to be a nationwide effort. Selecting proper sites for construction was of crucial importance.

In September, before selecting Oppenheimer as Scientific Director, Groves chose a site in Tennessee for "Site X." Site X was located in Oak Ridge, Tennessee, and would come to include four separate research laboratories by the end of the Manhattan Project. In November, both Groves and Oppenheimer sought out "Site Y," and ultimately decided on Los Alamos, New Mexico, as the ideal location.

Workers at Oak Ridge

Each of these sites was selected in part for their isolation from major population centers. The Manhattan Project was a secret and needed to be removed from public interest. The U.S. Army Corps of Engineers went about creating literally new cities to house the facilities' workers, while the airspace over the facilities was heavily guarded and closed off. In Oak Ridge, a once sparsely inhabited valley saw its population jump from 3,000 in 1942 to 75,000 by the end of the war. Because of the sensitivity of the research being conducted, the sites also needed to be distant from international borders. Unsure of what their research would yield, Groves and Oppenheimer did not want a nuclear meltdown to take place in a location that could leak across international borders.

With these two initial sites of production selected, construction of laboratories quickly began at both locations. In the meantime, work continued at universities, much as it had before the centralized takeover of American nuclear research. During this time period, the most important breakthrough in nuclear science came from the laboratories of Enrico Fermi, in collaboration with Leo Szilárd, at the University of Chicago. There, the two created the first man-made nuclear reactor, known as Chicago Pile-1.

Chicago Pile-1 went into action successfully on December 2nd, 1942. The nuclear reactor, unlike almost all nuclear reactors since, did *not* have any cooling system or radiation shield. Fermi thought this was unnecessary and predicted that a self-sustaining nuclear chain reaction faced little threat of melting down. This was, of course, dangerously incorrect. In hindsight, Fermi's first controlled reaction put the city of Chicago in enormous danger. Luckily, after 28 minutes of operating Chicago Pile-1, Fermi closed down the reactor and all was fine. Had it spun out of control, however, a nuclear meltdown would have destroyed one of the nation's most densely populated cities, and a disaster would have certainly eliminated any public support or political will to continue the Manhattan Project.

In conveying to his colleagues around the country that the project was a success, the scientist simply stated that "the Italian navigator has landed in the New World." Secret codes like this ensured that the Manhattan Project remained known by only the nation's most elite scientists. It was quickly, however, becoming a national effort encompassing thousands of employees. By the end of the war, the Manhattan Project employed nearly 150,000 people.

At last the Americans were making significant headway in the production of nuclear weapons. President Roosevelt had given his seal of approval, but the British had soured on the idea of conducting a joint British-American effort. With more credibility now supporting the country's project, Roosevelt was ready to attempt closer transatlantic cooperation once again.

President Roosevelt and Prime Minister Churchill met in Quebec City, Canada, in August 1943 to discuss joint cooperation. While fortunes in Roosevelt's country had changed for the better between 1941 and 1943, progress had stalled in Britain. The British and their Empire were now under continual military assault, and all of their resources were being poured into fighting Nazi Germany. Building a nuclear bomb was important, but marshaling resources toward a bomb that existed only in scientists' imaginations was removed from the forefront in the interest of battling the Luftwaffe in Europe. Moreover, the British were having trouble moving forward on the project.

On August 19, 1943, President Roosevelt and Prime Minister Churchill signed the Quebec Agreement, a formal statement that laid out the terms of transatlantic cooperation on nuclear weapons research. The agreement not only allowed the British "Tube Alloys" program to join the Manhattan Project, but it also designated how the two nations and Canada would use nuclear weapons in the future. Specifically, the three nations agreed to never use nuclear weapons against each other, never to use them against another country without the consent of all three nations, and never to give the research to another nation without unanimous agreement among the three countries.

With the Quebec Agreement in hand, British scientists came to the United States to join American researchers working on the Manhattan Project. In reality, the two groups had been communicating throughout their respective projects, but the Quebec Agreement allowed them to do so officially. Separated from Japan and Germany by oceans, the U.S. was a much safer place to work on the project anyway, ensuring that the Project could remain a secret. And with more rural land with which to work, the United States also provided better space for conducting nuclear tests than the United Kingdom anyway.

With the addition of British scientists, the Manhattan Project expanded rapidly throughout 1943 and 1944. Construction on sites began not only at Oak Ridge and Los Alamos, but elsewhere across the country. The three most important sites were Oak Ridge and Los Alamos, and another site in Washington called the Hanford site. Oak Ridge served to enrich uranium, Hanford enriched plutonium and Los Alamos was the research site used for assembly of the bomb itself. The Manhattan Project, however, was not limited to these three sites. It expanded into dozens of locations across the United States and Canada at the Project's peak. Each site served a unique purpose, and all were under the central command of the Army Corps of Engineers, led by General Groves and Oppenheimer.

Sites where work was conducted on the Manhattan Project

In the fall of 1943, the production phase of nuclear weaponry moved on to the delivery aspect of the project. While scientists were working on the physics of a nuclear reaction, engineers needed to find a way to deliver nuclear energy in a manageable bomb format. In October of 1943, groups of Army engineers in Los Alamos and a site at the Wendover Army Airfield in Utah got to work designing the bomb itself. This project became known as Project Alberta, known colloquially as "Project A."

Project A not only designed the shape and size of the bomb, it also created measures to ensure that the bomb did not detonate prematurely or become vulnerable to induced detonation from a Japanese attack. The engineers also created devices to time the explosion and test the effects of high altitudes on nuclear reactions.

Project Alberta was a final stage in the creation of the nuclear bomb. For the first time, sites in

Japan were now being targeted for nuclear delivery, and the design of the bombs took these targets into account.

1944 brought enormous progress with the construction of the nuclear bomb, though not without some initial failures. First among these setbacks was the discovery in April that the "gun-type" fission weapon would probably not work. A man named Emilio Segrè, another Jewish-American who escaped oppression in fascist Europe, worked with enriched plutonium at Los Alamos. He discovered that plutonium was unsuitable to the "Thin Man" nuclear bomb prototype proposed by scientists at Oak Ridge. "Thin Man" proposed using fissionable plutonium to explode a bomb via a gun-like contraption within the bomb itself. Segrè discovered, however, that the fission rate of plutonium was too high and was unsuitable to this model.

Segrè

Two other models were also in development: another gun-type bomb using uranium, called "Little Boy," and an implosion-based bomb called "Fat Man". "Thin Man" was discarded after Segrè's discovery, and priority was thereafter given to the other two types of bomb. Lead-scientist Oppenheimer reviewed Segrè's discoveries and made the call to suspend development on the plutonium gun-type bomb.

By the middle of the summer of 1944, the Manhattan Project had developed the two prototypes that would eventually form the bombs dropped on Hiroshima and Nagasaki.

The design for Little Boy

The design for Fat Man

Franklin D. Roosevelt had been disabled for much of his adult life, but it still came as a surprise when he suffered a hemorrhage and abruptly died in April 1945. Vice President Harry Truman succeeded him. Incredibly, the Manhattan Project had been so secretive that the Vice President-turned-President did not even know of its existence. Following his first Cabinet meeting on his first day as President, Secretary of War Henry Stimson informed the President of the Project.

Despite the glaring oversight of failing to brief the Vice President, the Manhattan Project was unfazed by Roosevelt's death and continued undisrupted. The war itself was also mostly undisturbed by Roosevelt's death. Months earlier, with the Soviets racing toward Berlin from the east and the British and Americans pushing toward Germany from the west, Roosevelt had met with Churchill and Stalin at the Yalta Conference to plan out a postwar Europe. A month after the President's death, victory was achieved in Europe.

Construction of the bomb, however, did not stop with victory in Europe. There was widespread jubilation when Germany surrendered, but the Japanese were showing no sign of surrendering. In May 1945 the Americans and Japanese were engaged in an extremely deadly campaign at Okinawa, an island close enough to use for air attacks on the Japanese mainland. Facing kamikaze attacks and fanatic Japanese soldiers, the Allies suffered 50,000 casualties, leading American military officials to estimate upwards of a million Allied casualties if they had to invade the Japanese mainland. Besides, the nuclear bombs being constructed in Los Alamos were always intended to be used in Japan, and so the end of the war in Europe did not make the bombs any less necessary.

Under a new President, the Manhattan Project continued unabated. When Truman came to office, the Manhattan Project was on the brink of its final goal, a successful detonation of a nuclear device, which would come in a matter of months. At that point, President Truman would be left to make a fateful decision about using the most destructive weapon ever created.

The bomb was not yet officially complete, nor had it been tested, before President Truman and his advisors were being pelted by letters from scientists raising ethical objections to the use of the nuclear bomb. It was not making Truman's decision any less difficult.

The first of such letters came in June 1945 from James Franck, yet another Jewish escapee from Central Europe who came to the United States and worked on nuclear research. In his letter, Franck offered apt advice on the threat of a nuclear arms race should the U.S. use the weapon. He suggested that the weapon would be so powerful and so devastating that nations around the world would race to gain access to the technology themselves. Franck's solution was to either keep the nuclear bomb secret indefinitely or to test it in a barren desert before the United Nations, to show Japan and the world its devastating destructiveness. The letter was signed by Franck and other notable nuclear scientists, including Leo Szilárd and Glenn Seaborg, both early proponents of and contributors to the Manhattan Project. The letter was received and taken into account by a nuclear arms committee appointed by President Truman.

Franck

A second important letter came in July, less than a month before the nuclear detonations over Hiroshima and Nagasaki. Penned by Leo Szilárd, the document was signed by an additional 69 physicists and researchers. It explicitly opposed using the weapon against Japan unless that nation was offered surrender terms beforehand and rejected them. All 70 petitioners lost their jobs in the Manhattan Project, though the letter was received by the same committee that reviewed the Franck Letter.

In between the two petitions, the American nuclear bomb had finally come to fruition. On July 16, 1945, the first detonation of a nuclear device took place in Alamogordo, New Mexico.

The first bomb was nicknamed the "gadget," to avoid espionage attempts to discover that it was, indeed, a bomb. In some sense, the device detonated in July was not really a "bomb" anyway; it was not a deployable device, though it one that could be detonated.

The Trinity Test device was a "Fat Man" implosion type of nuclear device that relied on plutonium, not uranium. It featured a rounded capsule filled with a plutonium center surrounded by explosives. The explosives detonated simultaneously inward, forcing dense pressure onto the plutonium. This resulted in a nuclear explosion.

To conduct the actual test, a 100-foot tower was built, to which the bomb was hoisted at the top. Because the Trinity site was a huge desert, physicists scattered around the tower at no less than 10 mile distances, and everyone wore ultraviolet lenses to protect their eyes from damage.

At 5:10 p.m., the 20-minute countdown began. No one *really* knew what would become of the detonation; some speculated that the bomb would ignite the atmosphere of the entire planet, killing all life on earth. That, however, was among the more extreme predictions. Other less extreme but still horrifying predictions guessed that all of New Mexico would be incinerated.

After waiting 20 minutes, however, all these fears were put to rest, when the world's first mushroom cloud was detonated over the desert sky. For a few seconds, all of the mountains within view of the detonation were reportedly brightly lit up, and the earth trembled.

The Trinity Test

With this success, word reached President Truman, who was then attending an Allied Conference in Potsdam. There, he presented the news to Soviet leader Josef Stalin. Stalin feigned surprise; espionage missions had revealed American nuclear research to the Soviets before it had even reached then-Vice President Harry Truman.

The physicists present at the detonation inspected the site a few weeks later. Little did they know that nuclear fallout had infected some parts of New Mexico, though no densely populated regions were affected. Upon inspection, they found sand that had been turned to glass by the enormous force of the world's first nuclear explosion.

Oppenheimer and Graves inspect the detonation site

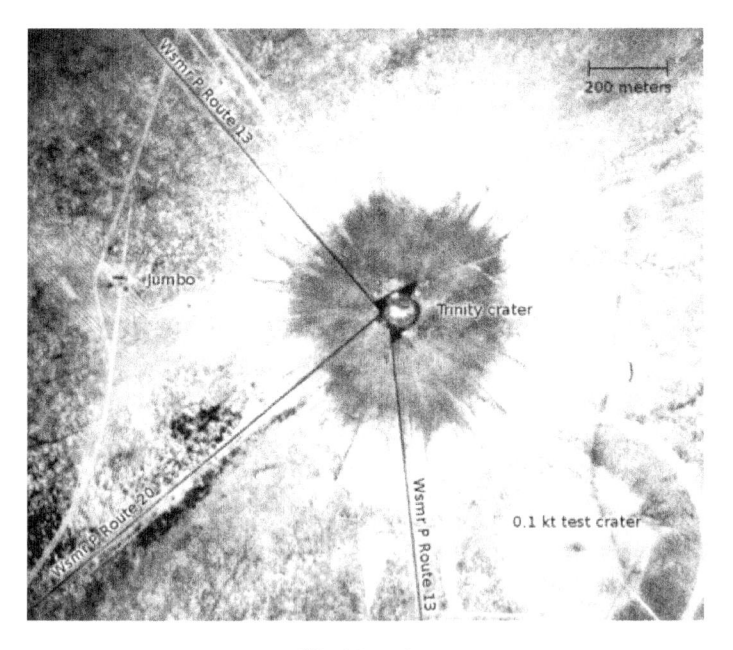

The blast site

Before making his decision to use the bomb, Truman considered some of the ethical advice submitted by American physicists. In particular, he took the idea of informing the Japanese beforehand to heart. At the Potsdam Conference on July 26th, Truman, the United Kingdom and China issued the Potsdam Declaration, giving the Japanese an ultimatum to surrender or suffer "prompt and utter destruction."

Japan chose to ignore the ultimatum, and ultimately Truman chose to use the bombs. Truman took the scientists' concerns into account, but the deadly experience of Okinawa made clear that hundreds of thousands of Americans would be casualties in a conventional invasion of the mainland of Japan. Moreover, the fanatical manner in which Japanese soldiers and civilians held out on Okinawa indicated that the Japanese would suffer more casualties during an invasion than they would if the bombs were used. Pursuant to the Quebec Agreement, Canada and Great Britain consented to the use of the bomb. As a result, Truman authorized its use on two sites in Japan.

President Truman Ordering the Bomb to Be Dropped

Once Truman gave the go ahead to use the bomb, there was still a matter of picking out sites. Though largely forgotten today, the U.S. listed sites in Japan that had the most military value when choosing where to hit. Moreover, the Americans had to deal with weather conditions, which doomed Nagasaki on August 9.

The primary target for the use of the first bomb was the city of Hiroshima, located in south-central Japan and the largest in the Hiroshima Prefecture. The 509th Composite Group of the U.S. Air Force was created to deploy nuclear weapons, thus given the mission to hit Hiroshima. Lieutenant Colonel Paul Tibbets was selected for the mission well beforehand, and had been training at the remote Wendover Army Air Field in Utah. In the days leading up to the use of the bomb, the Air Force dropped leaflets telling residents of Hiroshima to flee, a warning about half the residents heeded.

On August 6, three planes set off from the island of Tinian to make the 6 hour flight to Hiroshima. Tibbets led the mission, flying the *Enola Gay*, a plane named after his mother that carried the nuclear "Little Boy" uranium gun-type nuclear bomb. Two other planes, *The Great Artiste* and *Necessary Evil* accompanied the mission. All three planes were B-29's.

Tibbets about to take off in the *Enola Gay*

At approximately 8:15 a.m. on August 6th, 1945, the bomb was dropped from the *Enola Gay*, almost exactly as planned. The bomb missed its precise target by 800 feet, an insignificant distance given the bomb's destructiveness.

With the detonation of "Little Boy," the destruction of Hiroshima was far from "little." Japanese officials estimated that approximately 70% of the city's buildings were completely destroyed and another 5-10% were severely damaged. 80,000 people were killed instantly, and another 70,000 severely injured. The entire world had witnessed the devastation of the world's most powerful weapon.

Wreckage in Hiroshima after the Bomb

Hiroshima would not be the only Japanese city to be destroyed by an American atomic bomb. President Truman reiterated his plea for an unconditional surrender after Hiroshima, cautioning that failure to do so would result in an additional "rain of ruin from the air, the like of which has never been seen on this earth." Making matters worse for Japan, the Soviet Union broke its Soviet-Japanese Neutrality Pact and declared war on Japan on August 9, as part of an agreement the Soviets had reached with the Allies.

Still, Japan refused to surrender. Instead, the Japanese government instituted martial law within the country to prevent anyone from surrendering. As such, Truman's "rain of ruin" continued. The second site targeted was the city of Kokura, in Southern Japan. This time, a plane called the *Bockstar* was to deliver the bomb, piloted by Major Charles Sweeney.

Luckily for the residents of Kokura, its name would remain irrelevant in the narrative of World War II. The nuclear bombing required the pilot to be able to see the ground, but Kokura was obscured by dense cloud cover on the date of the bombing. Thus, Sweeney made the call to divert to the secondary target, a city farther south called Nagasaki.

There, too, the city was covered in clouds, but a very brief break in the cloud cover at about 11:00 a.m. on August 9 allowed *Bockstar* to drop the "Fat Man" plutonium implosion-type bomb it was carrying. The bomb landed significantly north of its intended epicenter, about two miles to the north and west, in Nagasaki's industrial district. As such, Nagasaki was not as badly destroyed as Hiroshima, but over 40,000 people were still killed.

On August 14th, 1945, five days after the bombing of Nagasaki, Japan's Emperor Hirohito offered a capitulation and unconditional surrender. Despite some initial protest from Japanese militarists, the war was now definitely over. Hirohito cited the unprecedented nuclear attack as the primary reason for surrender, though the Soviet invasion was also a significant factor.

World War II was now officially over on both fronts. On August 28, the Supreme Allied occupation of Japan began, and the official surrender ceremony was completed on the USS *Missouri* on September 2. Interestingly, the official end of the state of war between the U.S. and Japan, however, did not come until 1952, with the Treaty of San Francisco being signed on April 28 of that year.

With the bombings of Hiroshima and Nagasaki marking the end of World War II, the Manhattan Project went from top secret to public knowledge. Just a year after the war's end, Congress began debating what to do with its newly-found nuclear arsenal and how to control the deadly technology.

An important component of the post-war discussion of atomic energy involved the military's lone control over nuclear technology during the war. Was this politically justified? Even after the war, the U.S. military alone had access to the secrets of nuclear technology and controlled the nation's arsenal, without any oversight by Congress. Amazingly, the U.S. Congress was largely unaware of the Manhattan Project during most of its history. For many Americans, this represented a major violation to the nation's concept of a civilian-controlled military.

Out of this came the Atomic Energy Act of 1946, proposed by Senator Brien McMahon of Connecticut. It passed the Senate unanimously and also passed overwhelmingly in the House. It was signed by President Truman on August 1, 1946, going into effect on January 1, 1947. The Atomic Energy Act created the United States Atomic Energy Commission to ensure that future developments in nuclear technology were overseen by Congress. The law also restricted the ability of the United States to share nuclear knowledge with other nations, a proviso that offended Great Britain and Canada, who had contributed to the Manhattan Project and had shared information with the U.S. during the war. As a result of the Atomic Energy Act, both nations were forced to decide whether or not to pursue their own separate nuclear energy programs. Congress had essentially voided the Quebec Agreement; because it was signed by Roosevelt in secret, it was not legally binding.

A raging debate over the ethics of the attacks on Hiroshima and Nagasaki lasts to this day. Were the nuclear attacks on those cities justified? Proponents of the bombings say that, had the U.S. not dropped the bombs, more Japanese and American citizens would have eventually died during continued fighting between the two countries. To this, critics insist the U.S. could have achieved victory on its own terms without killing as many innocent civilians. But it remains unclear how that could have happened. The U.S. obviously could not have achieved victory faster without using the nuclear bomb, which ended the war within a week of its use on Hiroshima. There's no question that a combined naval and military assault on Japan would have taken much longer. And the suggestions that the U.S. demonstrate the bomb's deadliness to Japan beforehand seems to fall flat, considering Japan rejected surrender terms and still refused to surrender after the bombing of Hiroshima.

In the end, the debate comes down to one of speculation. It's impossible to know how intense Japanese-American fighting would have been without the nuclear bomb, and how many people would have been killed as a result.

Another lasting issue that came out of the Manhattan Project involves the global nuclear arms race it ignited. On this, the Project's legacy is much more certain. Much as the Franck letter forewarned, the bombings of Hiroshima and Nagasaki *did* ignite a multi-decade arms race between the Soviet Union and the United States. Arms races sprung up elsewhere in the world, notably between India and Pakistan, and nations around the world vie to gain access to nuclear weapons \ today. The nuclear attacks on Japan solidified the idea that ownership of nuclear technology permanently insulated a nation from external attack. No nation would threaten to attack the United States out of fear of nuclear retaliation. Countries like Iran hope to gain that sort of invincibility today, while its enemies fear the consequences of letting antagonistic regimes get hold of such deadly weapons.

While the Manhattan Project undoubtedly spurred an arms race, the consequences of that race are more hotly debated. Is a global nuclear arms race necessarily a bad thing? After the World War, two global superpowers, the Soviet Union and the United States, avoided war for decades, despite unprecedented hostilities. Nuclear weapons are given significant credit for this lasting state of peace. The weapons served as a significant deterrent; neither nation could conceivably go to war with the other without risking nuclear annihilation. Similar peace has been kept elsewhere in the world because of the strategic balance created by opposing sides holding nuclear weapons.

Finally, it's important to remember the legacy of the Manhattan Project is not limited merely to political issues of war and peace. Having broken enormous ground in the science of atomic energy, the Manhattan Project has given the world a new and powerful source of energy. While the risks of nuclear power are many, the reality is that few meltdowns have occurred and nuclear energy remains a clean and promising way of powering an information-age society. At its start, the Manhattan Project in the United States was devoted more to this use of uranium and plutonium. In the end, domestic energy serves as one of the brightest contributions the Manhattan Project offered to global society.

Further Reading

Appleman, Roy Edgar; Burns, James M.; Gugeler, Russel A.; Stevens, John (1948). Okinawa: The Last Battle. Washington DC: United States Army Center of Military History. ISBN 1-4102-2206-3. full text online

Astor, Gerald (1996). Operation Iceberg: The Invasion and Conquest of Okinawa in World War II. Dell. ISBN 0-440-22178-1.

Battle of Iwo Jima: Japanese Defense – www.battle-fleet.com/pw/his/Battle-Iwo-Jima-Defenses.htm

Burrell, Robert S., "Breaking the Cycle of Iwo Jima Mythology: A Strategic Study of Operation Detachment", in *Journal of Military History*, Vol. 68 No. 4 (October, 2004)

Buckner, Simon Bolivar, Jr. and Joseph Stilwell. Seven Stars: The Okinawa Battle Diaries of Simon Bolivar Buckner, Jr. and Joseph Stilwell ed. by Nicholas Evan Sarantakes (2004)

Caidin, Martin (1960). A Torch to the Enemy: The Fire Raid on Tokyo. Balantine Books. ISBN 0-553-29926-3. D767.25.T6 C35.

Christ, James F. *Iwo, Assault on Hell*, Battleground Publishing: Chandler, 2010

Coffey, Thomas M. (1987). Iron Eagle: The Turbulent Life of General Curtis LeMay. Random House Value Publishing. ISBN 0-517-55188-8.

Crowl, Philip A. *Campaign in the Marianas.* Harrisburg, 1994.

DeGroot, Gerard J. *The Bomb: A Life.* Cambridge: Harvard University Press, 2005.

Boston: Little, Brown and Company, 1967.

Denfeld, D. Colt. *Hold the Marianas: The Japanese Defense of the Islands.* Shippensburg, 1997.

Feifer, George (2001). The Battle of Okinawa: The Blood and the Bomb. The Lyons Press. ISBN 1-58574-215-5.

Fisch Jr., Arnold G. Ryukyus. World War II Campaign Brochures. Washington D.C.: United States Army Center of Military History. ISBN 0-16-048032-9. CMH Pub 72-35.

Frank, Benis. *Okinawa: Touchstone to Victory.* New York, NY: Ballantine Books Inc., 1969.

Frank, Richard B. (2001). Downfall: The End of the Imperial Japanese Empire. Penguin. ISBN 0-14-100146-1.

Gailey, Harry. *The Liberation of Guam: 21 July – 10 August 1944.* Novato, 1997.

Gandt, Robert (2010). The Twilight Warriors. Broadway Books. ISBN 978-0-7679-3241-7.

Goldberg, Harold J. *D-Day in the Pacific: The Battle of Saipan.* Bloomington, 2007.

Gow, Ian. *Okinawa 1945: Gateway to Japan.* Garden City, NY: Doubleday & Company, Inc., 1985.

Grayling, A. C. (2007). Among the Dead Cities: The History and Moral Legacy of the WWII Bombing of Civilians in Germany and Japan. New York: Walker Publishing Company Inc. ISBN 0-8027-1565-6.

Groueff, Stephane. *Manhattan Project: The Untold Story of the Making of the Atomic Bomb.*

Hallas, James H. (2006). Killing Ground on Okinawa: The Battle for Sugar Loaf Hill. Potomac Books. ISBN 1-59797-063-8.

Hanley, Brian, "The Myth of Iwo Jima: A Rebuttal", in *The Journal of Military History,* Vol. 69 No. 3 (July 2005)

Hastings, Max (2007). Retribution – The Battle for Japan, 1944–45. New York: Alfred A. Knopf. ISBN 978-0-307-26351-3.

Iwo Jima.com – *Japanese Iwo Jima Strategy*

Lacey, Laura Homan (2005). Stay Off The Skyline: The Sixth Marine Division on Okinawa—An Oral History. Potomac Books. ISBN 1-57488-952-4.

Leckie, Robert. *Okinawa: The Last Battle of World War II*. New York: Penguin Books, 1996.

Leckie, Robert. *Strong Men Armed: The United States Marines Against Japan.* Cambridge, 1990.

Linenthal, Edward T.: Review of "Iwo Jima in American Memory" of Karal Ann Marling, John Wetenhall

Manchester, William (1980). Goodbye, Darkness: A Memoir of the Pacific War. Boston, Toronto: Little, Brown and Co. ISBN 0-316-54501-5.

Meyers, Bruce F. *Fortune Favors the Brave: The Story of First Force Recon.* New York, 2004.

Morison, Samuel Eliot (2002 (reissue)). Victory in the Pacific, 1945, vol. 14 of History of United States Naval Operations in World War II. Champaign, Illinois, USA: University of Illinois Press. ISBN 0-252-07065-8.

Nichols, Charles Sidney; Henry I. Shaw Jr. (1989). Okinawa: Victory in the Pacific. Battery Press. ASIN B00071UAT8.

O'Brien, Cyril, *Iwo Jima Retrospective* – www.military.com

O'Brien, Francis A. *Battling for Saipan.* New York, 2003.

Oral History, *Iwo Jima: The Flag Raising, John Bradley Interview* – www.history.navy.mil/flags/faq87-31.htm

Oral History – www.history.navy.mil/faq61-2.htm

Prefer, Nathan N. *The Battle for Tinian: Vital Stepping Stone in America's War Against Japan.* Havertown, 2012.

Rottman, Gordon (2002). Okinawa 1945: The last Battle. Osprey Publishing. ISBN 1-84176-546-5.

Rottman, Gordon L. *Saipan & Tinian 1944: Piercing the Japanese Empire.* Botley, 2004.

Sherrod, Robert Lee. *On to Westward: War in the Central Pacific.* New York, 1945.

Sledge, E. B.; Paul Fussell (1990). With the Old Breed: At Peleliu and Okinawa. Oxford University Press. ISBN 0-19-506714-2., famous Marine memoir

Sloan, Bill (2007). The Ultimate Battle: Okinawa 1945—The Last Epic Struggle of World War II. Simon & Schuster. ISBN 0-7432-9246-4.

The Battle for Iwo Jima: Military Service Records – www.myheritage.com/MilitaryRecords

The Navy Department Library, *Battle for Iwo Jima, 1945.* – www.history.navy.mil/library/online/battleofiwojima.htm

Tillman, Barrett. *Battle in the Philippine Sea: The Marianas Turkey Shoot, June 19-20, 1944.* St. Paul, 1994.

USS Enterprise: 1945 Iwo Jima – www.cv6.org/1945/iwo-2.htm

Yahara, Hiromichi (2001). The Battle for Okinawa. John Wiley & Sons. ISBN 0-471-18080-7.-Firsthand account of the battle by a surviving Japanese officer.

Zaloga, Steven J. Japanese Tanks 1939–45. Osprey, 2007. ISBN 978-1-84603-091-8.

Free Books by Charles River Editors

We have brand new titles available for free most days of the week. To see which of our titles are currently free, click on this link.

Discounted Books by Charles River Editors

We have titles at a discount price of just 99 cents everyday. To see which of our titles are currently 99 cents, click on this link.

Printed in Great Britain
by Amazon